ISBN 978-0-483-39251-9
PIBN 10447058

THE HASTINGS CONSERVER.

VOLUME III.---NO. 21. HASTINGS, DAKOTA COUNTY, MINNESOTA, TUESDAY, SEPTEMBER 1, 1863. $2 00 PER YEAR.

THE CONSERVER.

BY IRVING TODD.

TUESDAY, SEPTEMBER 1, 1863.

Single copies of the CONSERVER may be obtained at this office, or at the Bookstore. Price Five Cents.

Republican Union Ticket.

For Governor,
STEPHEN MILLER,
of Stearns County.

For Lieutenant Governor,
CHARLES D. SHERWOOD,
of Fillmore County.

For Secretary of State,
DAVID BLAKELY,
of Olmsted County.

For Auditor of State,
CHARLES McILRATH,
of Nicollet County.

For State Treasurer,
CHARLES SCHEFFER,
of Washington County.

For Attorney General,
GORDON E. COLE,
of Rice County.

For Clerk of the Supreme Court.
GEORGE F. POTTER,
of Houston County.

County Convention.

The republicans and all other unconditional union men of Dakota County, who are in favor of sustaining the administration in its efforts to suppress the rebellion, are invited to send delegates to a county convention to be holden at Teutonia Hall, in the city of Hastings, on Saturday, Sept. 12th, at 2 o'clock P. M., for the purpose of nominating the following county officers to be supported at the ensuing election:

State Senator,
Two Representatives,
Treasurer,
Sheriff,
Register of Deeds,
Attorney,
Commissioners in the 2d and 3d Districts,
Surveyor,
Coroner.

The different townships will be allowed representation as follows:

Hastings 7; Ravenna 2; Nininger 3; Inver Grove 4; West St. Paul 5; Mendota 3; Eagan 3; Rosemount 2; Burnsville 3; Lakeville 2; Eureka 3; Empire City 2; Sciota 2; Waterford 2; Green Vale 2; Castle Rock 3; Lebanon 2; Marshan 2; Randolph 2; Douglass 1; Vermillion 2; Hampton 3.

It is recommended that the primary meetings be held on Thursday evening, Sept. 10th, at such public places as may be most convenient.

By order of County Committee.
IRVING TODD, Chairman.
Hastings, Sept. 1st, 1863.

The Democratic State Convention.

The delegates met in St. Paul on the 26th inst., and after, a considerable wrangling, succeeded in grinding out the following ticket:

Governor,—H. T. Welles, of Hennepin.

Lieut. Governor,—A. D. LaDue, of Dodge.

Sec. of State,—A. E. Welch, of Goodhue.

State Auditor,—J. A. McKinney, of Fillmore.

State Treasurer,—Peter Wilkin, of Le Sueur.

Attorney General,—W. H. Grant, of Ramsey.

Clerk of Supreme Court,—Hugo Petzhold, of Ramsey.

We are glad of one thing—the democracy of this state have finally shown their hand. The copper is plainly visible. And their candidates are in keeping with their principles—rotten, pusillanimous. Just compare the two tickets, and note the difference. We are not afraid to trust the issue with the voters.

We can give no better idea of the condition of things than to quote the following article from the St. Paul *Pioneer* (dem.), of the 27th inst.:—

"The democratic state convention, held in this city yesterday, would have been a farcical spectacle, if the circumstances of the times did not make it humiliating and disgraceful. With the exception of the nominee for governor and secretary of state, the candidates are mere burlesques. Not one of the others has reputation or capacity for his position.

"The candidate for governor, Mr. Welles, is an amiable gentleman, of moderate, every-day ability, and of immoderate, copperhead proclivities. The candidate for secretary of state, Maj. Welch, of the Fourth Regiment, is a gallant soldier, of too much promise as such, and as a man, to suffer him to accept the doubtful compliment which the convention sought to bestow upon him.

"The platform is a milk-and-water affair, asserting absolutely nothing bad, and embodying nothing which can appeal to the sympathies, or stir the blood of the loyal citizen. It is cold-blooded copperheadism, thinly disguised with a covering of pretended devotion to the constitution and the Union.

"We print elsewhere the proceedings of this convention in full. The reader is referred to that for details. The democracy of this state, if this convention is to be taken as a fair representation of its principles and men, has about run itself out; and the sooner it is buried out of sight, the better it will be for the honor of the state, and the healthiness of its politics. It has been 'growing small by degrees, and beautifully less,' these three years past; and, if the people don't whittle it down to a point this fall, we shall distrust their loyalty and their intelligence."

North-Western Fair for the Sanitary Commission.

The continued need of money has suggested to many of the active and patriotic women of the north-west the necessity of holding a grand north-western fair in the fall, for the benefit of the sanitary commission. After a correspondence of nearly two months with some of the principal aid societies and union leagues of the north-west, aided in many instances by personal interviews, it has been decided to hold a northwestern fair in Chicago, during the last week of October and the first of November, the proceeds to be devoted to the relief of our sick and suffering soldiers. Assurance have been received that the states of Illinois, Michigan, Wisconsin, Iowa, and Minnesota will generally join in this project, and substantial offers of aid have been proffered by leading persons in these states. A mass meeting of ladies has already been held in Chicago, at Bryan Hall, when an executive committee of sixteen ladies was appointed to make such arrangements for the holding of the fair in that city as might be necessary. It was also decided to call a convention of the delegates from the aid societies and union leagues of the above mentioned states to meet in Chicago, at Bryan Hall, to-day, at 10 o'clock, A. M., to make necessary arrangements for the fair, which shall be alike agreeable to all parties. The order of Good Templars, an extensive temperance organization, which has rendered very efficient help to the sanitary commission, by donations of money and supplies, generously volunteer their aid in this enterprise, and are included in this call.

Already great enthusiasm is manifested concerning the fair. A piano, two or three first class sewing machines, a knitting machine, washing machines, wringing machines, a safe, cabinet ware, oil paintings, wax work, and a variety of lesser articles are offered. The affair has greatly increased in magnitude since it was first discussed, until now it promises to eclipse any occasion of the kind ever before held in the north-west. It is hoped and expected that gifts of all kinds will be donated. Anything rare, useful, curious, or elegant in nature or art, is solicited, and it is greatly desired that the fair shall be indebted to the handiwork of men as well as women, for its enriching.

It is also proposed to gather a large collection of relics and mementoes of the present war, for a cabinet, which shall be sold at the fair to the highest bidder. Persons, therefore, who possess relics of the battle-field, mementoes of persons and places made historic by this war, or any of the thousand specimens or curiosities which have found their way to the North, from the seat of war, during its progress, are invited to donate them for the furnishing of this cabinet.

An earnest appeal is made to aid societies and union leagues for assistance. Boxes containing offerings, labelled with name and residence, may be sent direct to the care of the Chicago Sanitary Commission.

St. Paul and Winona Railroad.

It is with gratification that we are able to assure our readers that the survey of this important route has been completed, and with the most satisfactory results. We received a call last week from Mr. Chas. A. F. Morris, chief engineer of the St. Paul and Pacific Railway, and an assistant, from whom we learn several important items connected with the expedition. The entire distance from the railroad track in St. Paul to the track of the Winona and St. Peter railroad at Winona is one hundred and three miles by the proposed route, with a fall of only thirty-eight feet between the two points. For the most part the line selected contains no serious obstacles, and is decidedly favorable to the construction of the road.

The party, or a portion of them, returned to this place for the purpose of running a second line through to Red Wing, this time keeping nearer to the river. Before, they struck back across the prairie, it being thought a better route. The engineers estimate the average cost of grading, ready for the rails, at $5,000 per mile. The most serious obstacles are two miles at Dayton's Bluff, near St. Paul, and three miles near Hastings, which will cost in the neighborhood of $10,000 a mile. We are now able to substantiate our faith in the undertaking by the figures, and hope soon to see the iron steed pawing his way up the Mississippi Valley.

Ballots for the Soldiers.

Solomon Snow, of Austin, and J. P. Kidder, of St. Paul, commissioners appointed for the purpose of taking the votes of all Minnesota volunteers in the service of the United States in the Army of the Potomac, give notice that they will leave the state for that purpose on the 21st of September next, and that all ballots for officers to be voted for in the coming election, to be used in said army, must be delivered to the commissioner at St. Paul, or to the commissioner at Austin, on or before the 20th day of said September.

Leaving the Sinking Ship.

Maj. Welch, nominee of the copperhead convention for secretary of state, and Hugo Petzhold, nominee for clerk of supreme court, have published cards declining the *honor* conferred on them, and refusing to lend their names to such a questionable proceeding. We presume others will follow their example, probably all but Le Duc and "Thrippenny" Grant. These will make a ticket of themselves.

The Fall of Charleston.

The telegraph reports the downfall of Forts Wagner and Sumter, and probably, ere this, Charleston, the hot-bed of secessia, has fallen into our hands. Gen. Butler has been appointed to the command of the city as soon as we obtain possession.

Anatomists say that men change every seven years. Presume this is the reason why debts become outlawed in some states after that period of time has elapsed. The logic is self evident and conclusive; if he has changed, then he is not the man, and consequently not liable to pay.

ALL IS WELL THAT ENDS WELL.—Thus exclaimed many thousands after trying the celebrated Chemical Saleratus of DeLand & Co. They say it works like a charm, and they always have nice light bread, biscuit, cakes, etc. It never fails.

The *Democrat* should not feel so bad about our state nominations. If the ticket is so weak, as it says, it will be all the easier for them to beat, and therefore it should rejoice. Be consistent.

SUCCESSFUL ENGINEERING.—Three gentlemen of high aspirations in the democratic party, attended its state convention, lately held, for the purpose of so engineering it that they could secure nominations and elections to the supreme bench, next year. These were Judge Wilder, of Goodhue County, Judge Chatfield, of Scott County, and Judge Hamlin, of Benton County. They took the management of affairs into their own hands, placing the first in the chair, the second on the committee on organization, and the latter on the platform committee; and the talent of the trio was concentrated on the candidates.

The result of their combined wisdom is before the people, in a platform which is tinctured with disloyalty, and, in a ticket which if its members be boiled down into a single person, it would disgrace any gentlemen to be found in familiar contact with. Crediting these judicial aspirations with the result attained through the democratic convention, and it must be admitted that they have made successful strides towards the goal of their ambition.—*Pioneer.*

A breezy old copperhead tried his affections yesterday on a loyal German near Lang's saloon.

Copperhead—"D'you know that this war is going to free all the d——d niggers in the South?"

German—"Yaw."

Copperhead—"And you want to make the niggers your equal, do you?"

German—"Yaw."

Copperhead—"Then you want your daughter to marry a d——d nigger?"

German—"I'd sooner she'd marry a nigger than a copperhead!"

Copperhead mizzled.—*La Crosse Republican.*

DIED.

In this city, Aug. 25th, 1863, HENRY ALBERT, only child of A. T. NORTON, aged 3 months and 18 days.

LOCAL AFFAIRS.

P. O. Notice.—Summer Arrangement. Mail going East closes at 11 o'clock, A. M. Way mail down closes at 8 o'clock, P. M. Mail for St. Paul closes on the arrival of the boat from below in the afternoon. Faribault mail leaves at 6 o'clock A. M., closes at 9 o'clock P. M. Office hours from 8 A. M. to 8 P. M.

WM. H. SKINNER, Post-Master.

THE MAGAZINES.—*Godey* and the *Atlantic* for September are on our table, full as usual of good things. For sale at STANLEY's on Ramsey Street.

POSTPONED.—By reason of the space occupied by the proceedings of the State Teachers' Association, the educational column of Prof. THICKSTUN has been deferred until next week.

NOTICE.—The Young Peoples' Prayer Meeting will be held in the Methodist Church on next Sunday afternoon at 4 o'clock. A general invitation is extended.

FESTIVAL.—The festival on Friday evening at Teutonia Hall, for the benefit of the Baptist denomination, was well attended, and a complete success. Some $80 we believe were taken in.

PLUMS.—Wild plums are very plenty in market, and consequently quite cheap. They make excellent preserves, and are a great addition to the culinary department.

FROST.—This section of country was visited by a severe frost on Friday night, damaging corn, vines, and things generally. Some fields of corn are entirely ruined.

GOING EAST.—Most of our merchants have left, or are about leaving for below to purchase their usual fall stocks of goods. Business promises to be brisk the coming season.

THE BLACK SWAN, who has been singing with so much success up the river, is expected here in a few days. Timely notice of her appearance will be given to the public.

CLOTHING.—Leave your orders at PRATT's for a suit of good clothes, and you will get them. We are positive on the subject, for we have tried it to our entire satisfaction. Shop next door to post-office.

NEWMAN's new store is nearly finished, and is one of the best rooms for business in town. Moreover he has one of the best and largest stocks of dry goods to put in to it. Call and see him after he gets moved.

COMMISSIONERS' MEETING.—The annual meeting of the county commissioners takes place to day, at their rooms in the county building. Persons having business to transact should lay it before them as early as practicable.

STATE TEACHERS' ASSOCIATION.—This body met in Hastings on Wednesday and Thursday of last week, and the exercises passed off very pleasantly and profitably, and was quite well attended. A full report of the proceedings is given elsewhere.

RETURNED.—We are informed that the gallant Col. ADAMS, of the 1st Regiment, dangerously wounded at Gettysburg, and for a long time not expected to live, has returned home. He is able to get about on crutches, and there is fair prospects of his entire recovery.

ENGRAVING.—It can be truly said that we have one of the best engravers in the West, and any one skeptical on the subject may be convinced by calling at ANDREWS' on Second Street, and examining specimens of his work. All kinds of repairing done to order, on short notice.

FOR SALE.—The *Independent* publishes a list of the republican union candidates, and says: "We shall continue, as heretofore, to occupy an independent position." That is, in other words, remain on the fence, waiting for an offer. Who bids and how much, gentlemen! Going, going, can't dwell, gentlemen, going, g-o-i-n-g, g-o-!

THE GREAT AMERICAN NAVY SOAP.—Two suspicious looking personages were about town a few days ago selling this wonderful preparation, *warranted* to remove "rust, ink, paints, mildew, and grease" from clothing. It is a very fair article of rosin soap, and may be purchased at wholesale at any grocery for ten cents a bar.

CHOPFALLEN.—The delegates to the democratic state convention returned very quietly, and have little to say. We learn that tail-feathers are abundant on the road between here and St. Paul, and occasionally a belated oath comes whistling by. Yer did n't come it, did yer? What do you think about 10,000 majorities now? Evidently democratic stock is below par.

State Teachers' Association—Third Annual Session.

FIRST DAY.

The association assembled at the University, at Hastings, on the 26th inst., at 10 A. M. In the absence of the president; the vice president, Prof. T. F. Thickstun, presided. Mr. J. W. Stearns, of Winona, was chosen secretary.

Opened with reading of scriptures and prayer by Rev. D. Burt, of Winona.

On motion, Messrs. Dale, Etheridge, Shandrew, and Meacham were appointed a committee to arrange and conduct the singing during the convention.

The minutes of last meeting were read by Prof. Thickstun.

Messrs. Twitchell, Meacham, and Etheridge were appointed a committee to obtain the names of the members present, and the following were thus enrolled.

Prof. Samuel R. Thorp, Red Wing.
Mr. A. J. Meacham, " "
Miss Belle S. Webster, " "
Miss Larina Meacham, " "
Miss Martha E. Densmore, " "
Prof. Jabez Brooks, " "
Mrs. Wellington, " "
Miss Ellen J. Sherman, " "
Miss Laura Parkhust, " "
Mr. H. C. Harden, " "
Mrs. C. E. Thorp, " "
Prof. J. W. Stearns, Winona.
Mr. F. E. Shandrew, "
Rev. D. Burt, "
Rev. L. B. Tefft, "
Dr. Jno. D. Ford, "
Miss R. M. Thorne, "
Miss E. F. Thorne, "
Miss Lizzie Ford, "
Mrs. F. E. Stearns, "
Miss Mary E. Winters, "
Mrs. M. E. Gault, "
Miss M. L. Worthington, "
Miss Hattie J. Brierly, St. Paul.
Miss Helen E. Morrow, "
Miss Mary J. Cramsie, "
Miss L. J. Bray, "
Miss M. E. Hoffman, "
Miss Sarah Etheridge, "
Prof. A. D. Williams, Wasioja.
Miss J. F. Armstrong, Trimbelle, Wis.
Miss C. L. Armstrong, " "
Prof. E. J. Thompson, Chatfield.
Miss Flora J. Sargent, Faribault.
Miss E. D. Harn, Minneapolis.
Mr. J. J. Copp, Groton, Conn.
Mr. J. Haskell, Afton.
Mr. M. M. Countryman, Nininger.
Mr. L. N. Countryman, "
Miss Anna A. Reel, "
Mrs. Ada Sprague, "
Mr. A. H. Truax, "
Miss Lucy A. Reed, "
Miss Martha Countryman, "
Miss Rosella Plummer, Castle Rock.
Miss Ellen A. Rice, " "
Miss Mary E. Bollock, Lewiston.
Miss Jennie M. Daniels, "
Miss Esther M. Sprague, Peoria, Ill.
Mr. D. P. Sackett, Waterford.
Mr. A. A. Beman, Rochester.
Miss Evelyn E. Ireland, "
Mr. J. M. Gates, Wabashaw.
Prof. W. P. Dale, New York City.
Mr. W. A. Wright, Prescott, Wis.
Rev. Charles Thayer, "
Rev. J. W. Miller, "
Miss Lucy H. Howes, "
Miss Mary P. Collins, "
Prof. R. L. Reed, "
Miss Ira D. Nowell, "
Prof. W. T. Hatch, "
Miss Chloe E. Hatch, "
Miss Ellen Johnston, "
Mr. J. M. McKee, "
Mr. J. M. Copp, "
Mr. B. F. Copp, "
Mr. W. M. Howes, "
Mr. E. V. McLeod, "
Mr. B. F. Miller, Monticello.
Gov. W. Holcombe, Stillwater.
Mr. Joel Townsend, "
Mr. Frank Slocum, Cannon Falls.
Miss Augusta M. Marshall, Hastings.
Miss Jennie Buell, "
Miss Sarah L. Johnson, "
Mrs. J. W. Pratt, "
Mrs. J. A. Morton, "
Mrs. C. A. Hesketh, "
Mrs. A. W. Canning, "
Mrs. K. B. Webster, "
Rev. Charles LeDuc, "
Mr. A. D. Haynes, "
Mr. F. B. Van Hoesen, "
Mr. John White, "
Mr. Irving Todd, "
Mr. Robert S. Lemon, "
Miss Maggie Mc Hugh, "
Miss Amelia E. Jones, "
Mrs. M. A. Boynton, "
Mrs. S. J. Corson, "
Miss Emma Lewis, "
Miss Susie E. Corson, "
Mr. L. L. Twitchell, "
Miss Nettie P. Van Hoesen, "
Mrs. M. J. Plumstead, "
Mrs. Abba L. Green, "
Mrs. Eliza W. Merrill, "
Mrs. M. P. Woodbury, "
Mrs. S. M. L. Thickstun, "
Mrs. A. C. Smith, "
Miss S. P. Ketchem, "
Miss Kate E. Stowell, "
Miss Celia T. Gardner, "
Mrs. M. Clematine Ward, "
Miss Sallie C. Pyle, "
Miss Belle Patch, "
Mrs. Charles Etheridge, "
Miss Louisa C. Groff, "
Mrs. J. C. Pride, "
Mrs. Wm. E. Maddocks, "
Mrs. Byron C. Howes, "
Miss Lizzie LeDuc, "
Miss Mary E. LeDuc, "
Miss Sarah M. Lancaster, "
Mrs. M. F. Armington, "
Miss Abbie Gibson, "
Mrs. M. A. Bennett, "
Miss Angie Patch, "
Mrs. L. W. Mather, "
Mrs. M. B. Tozer, "
Miss Laura E. Corson, "
Miss Ada Thomas, "
Prof. T. F. Thickstun, "
Mr. C. B. Lowell, "
Mr. Homer Hatch, "
Mr. Nelson B. Holmes, "
Mr. Charles Etheridge, "
Mr. James H. Etheridge, "
Mr. C. Stebbins, "
Mr. M. D. Merrill, "

On motion of Prof. A. D. Williams, of Wasioja, the order of last year for meeting and adjournment was adopted.

On motion of Prof. Brooks, of Red Wing, a committee of five on resolutions was appointed, consisting of Prof. Brooks, Dr. Ford, of Winona, Mr. Thompson, of Chatfield, Miss Patch, of Hastings, Miss Brierly, of St. Paul.

The executive committee then reported an order of exercises for the afternoon.

On motion, the lecture of the evening was announced to be held in the Presbyterian Church.

Adjourned till 2 P. M.

AFTERNOON SESSION.

Association met pursuant to adjournment.

The following committees were announced:—

On Teachers Institutes.—Prof. Brooks, of Red Wing, Mrs. Sprague, Nininger, Rev. J. W. Miller, Prescott, Miss F. J. Sargent, Faribault, Miss C. E. Hatch, Prescott.

On Common Schools.—Rev. D. Burt, Winona, Mrs. Wellington, Red Wing, Ex-Gov. Holcombe, Stillwater, Miss S. E. Corson, Hastings, Mr. B. F. Miller, Monticello.

On Normal Schools.—Prof. A. D. Williams, Wasioja, Prof. S. R. Thorp, Red Wing, Rev. L. B. Tefft, Winona, J. H. Haskell, Afton, Gov. Holcombe, Stillwater.

On Qualifications of Teachers.—Prof. A. D. Williams, Wasioja, Prof. S. R. Thorp, Red Wing, Rev. L. B. Tefft, Winona, Miss E. D. Harn, Minneapolis, Prof. W. T. Hatch, Prescott.

Report of executive committee was then read by Prof. A. D. Williams, and accepted. The discussion of its recommendations was made the special business of Thursday morning.

Mr. C. Stebbins introduced a resolution on the subject of the state superintendency, referred to committee on resolutions.

Prof. S. R. Thorp, of Red Wing, then read a paper on Mathematics. Discussion of the topic deferred.

A committee of five, consisting of Gov. Holcombe, Irving Todd, Rev. Chas. S. Le Duc, Rev. Chas. Thayer, and Mr. R. S. Lemon, was appointed to nominate officers for the ensuing year.

Adjourned till 7½ P. M.

EVENING SESSION.

Association met at Presbyterian Church. Opened with singing by the choir. Reading of Scriptures and Prayer by Rev. J. W. Miller, of Prescott.

Another song by the choir. Rev. D. Burt, of Winona, then delivered a lecture; subject, Methods of Improving our System of Public Instruction.

Closed with the singing of America by the choir.

SECOND DAY—MORNING SESSION.

Association convened at 9 A. M. Religious exercises, by Prof. Williams.

Prof. Williams introduced a resolution in reference to the school for deaf mutes, which was referred to the committee on resolutions.

Report of executive committee was then taken up, and the first recommendation was generally discussed. On motion of Mr. J. W. Stearns, the following resolution was adopted in place thereof:

Resolved, That a committee be appointed to urge upon the legislature, among other improvements in our school system, the following objects:

1. The appointment of a superintendent of public instruction.

2. The appointment of a local superintendent of public instruction for each of the judicial districts of the state.

3. The appropriation of money sufficient for the efficient and successful conduct of the normal school already established and for the foundation of others in contemplation as soon as expedient.

On motion of Rev. Charles S. LeDuc, Gov. Holcombe, Prof. Brooks, and Dr Ford were named as the committee to memorialize the legislature. On motion of Mr. Shandrew, the committee were empowered to appoint substitutes.

The second recommendation was, on motion, laid on the table.

The third was referred to committee on teachers institutes.

The following resolutions, introduced by Rev. L. B. Tefft, were adopted in place of the fourth recommendation:

Resolved, That we believe that great advantages would accrue to the teachers and people of the state from the establishment and hearty support of a state educational journal, and that we will hold ourselves ready to undertake such enterprise as soon as circumstances will permit.

Resolved, That for the present we recommend to Prof. Thickstun to continue to publish his quarterly journal, assuring him of our sympathies and pecuniary support to an amount not less than $30.

On motion of Dr. Ford, report of executive committee was referred to committee on common schools.

On motion of Dr. Ford, the following committee was appointed to recommend a singing book for the use of common schools:

Dr. Ford, Prof. Dale, A. J. Meacham, D. E. Eyre, and Miss C. E. Hatch.

Prof. Thompson then read an entertaining paper entitled Experiences of a Pedagogue in Vermont.

Arrangements for afternoon session were then reported by committee.

Adjourned till 2 P. M.

AFTERNOON SESSION.

Association met at 2 P. M. The secretary being absent, Rev. L. B. Tefft was appointed secretary *pro tem.*

Considerable discussion then arose as to designation of next meeting of the association. Red Wing and Winona were suggested, and, on motion, it was agreed to be held at Red Wing.

Prof. Williams, from committee on normal schools, reported as follows:

Resolved, That the principles of our school system and the wants of our schools imperatively require the immediate prosecution by our state of the normal school system.

2. That the proffered pledges of the state and the generous acceptance of them by the citizens of Winona demand a resuscitation and permanent establishment of the state normal school at Winona.

3. That we highly approve the action of the normal board to receive only a limited number of pupils from a given district, and recommend that it be made a thorough normal school.

4. That the system of normal schools should be extended as rapidly as possible till sufficient provision be made for giving well instructed common school teachers to the whole state.

On motion, they were adopted.

Song by the choir.

Prof. Brooks, from committee on teachers institutes, made a report, which was adopted, as follows:

Resolved, That the convention regards the holding of teachers institutes as an agency eminently promotive of the improvement of teachers, and of arousing an interest on educational matters in the community in which they may be held.

Resolved, That we urge upon the teachers in the several counties and towns of the state to hold county and town teachers' institutes in their several places of labor.

Prof. Brooks, from committee on resolutions, made the following report, which was adopted:

The resolutions on state superintendency and state institution for the education of deaf mutes referred to your committee we beg leave to report back with slight alterations to the convention, with the recommendation that they be adopted:

Resolved, That we, the teachers of the state of Minnesota, most unqualifiedly give it as our opinion that a state superintendent of public instruction, disassociated from any other state office, is an absolute necessity in making our school law effective, and every moment's delay in securing that important school officer is prejudicial to the educational interests of the state.

Resolved, That we hail with joy the commencement in our state of a state institution for the education of deaf mutes, and to Prof. R. H. Kinney we extend a warm and hearty greeting as a fellow teacher.

The committee would also report the following for consideration:

1. That the situation of the teacher must be made desirable by adequate compensation, by good treatment, by suitable accommodations, by limiting his labors to the requirements of health and self-improvement.

2 That in the selection of teachers, merit should be preferred to any other consideration, and free competition should be allowed to determine such merit.

3. That this convention recommend that the people commit the interests of our common schools to persons both in our legislature and school committees who are in hearty sympathy with an effective school system.

4. That the thanks of this convention be and are hereby tendered to the steamboat companies who have passed the members of this convention at half fare.

5. That the thanks of the convention are hereby tendered to the committee on music for the excellent music discoursed during the session.

6. That the thanks of this convention be and are hereby tendered to the ladies and citizens of Hastings for the cordial and generous welcome given to its members.

Rev. D. Burt, from committee on common schools, made the following report which was adopted as amended by Prof. Brooks:—

Your committee on common schools find the subject so comprehensive that only a few of the many topics included in the theme can at this time be noticed. While hoping that our school laws will soon be reconstructed so as to admit into our educational system the prominent features already recommended by the convention, we would suggest that our teachers should work as reformers in their intercourse with the people. We earnestly urge them to become

Continued on Fourth Page.

THE CONSERVER.

BY IRVING TODD.

Office Over the Bank of Hastings, Exchange Block, Second Street.

Our Platform.

Resolved, That we, chosen to represent in convention the unconditional union men of Minnesota, grateful to Almighty God for the success which has hitherto crowned the arms of our country and for the prospect thus opened of a speedy, honorable, and lasting peace, do hereby, for ourselves and our constituents, reaffirm our determination to support our government by every means in our power in the vigorous prosecution of this war,—on our part, holy, just, and forced upon us by the criminal acts of others,—until not an enemy in arms shall be found within our borders. And to this we pledge our lives, our fortunes, and our sacred honor.

2. That we tender our grateful thanks to the survivors of our glorious armies, and our warm sympathy to the relatives of their gallant dead, who have won for the country so glorious victories, for themselves imperishable renown, and for us all an assurance of liberty and safety, for ourselves and our children, under our beloved and now well-tried government.

3. That with especial pride we point to the gallant achievements on many a hard-fought battle-field, of our Minnesota regiments. Their bravery, discipline, and patriotism have won for them a name that shall never die, and made forever honorable to a citizen of Minnesota.

4. That, without claiming for it exemption from error, we heartily endorse the general policy and conduct of our national administration; and we point to the recent magnificent triumph of our armies as its best vindication from the charge of incapacity so freely brought against it by those who prefer national ruin to success under the present administration. Especially do we approve the emancipation proclamation, and the raising of black troops, as being among the best possible measures to weaken the enemy and strengthen ourselves.

5. That our state administration and congressional delegation deserve our hearty approbation for the zealous and efficient co-operation they have afforded the national authorities in carrying on the war.

6. That we call upon those in authority to take such measures, by retaliation or otherwise, as shall effectually prevent brutal and barbarous treatment by the enemy of our soldiers, of whatever color.

7. That it is due to our shattered armies in the field, as well as to the sacred cause which they uphold, that their ranks should as speedily as possible be filled up by every means in our power. It is due to the country that the mobs raised to resist and prevent the draft, should not even seem to have succeeded a day longer than is necessary to enforce the laws.

8. That the way to peace is, and ever has been, open to the rebels; the only condition we have ever sought to impose is that they should lay down their arms and submit to the authority of the general government. We protest against the making of any terms with them in advance as to their *status* in communities, when they shall have returned to their allegiance. Having been declared "public enemies" by a recent unanimous decision of the Supreme Court of the United States, they must accept the consequences that legitimately flow from having placed themselves in that position.

The Mankato *Union* and the *Press* both recently gave the Hon. Senator Wilkinson credit for having secured to the school land fund of the state the 16th and 36th sections of the Winnebago Reservation, and report that that was Senator Wilkinson's business to Washington recently. We would not pluck a leaf from the well earned laurel wreath which binds the brow of our honored senator; but it is due to justice and fairness that honor should be rendered to whom honor is due, and the honor of having secured this valuable addition to the school lands of the state is due mainly to Attorney General Cole. Will the *Union* and *Press* please be just as well as generous?—*Central Republican.*

The Nashville *Union* is officially authorized to state that Gov. Johnson proposes to issue writs of election for a legislature, at the very earliest practical day; that is, when the progress of military operations is such that loyal citizens can go to the polls in *safety*, and when sympathizers with the rebellion will no longer dare, backed by the presence of rebel troops and by guerilla terrorism, to control the policy of the state. Regard will also be had to the disposition manifested by the people to resume their former privileges in the federal union. They must, it says, indicate in some way a desire to vote for their officers as loyal citizens. Elections will not be forced upon them against their will.

A box of rattlesnakes was put on the train for New Haven at New York, the other day, and during the trip one of the delightful reptiles got out and gave the baggage man and mail agent some very original ideas of gymnastics with the rattles thrown in. They flew around pretty lively—baggage man, snake, and mail agent, and "things was promiscuous" for a short time, but no essential damage was done except to the young men's sensibilities.

The following is reported as a fact: A Louisville union lady, a few days since, called upon a secesh friend, and felt compelled to listen to her tirade. On rising to leave she noticed and praised a portrait of Gen. George Washington, whereupon the rebel lady remarked: "I intend to get the portraits of Jeff Davis and Beauregard and hang one on each side of that." "Do," said union, "we read in the Bible that our Savior was hung between two thieves."

Translated from democratic hieroglyphis into plain English, the disloyal argument is this: "We propose to restore the union, and obtain an honorable peace by a feeble prosecution of the war." The absurdity of this argument, when expressed in syllogistic form, is its own refutation.

Going to Newport.

"Now, Inez, do n't be a goose! Give me a kiss, and say you'll make yourself contented at home, as a good little wife should do. Newport, indeed! the idea is perfectly preposterous!"

As Mr. St. John concluded this speech, he bit off the end of the cigar intended to comfort him on his way to Wall Street, and looked around towards the window where his wife stood. Her face was averted, but you could see from the rounded curves of the throat and chin that it was a very, very pretty one, and the hand that rested on the window lintel was small and white and loaded with sparkling rings.

"I do n't see anything is very preposterous in my wishing a little gay society," she pouted; "I'm tired to death of this monotonous life!"

"Home, and your husband's society, then, have lost their charm!" said St. John, gently, as he passed his arm around her waist, and drew her face towards him. But she disengaged herself with a petulant jerk.

"Everybody else is going to Newport—and I want to go, too!"

"You are aware that business arrangements renders it impossible for me to accompany you?"

"Well, what then? I can go with the Merringtons."

"And leave me here alone!"

"Oh, I dare say you'll find ways and means of amusing yourself," laughed Inez, her bright eyes beginning to sparkle at the prospect of winning her point at last. "I do n't believe in husband and wife being so entirely dependent on one another for society! Say I may go, George, that's a darling."

She put up her coral mouth for a kiss, as a spoiled child might have done. St. John opened his purse and silently placed a roll of bank bills in her hand.

"They are all right," he murmured to himself, as she skipped joyfully away. "I have spoiled her with my foolish, unreasonable indulgence; but I never fancied before that she was selfish and heartless too. Pshaw. I will not entertain the thought for a moment—yet if I could but find the key to that strange, sweet, wilful nature."

All day long George St. John was singularly absent and thoughtful—so much so that the clerks in his down-town office secretly marvelled whether or no "Mr. St. John was going to fail." But they were wrong in their shrewd conjectures for once. St. John's abstraction was owing to quite another cause.

Sunset on the broad, white beach at Newport—sunset edging the green, tumultuous waves with liquid lines of gold, and turning the ripped sands to acres of diamond sparkles—and the salt sea breeze fresh from the grand old Atlantic, lifted the long white plume that drooped from Inez St. John's jaunty Spanish hat, and gave a deeper crimson to her beautiful flushed cheek.

She was in her element at that moment—surrounded by gentlemen who bowed at the shrine of her exceeding beauty, and ladies who envied, yet could not choose but admire. For Inez St. John knew just how to set off her fresh loveliness to the best possible advantage.

"By the way, Mrs. St. John," observed a gay little brunette widow, who is this dashing fellow who is getting up so many flirtations with the belles at the 'Atlantic!' He's as handsome as Appollo, and rides as charmingly. Some relation of yours, perhaps—his name is St. John."

Inez shook her head with cool indifference.

"I'm sorry I can't claim any relationship—the only person of that name whom I know is my husband, at this moment probably looking over the stock lists in Walll Street."

"Indeed!" said the brunette widow. "How delightful it must be to be so confident of the whereabouts of one's better half!"

Inez only laughed—she could afford to set the little lady's shafts of sarcasm at defiance.

"I declare!" ejaculated the widow, putting up her eye-glass, "there he is now—no mistaking those superb grays! Kate Appleton is with him! Well, if he likes a desperate flirtation, Kate's the girl for him! I only wish he'd ask me to drive with him!"

Inez looked up with a sort of careless interest—but all of a sudden her cheek glowed scarlet, and she gave a quick little start.

"George!"

"Inez—is that you? Miss Appleton—my wife! How are you getting along here, my love? Any funds wanted?"

Inez stood speechless and dismayed. Was *this* gay, nonchalant fellow the devoted husband whose life had been one long slavery to her smiles.

"I'll run round to see you for a few moments this evening," said the gentleman, coolly gathering up his reins. "I'm rather in a hurry just now—Miss Appleton wants to see the sun set from Silver Point; so, *au revoir!*"

And in a moment the grays were out of sight.

"So he's her husband," whispered the widow, maliciously, behind her jewelled fan. "Upon my word, flirtation seems to run in the family."

"But Inez had neither heart nor spirit to take up the wordy challenge.

"Well, dear," was St. John's careless salutation, as he lounged into the crowded hotel parlors that night, about nine o'clock. "I can't stay long, for I've promised Mrs. Fessenden to take her to the hop this evening. Gay season, is n't it?"

"You have been here a week, George—why did you not come to see me sooner?"

"Oh—why—I do n't know—what was the use? You were having a nice time, and so was I. Our Darby and Joan days are over. What a splendid girl Kate Appleton is, eh?"

"But, George, I—I wish you would n't go with her quite so much."

"Why not? Where's the harm? Do I find fault with your manifold flirtations? Now, my dear little wife, do n't make yourself ridiculous. I must improve every opportunity, for I am obliged to be at home by Wednesday."

Inez St. John lifted her tear-filled eyes to her husband's face.

"George, will you take me home, too?"

"Home! So early in the season. Why, I thought you meant to stay until September."

"So I did, but—the truth is, George, I am weary of Newport—oh, so weary."

Mr. St. J whistle.

'There's no accounting for a woman's freaks," he said. "However, do as you like—its a matter of no consequence to me."

'Of no consequence." How the words rang in Inez's ears during the slow, creeping hours of that long, sultry night. For she had never known how tenderly she prized her husband's love until the shadow of its loss brooded over her life.

She was sitting there, and dressed for the home journey on Wednesday morning, when an elderly gentleman, an old familiar friend, walked in.

"Ready, Mrs. St. John?"

"Yes, and only waiting for George, Mr. Spellman.

"The fact is," began the old gentleman, with some embarassment in his manner, "he finds his engagements will not permit him to return until to-morrow, and as he concludes you are anxious to reach home, and I am returning to New York, he requested me to act as your escort."

Inez rose, pale as death, and silently placed her arm within that of Mr. Spellman, while the bitter cry of despair went up from her secret heart.

"O! if I had never come to this dreadful place!"

It was late at night when she entered her own familiar sitting room, spiritless and weary, with her eyes red with tears, and her check pale and wan. She had fancied it would be dark and deserted; instead, there were cheerful lights burning; and there, beside the table, stood—her husband!

"George."

"Inez—my darling little wife."

He had drawn her to his breast with all the tenderness of old—he was whisling the sweet words that had never seemed so sweet before.

"The troubled dream is over, dearest—we are at home once more."

Yes, it was indeed home—and from that hour Inez never sighed to leave it more. The remedy had been severe, but it was also efficacious. George St. John had found the key to his little wife's heart.

A WOMAN'S OPINION.—From the Parlor and Sidewalk Gossip of that most admirable of all New York city weeklies the *Sunday Times* we clip the following racy paragraph. The author is "Jennie June," the *nom de plume* of Mrs. Croley, formerly an editress of the Rockford *News*, one of the most original and readable journals ever published in the west:

"We confess to liking occasionally to give men a scolding when they do not come up to the mark; but we cannot bear to have anybody else to do it. We should not care to live in this world if there were no men in it. We may have been unfortunate in the specimens connected with us by intimate associations, but take them all together we consider them an immense institution. Who would pay the stage and cab fare? Who would bring home pockets full of newspapers and magazines and bouquets and oranges on Saturdays and birthdays if the men were all gone? Who would care whether one was good-looking or well or ill-dressed, or what the baby said when it first began to talk, or how much handsomer it was than Mrs. So-and-So's baby, if only women inhabited this hemisphere? Above all, who would carry the umbrella or do the errands down town when it rains, or assist in stowing carpet bag and reticule and little basket and parasol and bundle and extra shawl away in the railroad cars and produce at the very last moment from the depths of a capacious pocket the last "Atlantic" uncut and a paper of bananas to eat on the way? Who would do all this—and much more that we cannot enumerate—if men were voted out of existence? Where would be our chances for opera and lecture and concert and summer trips, and to come down to more materialities, new bonnets and bread and butter? Echo answers; they will be very dim indeed.

The copperheads complain of military interference in the Kentucky election, and charge the result would have been different had not voters been kept away from the polls. Bramlette received over 75,000 votes for governor. The whole vote for president in 1860, was 146,216. So Bramlette received a clear majority of the entire vote of the state. Of course the copperhead pretense is false.

Seventeen conscript soldiers of the French army in Bonaparte's time raised themselves by their bravery and talent to the following distinguished stations: Two became kings; two, princes; nine, dukes; two, field marshals; and two, generals.

Gen. Van Dorn said to a federal officer after the battle of Corinth, "Tell Gen. Rosecrans that he beat me by a damned Yankee trick, but you may tell him, too, that he is the only general in the country who could have done it."

AGRICULTURAL.

Blooded Stock vs. Native.

A subscriber asks the pertinent question, will a blooded or grade animal sell for more in the cattle market than one of the same weight of native stock? We answer yes, usually, for the reason that high-bred cattle have their weight developed on desirable points. Bones are valuable for many purposes, but no butcher will pay 9 to 12 cents per pound for them, when he can obtain an equal amount of good meat for the same price. Native animals occasionally show great symmetry of form, well developed muscle, and meat laid on where the butcher and epicure like to find it. In such cases the market value of the animal will not differ materially from that one having a good pedigree. Usually, however, it is found that native breeds give more of offal and coarse meat, than those bred for generations back with a view to fitting them for the shambles, and hence their value for slaughtering decreases correspondingly. It should be constantly kept in mind, that it is not the peculiar excellence of single animals that wholly determines their value upon the farm. A perfectly well-formed native cow yielding a generous supply of milk, is justly prized for her individual qualities; but the owner can not, with any degree of certainty, expect her good qualities to be transmitted to the next generation. Of course her calf will be more likely to prove good than one from an ill-favored dam, but the deficiencies of her ancestors may crop out in an unlooked-for degree, and render the progeny comparatively worthless as a breeder. It requires many years of careful management to fix the qualities of a breed of animals, so that they shall be repeated in the progeny. There must be a counter-balancing of points, and overcoming of deficiencies, by proper selection of sire and dam, for many successive generations. Unquestionably this may be done by starting with a promising native pair, and continuing to breed sufficiently long with reference to the development of desirable points. But few are found possessed of sufficient means, time, patience and perseverance, to carry the process to a successful termination. A few have done so in other countries, especially in England, and the world is sharing the benefit of their endeavors. Again, even supposing success attainable by starting with native animals, it seems more feasible to begin with animals already possessing fixed qualities of excellence, and to super-add to these, by proper breeding, whatever may be wanting. Intelligent cattle raisers are pursuing this course, and already this country can furnish no mean show of blooded stock compared with that of any other land. To every farmer who proposes to raise but a single calf, we would say secure the services of the best blooded bull attainable, and continue to do so; in ten years you will find your account in it.—*Agriculturist.*

How to Cure Indian Corn for Fodder.

In order to have the fodder good, the corn should be cut up while it is yet green—that is, before the leaves and stalks begin to dry. Any time after the corn becomes hard (or glazed) the corn may be cut without injuring to the grain.

I make a stanchion for the shock by tying the tops of four hills together—then the fodder should be set up in the angles as nearly perpendicular as possible. After setting up six or eight hills, the tops should be tied together with a wisp of grass or stalk; this makes a firm begining for a shock. The shock should contain at least 144 hills, as the larger it is the less proportionately it will be exposed to the weather. Bear it in mind that the stalks should be set up as nearly perpendicular as possible. Lastly, the shock should be well tied at the top with a band of rye straw.

Corn put up in this manner will not fall down before husking time. I usually husk my corn in from four to six weeks after cutting it up. When the corn is husked, the fodder should be tied with straw in convenient sized bundles for pitching, and it is better to put the stalks from two shocks into one, and tie the tops as before; then, if the weather is dry, it may be hauled at any time and put in stacks convenient to barn. There is no safety in putting it in the mow, however dry it may appear, for the pith in the butt of the stalk is a great absorbent, and as long as the stalks stand on the ground it will retain moisture enough to spoil the stalks if put into a mow, but when they are stacked up so that the buts come to the sun and air, the stalks will not spoil.

I make my stacks in the following manner, so that we can always haul in an entire stack at a time: Take a pole, from 4 to 6 inches thick and from 15 to 18 feet long, and set it firmly in the ground; then build the stock around it, laying the tops in against the pole and the butts out, keeping the middle full as in other stacks. At the top I make a cap of a bundle of stalks.

Corn that is sown for fodder should be treated as nearly in the same manner as possible, and you will have good sweet food for your cattle, which they will need no coaxing to eat.—*Ira M. Allen, in Country Gentleman.*

The discovery of a tin mine in Missouri is announced by a correspondent of the *Scientific American*. If the report be true, no more important discovery has been recently made public. We have heretofore been entirely dependent upon England and the East Indies for our supply of this metal.

A correspondent of the *Boston Cultivator* says: "Cover the bottom of a large jar with coarse salt. Put the butter in a bag, place it in the jar in a north room, and the salt will keep the butter nearly as cool, through the summer, as a common cellar."

BATCHELDER'S COLUMN.

GREAT ATTRACTIONS

AT THE

OLD STAND.

GEO. F. BATCHELDER,

(Successor to North & Carll)

WHOLESALE

AND

RETAIL

Dealer in

DRY GOODS,

GROCERIES,

Boots and Shoes,

HARDWARE, ETC.,

HASTINGS, MINN.

Having laid in an unusually heavy stock of staple wares, would invite the attention of the public to my large assortment of

GOODS,

Consisting of Imported and Domestic

SILKS, DELAINES,

LAWNS AND

CALICOES,

also to my stock of Foreign and Domestic

SHEETINGS,

These goods were purchased at exceedingly low rates, and am therefore enabled to sell at prices to suit the times.

A well assorted stock of

Hats and Caps,

for Men and Boys, of the latest styles.

READY-MADE

CLOTHING,

a fine assortment, custom made, from the best of cloths, bought expressly for this market, and will be sold at reasonable figures, for cash only.

A choice stock of pure and fresh

GROCERIES

Just received from the East, where especial attention was paid to their selection.

A fine lot of assorted

Boots and Shoes,

comprising Gent's, Ladies', Boy's, and Misses', of all varieties. The especial attention of farmers is invited to a large and complete stock of

HARDWARE.

The celebrated Moline Plow always on hand.

A long experience in and close supervision of the business, and personal attention to the buying of goods, gives confidence that entire satisfaction will be rendered to patrons. Customers will be waited on by experienced and accommodating salesmen; and their wishes promptly attended to. All goods warranted as represented.

GEO. F. BATCHELDER.

Hastings, June 9, 1863. 9-tf

THE CONSERVER.

Published every Tuesday Morning at HASTINGS, DAKOTA COUNTY, MINNESOTA.

Terms.

Single copy one year	$ 2 00
" " six months,	1 00
" " three months,	50
Five copies, to one address,	8 75
Ten " " "	15 00
Twenty " " " and one to getter up of club,	30 00

Payment invariably in advance.

RATES OF ADVERTISING.

1 square	1 week	$1 00	2 squares	8 months	9 00
"	2 weeks	1 50	"	1 year	15 00
[illegible]	[illegible]	[illegible]	[illegible]	[illegible]	[illegible]

One inch in space will be counted as a square of solid matter.

Business cards on second page, not exceeding seven lines, seven dollars per year; each additional line one dollar.

Legal advertisements inserted at the rates prescribed by statute, and attorneys ordering such advertisements will be held responsible.

Special notices 15 cents per line for first insertion and ten cents for each subsequent insertion.

Transient advertisements must be paid in advance—all others quarterly.

Advertisements not otherwise ordered, will be continued until they are ordered out, and charged accordingly.

Sleep On.

Sleep on—sleep happily on,
Untroubled by the cares of day,
While thy free spirit wings its way
Then to me!

Dream on—but dream of me!
As all my dreams of dear delight,
Through the sweet slumbers of the night,
Are of thee!

Rev. Dr. B—dm—n, of this city, is a brick. No divine on the continent stands higher either as a theologian, a christian, or a gentleman. Dr. B. has two churches, and preaches one sermon for each every Sunday. Among Dr. B——'s congregation is a Mr. H——, a gentleman who some twelve months ago married a gay, dashing, and beautiful girl, very much such a looking lady as your correspondent "Getty Gay." A few days ago Mr. H. visited the doctor at his study. Mr. H. looked sad, while his face was as long as though a cannon ball was hung to his chin. The following conversation then opened up:

"Doctor B——, I came to consult you on a serious matter."

"I am all attention," replied the doctor, as he bowed his visitor into a seat.

"The fact is, sir; I am apprehensive of trouble. I fear I've done wrong in marrying Maria."

"I trust not, sir. I have ever held her in high esteem. Pray what appears to be the difficulty?"

"Well, doctor, Maria is very unsteady—very volatile—very—"

"But my dear sir," urged the doctor, "consider the natural flow of spirits in a young person."

"I do, sir; but I do n't want that flow of spirits to shape itself into a preference for balls and parties, to my society."

"Of course not; but is that all you have to complain of?"

"It is at present, and it's enough to complain of, I think." Then shifting his position on the chair, he continued: "Do n't you think, doctor, that if you were to preach a sermon against this sort of thing—against going out to parties and other humbugs—it would be a first rate thing?"

"Well no, sir, I doubt its effect. But I can suggest a better remedy—a remedy that will at once cure your good lady of her roving propensity."

"Name it, sir, and receive my everlasting gratitude."

"I will, sir. Provide her with a baby. A blue eyed boy will do more towards inculcating the commandments in the breast of a live woman, than all the homilies ever uttered in the pulpit."

Mr. H.'s countenance did n't light up, though the gass did just at that moment. Mr. H. arose,

He folded his tent like the Arabs
And silently stole away.

The remark of Dr. B—dm—n conveyed no encouragement to Mr. H. Something must be the matter in that quarter. What it is remains to be discovered.—*Ex.*

A gentleman from Cheat Mountain tells the following: A squad of Indiana volunteers, out scouting, came across an old woman in a log cabin in the mountains. After the usual salutations one of them asked her,

"Well, old lady, are you secesh?"
"No," was her answer.
"Are you union?"
"No."
"What are you then?"
"*A Baptist, and al'ys have been.*"

A boy makes a huge snowball to show his skill and perseverance, and as something to wonder at, not that he can swallow it as an ice or warm his hands at it; and the man accumulates a pile of wealth for pretty much the same reason.

A husband recently cured his wife of divers ills by kissing the servant girl and allowing his wife to catch him at it. He says she was up at an instant, forgetting all her complaints, while he has never had to pay a cent for help since.

A jolly fellow being asked as he lay sunning himself on the grass what was the height of his ambition, replied: "To marry a rich widow with a bad cough."

"The devil's dead, minister," said two gents, scoffingly, at an old clergyman. "Ay, so I heard," replied the assailed, "and I'm wae for ye, twa pair fatherless bairns."

HARDWARE.

ATTENTION EVERY BODY!

Buy Where You Can Buy Cheapest and get Good Articles.

If you want good hoes and forks, go to Thomas' Hardware Store.

If you want good scythes and snaths cheap, go to Thomas'.

HARDWARE.

If you want fine table and pocket cutlery, go to Thomas' Cheap Store.

If you want nails or iron cheap, go straight to Thomas', and no where else.

If you want any kind of tools cheap and good, go to Thomas.

If you want hatchets or axes of the best quality, go to Thomas' Cheap Store.

If you want kerosene oil cheap and good go to Thomas.

HARDWARE.

If you want stoves and tinware of the best quality and cheap as the cheapest, go to the cheap hardware store of John Thomas.

If you want locks, latches, butts and screws, or any kind of house trimmings, Thomas' is the place to buy.

If you want sheep shears, gopher traps, smooth irons, iron bench screws, augurs, augur bitts, hand bells, cow bells, or any article kept in a hardware store, go to Thomas' and get it cheap and of the best quality.

HARDWARE.

Try it and see if you cannot make money at it.

JOHN THOMAS.

Hastings, May 14, 1863. 5-tf

HARDWARE.

M. MC HUGH,

Dealer in

HARDWARE,
TINWARE,
STOVES, ETC.,

Corner of Second and Vermillion Streets, Hastings, Minnesota,

has on hand and is constantly receiving a general assortment and a full supply of

Iron,
Nails,
Tinware,
Glass,
Sash,
And
Putty,

Also the best stock of

CUTLERY

ever before exhibited in this market. These goods have been bought expressly for this trade, and will be sold on the most reasonable terms for cash.

I am also agent for, and have on hand, the celebrated

STEWART COOKING STOVE,

known to be the best cooking stove manufactured.

Hastings, May 14, 1863. 5-tf

H. H. PRINGLE,

Wholesale and Retail Dealer in:

HARDWARE, IRON, NAILS,

STOVES AND TINWARE,

Mechanics' Tools,

Building Materials,

AGRICULTURAL IMPLEMENTS,

PAINTS, OILS, GLASS,

SASH, DOORS, BLINDS, ETC

HASTINGS, MIN.

TIN,

SHEET IRON & COPPER W'K

ON HAND OR MADE TO ORDER.

BRICK DRUG STORE,

R. J. MARVIN.

Dealer in

DRUGS,
MEDICINES,
CHEMICALS,
ETC., ETC.

On hand a large stock of

PAINTS,
OILS,
COLORS,
GLASS, AND
PAINTERS'
STOCK GENERALLY.

Also

Garden and Field

SEEDS.

Please give me a call before purchasing. Try my goods and prices, which is a better test than blowing.

May 1, 1863. 2-tf

PRINTING.

ALL KINDS OF

PRINTING

Neatly and Cheaply Executed

AT THE

CONSERVER OFFICE.

Cards,

Programmes,

Bill-Heads,

Circulars,

Posters,

Etc.,

Printed to Order and at

SHORT NOTICE.

Having received a choice supply of

NEW MATERIAL

from the East, am prepared to do

PLAIN AND FANCY WORK,

in styles to defy competition.

Orders from the country promptly attended to.

IRVING TODD.

FURNITURE.

H. BUTTURFF,

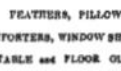

Manufacturer and Dealer in

FURNITURE, UPHOLSTERY,

DOMESTIC WILLOW WARE,

CRIBS, HOBBY HORSES,

PROPELLERS, BABY-JUMPERS,

FEATHERS, PILLOWS, MATRESSES

COMFORTERS, WINDOW SHADES,

TABLE and FLOOR OIL CLOTH,

CARPETS, CURLED HAIR, etc. etc.

PARLOR FURNITURE,

Cane Seat and Common Chairs, Extention, Dining and Centre Tables, Rocking Chairs, Bedsteads, Wardrobes, Bureaus, Tin Safes, Picture Frames and Looking glasses.

I keep employed the best of workmen, and manufacture to order, with neatness and dispatch.

N. B. Coffins on hand and made to order.

Hastings, Nov. 20, 1862. 32-tf

THE LIVING AND THE DEAD CAN be supplied at

Herzog & Corson's

with all kinds of

Sash, Doors,
Blinds, Chairs,
Cabinet Ware,
Planing, Matching,
Sawing, Turning
Etc., Etc.

Coffins of all kinds and styles, a large lot always on hand. Sole agents for

THE METALLIC BURIAL CASES.

Come and buy a good article cheap for cash or produce. Wood, Lumber, Pork, etc. taken in exchange for work.

Sale Rooms and Factory corner of Second and Eddy Streets, west of S. Eager's store. HERZOG & CORSON.

Hastings, Jan. 1, 1863. 38-tf

MISCELLANEOUS.

P. VAN AUKEN. H. H. LANGLEY

VAN AUKEN & LANGLEY,

STORAGE,

FORWARDING & COMMISS'N

MERCHANTS,

Dealers in Produce, and Agents for

Threshing Machines and Reapers,

RAILROAD & STEAMBOAT

TICKET AGENTS.

EQUITABLE LIFE ASSURANCE SOCIETY,

OF NEW YORK.

CASH CAPITAL,	$100,000
NET SURPLUS,	$138,000

Dividends on capital limited by its charter to seven per cent per annum—the entire profits go to the policy holders.

R. W. MONTGOMERY, Agent.

Hastings, Minn. Office on First Street in Gardner's new stone block. 42-1y

BLACKSMITH SHOP.

PLOWS! PLOWS!! PLOWS!!

I have just established myself in the above business on Second Street, above Herzog & Corson's Furniture Factory, and am prepared to do all kinds of Blacksmithing.

Also, constantly on hand all kinds of plows of the most approved patterns and made of the best material. I shall be obliged for a share of public patronage, and shall always warrant my work to be of the best quality. JOHN BATEMAN.

Hastings, Nov. 20, 1862. 32-tf

BOOKS AND STATIONERY.

W. P. STANLEY,

DEALER IN

Books and Stationery,

Paper Hangings, Curtains, Fixtures, Cord, and Tassels; buff and green Holland, oil green cloth for shades; Photographs of our generals and other distinguished individuals and albums to put them in; Yankee Notions, all the leading Magazines and Newspapers, Eastern and Western, St. Paul Dailies; agent for Prince & Sons Melodeons. 41-tf

CAPITAL NEW BOOKS, JUST PUBLISHED BY

JOHN BRADBURN,

(Successor to M. DOOLADY,)

Bookseller, Publisher, and Wholesale Book Jobber,

49 WALKER STREET,

(near Broadway,)

NEW YORK CITY.

Leaves from the Diary of an Army Surgeon.

By DOCTOR THOS. T. ELLIS,

Late Post Surgeon at New York, and acting Medical Director at White House, Va.

Cloth. 350 pages. 12mo. Price $1.

A Liberal Discount to the Trade.

Each copy contains an autograph letter from Gen. McClellan.

DR. CUMMING'S REPLY TO BISHOP COLENSO.

Bishop Colenso Fully Answered.

His Errors refuted, and the Mosaic authorship of the Pentateuch clearly established, by the Rev. John Cumming, D. D., in a series of lectures.

Cloth. 271 pp. Price $1.

The Actress in High Life.

AN EPISODE IN WINTER QUARTERS.

By a lady of South Carolina.

Cloth. 461 pp. 12mo. $1 25.

Adventures by Sea and Land of the Count de Gonay;

OR, THE DEVOTION AND FIDELITY OF WOMAN

An Episode of the Colonization of Canada.

By H. EMILE CHEVALIER.

Cloth. 312 pp. 12mo. $1.

Les Miserables.

By VICTOR HUGO.

Five Volumes in One.

Fantine, Cosette, Marius, St. Denis, Valjean.

Cloth. 476 pp. 8vo. $1 50.

Hans of Iceland;

THE DEMON OF THE NORTH.

A Romance.

By VICTOR HUGO.

Cloth. 187 pp. 8vo. 50c.

Arbitrary Arrests in the South.

SCENES IN THE EXPERIENCE OF AN ALABAMA UNIONIST.

By R. S. THARIN, A. M.

Native of Charleston; for thirty years a resident of the Cotton States; and commonly known in the West as "the Alabama Refugee."

Cloth. 245 pp. 12mo. $1.

Lives and Letters of Abelard and Heloise.

By O. W. WIGHT.

Cloth. 319 pp. 12mo. $1.

Three Years in Chili.

Cloth. 158 pp. 12mo. 75c.

Woods and Waters.

THE SARANACS AND RACKET.

By ALFRED B. STREET.

Cloth. 341 pp. 12mo. $1 25.

Stories of Frontier Adventure in the South and West.

By W. T. COGGESHALL,

Author of Home Hits and Hints, Poets and Poetry of the West, etc.

Cloth. 313 pp. 12mo. $1.

The Battle of Waterloo.

By VICTOR HUGO.

Paper Covers. 75 pp. 16mo. 15c.

Trips in the Life of a Locomotive Engineer.

Paper Covers. 224 pp. 12mo. 50c.

Cloth, $1.

Our Farm of Four Acres,

AND THE MONEY WE MADE BY IT.

From the 12th London Ed. by Harriet Martineau.

Paper Covers. 148 pp. 12mo. 25c. Cloth 50c.

These Books may be obtained at Retail, in this town, from the store of W. D. STANLEY, on Ramsey Street. 16-1m

THE ATLANTIC MONTHLY.—BEGINNING of a new volume. The number for January, 1863, begins the eleventh volume of the *Atlantic Monthly*. From the commencement, in 1859, the *Atlantic* has rapidly increased in circulation, and it now has the largest class of readers since its beginning, five years ago. Its prosperity steadily augments, and it continues, amid all the fluctuations and dangers incident to our national crisis, to gain ground in the estimation of the public. At a time so pregnant with events which touch the future destinies of America in every vital particular, the publishers and editors do not deem it necessary to promise that its pages will never swerve from the honest paths of loyal patriotism and universal freedom. Its opinions have always been on the side of Liberty, Progress, and Right, and the course it first adopted in its early career will ever be faithfully maintained.

The staff of writers regularly contributing to the *Atlantic Monthly* embraces many of the best known authors in American literature, and warrants the publishers in promising to its readers the best essays, the best stories, the best poems, which American talent can furnish.

LIST OF REGULAR CONTRIBUTORS.

In prose and poetry the *Atlantic* staff of writers is unequaled. The following authors are still among the regular contributors: James Russell Lowell, Henry W. Longfellow, Louis Agassiz, Ralph Waldo Emerson, Nathaniel Hawthorne, T. W. Higginson, Author "Margret Howth," Oliver W. Holmes, John G. Whittier, E. P. Whipple, Bayard Taylor, George S. Hillard, Mrs. H. B. Stowe, "The Country Parson," Rose Terry, Harriet E. Prescott. The *Atlantic's* list of contributors includes many of the leading writers of America.

TERMS.—The *Atlantic* is for sale by all book and periodical dealers. Price 25 cts a number. Subscriptions for the year $3, postage paid. Yearly subscriptions received or single numbers supplied by any dealer, or by the publishers. Specimen numbers sent gratis on application to the publishers. Inducements for subscribing, list of premiums, etc., furnished on application to the publishers.

TICKNOR & FIELDS, Publishers,
135 Washington Street,
44-tf Boston, Mass.

PUBLICATIONS.

THE CONTINENTAL MONTHLY.—The readers of the *Continental* are aware of the important position it has assumed, of the influence which it exerts, and of the brilliant array of political and literary talent of the highest order which supports it. No publication of the kind has, in this country, so successfully combined the energy and freedom of the daily newspaper with the higher literary tone of the first-class monthly; and it is very certain that the magazine has given wider range to its contributors, or preserved itself so completely from the narrow influences of party or faction. In times like the present, such a journal is either a power in the land or it is nothing. That the *Continental* is not the latter is abundantly evinced by what it has done—by the reflection of its counsels in many important public events, and in the character and power of those who are its staunchest supporters.

Though but little more than a year has elapsed since the *Continental* was first established, it has during that time acquired a strength and a political significance elevating it to a position far above that previously occupied by any publication of the kind in America. In proof of which assertion we call attention to the following facts:

1. Of its political articles republished in pamphlet form, a single one has had, thus far, a circulation of one hundred and six thousand copies.

2. From its literary department, a single serial novel, Among the Pines, has, within a very few months, sold nearly thirty-five thousand copies. Two other series of its literary articles have also been republished in book form, while the first portion of a third is already in press.

No more conclusive facts need to be alleged to prove the excellence of the contributions to the *Continental*, or their extraordinary popularity; and its conductors are determined that it shall not fall behind. Preserving all "the boldness, vigor, and ability" which a thousand journals have attributed to it, it will greatly enlarge its circle of action, and discuss, fearlessly and frankly, every principle involved in the great questions of the day. The first minds of the country, embracing the men most familiar with its diplomacy and most distinguished for ability, are among its contributors; and it is no mere flattering promise of a prospectus to say that this magazine for the times will employ the first intellect in America, under auspices which no publication ever enjoyed before in this country.

While the *Continental* will express decided opinions on the great questions of the day, it will not be a mere political journal: much the larger portion of its columns will be enlivened, as heretofore, by tales, poetry, and humor. In a word, the *Continental* will be found, under its new staff of editors, occupying a position and presenting attractions never before found in a magazine.

TERMS TO CLUBS.

Two copies for one year,	$ 5 00
Three copies for one year,	6 00
Six copies for one year,	11 00
Eleven copies for one year,	20 00
Twenty copies for one year,	36 00

Paid in advance. Postage 36 cents a year, to be paid by the subscriber. Single copies $3 a year, in advance. Postage paid by the publisher. 12-tf

JOHN F. TROW, 50 Greene St., N.Y.,
Publisher for the Proprietors.

ONLY $1 25 A YEAR IN CLUBS OF 4

Arthur's Home Magazine,

For 1863. Vols. XXI. and XXII. Edited by T. S. Arthur and Virginia F. Townsend. Contains novelets, stories, poetry, fashions, steel and wood engravings, needlework patterns in great variety, a mother's department, children's department, housekeeper's and health departments, with literary reviews, and all the accessories of a first-class magazine.

The Lady's Book bears this flattering testimony to the character of *Arthur's Home Magazine*:

"As we have often before said, it is, without controversy, the best $2 magazine published in the country; and this is the strongly outspoken testimony everywhere given by the press. We know of no periodical that so well deserves the praise bestowed. The editors never tire in their endeavors to give each month a rich and varied literary repast to their readers. Their work is kept fully up to the standard of their promise, is never dull, yet always full of instruction. We have often said, and repeat it again, that it should make a part of the reading of every household. We know of no better educator of the people, young and old. Of the editors we need not speak; their names are household words all over the country. In their hands no periodical can fail to reach the highest point of excellence."

A new serial by T. S. Arthur will be commenced in the January number entitled Out in the World.

Rare and elegant premiums are sent to all who make up clubs: 1. A large photographic copy of that splendid engraving Shakspeare and his Cotemporaries. 2. A large photographic copy from an engraving of Huntington's celebrated picture Mercy's Dream. 3. A similar copy of Herring's Glimpse of an English Homestead.

TERMS.—$2 a year in advance and one premium plate. Two copies $3. Three for $4. Four for $5. Eight and one to getter up of club for $10. One of the premium plates is sent to every getter up of a club, small or large. Three red stamps must be sent to pay the postage on each premium. Address

T. S. ARTHUR & Co.,
323 Walnut Street, Philadelphia.

THE INDEPENDENT, EDITED BY *Henry Ward Beecher*, is a religious newspaper, and a real newspaper. It affords its readers fair and thoughtful editorial discussions of the most important facts and occurrences and interests of this nation and of the world. A comprehensive record of facts, men and movements of the religious world. A full and careful weekly history of the progress of the rebellion. Ample chronicles of the important general news; home and foreign. Fair and careful accounts of new books; made on the express principle of serving as a safe guide to buyers. Interesting correspondence from Washington; from the West; from the army; from abroad. Six columns a week of carefully selected matter for family reading; being prose and poetry, suited to interest both the old people and the young people. A full chronicle of the progress of business and of the current prices of merchandise, produce and live stock in New York City

ONE SERMON EVERY WEEK

By Rev. Henry Ward Beecher. The following eminent writers are special contributors to its columns:—

Mrs. Harriet Beecher Stowe,
Rev. Theodore L. Cuyler,
Rev. Robert M. Hatfield,
Rev. George B. Cheever,
Horace Greely,
Bayard Taylor,
John G. Whittier.

TERMS.—$2 per annum, paid in advance. Specimen numbers sent gratis.

JOSEPH H. RICHARDS, Publisher,
No. 5 Beekman Street, New York.

For sale by news agents.

PATENT MEDICINES.

"To put up Vim entrench our power,
For the whole boundless Continent is ours."

DR. ROBACK'S

BLOOD PURIFIER

and

BLOOD PILLS

have been introduced to the public for more than six years, and have acquired an

Immense Popularity,

far exceeding any Family Medicines of a similar nature in the market.

An appreciating public was not long in discovering they possessed remarkable

Curative Properties,

and hence their

Rapid Sale

and consequent profit to the Proprietor, thus enabling him to expend

Many Thousands

of dollars each year in advertising their merits, and publishing the

Numerous Certificates

which have been showered upon him from

All parts of the Country.

The peculiarity of the

Blood Purifier and Pills

is that they strike at the root of Disease, by eradicating every particle of impurity

In the Blood,

for the life and health of the body depends upon the purity of the blood.

If the blood is poisoned, the body drags out a miserable existence. These medicines

Are Unequaled

for curing

Scrofula, Liver Complaint,
Skin Diseases, Female Complaints,
Salt Rheum, Rheumatism,
Dyspepsia, Syphilis,
Old Sores, Fever and Ague,
Leucorrhœa, Sick Headache,
Erysipelas, St. Anthony's Fire,
Tumors, Eruptions,
Fits, Scrofulous Consumption, etc.

ONE person writes, her daughter was cured of fits of nine years' standing, and St. Vitus' dance of two years.

ANOTHER writes, his son was cured after his flesh had almost wasted away. The doctors pronounced the case incurable.

ANOTHER was cured of Fever and Ague after trying every medicine in his reach.

ANOTHER was cured of Fever Sore which had existed fourteen years.

ANOTHER of Rheumatism of eight years.

Cases innumerable of Dyspepsia and Liver Complaint could be mentioned in which the Purifier and Pills

Work like a Charm.

The Blood Pills

are the most active and thorough pills that have ever been introduced.

They act so directly upon the Liver, exciting that organ to such an extent as that the system does not relapse into its former condition, which is too apt to be the case with simply a purgative pill.

They are really a

Blood and Liver Pill,

which, in conjunction with the

Blood Purifier,

will cure all the aforementioned diseases, and, of themselves, will relieve and cure

Headache, Costiveness,
Colic Pains, Cholera Morbus,
Indigestion, Pain in the Bowels,
Dizziness, etc.

Try these medicines, and you will never regret it.

Ask your neighbors, who have used them, and they will say they are

Good Medicines,

and you should try them before going for a physician.

Get a Pamphlet or Almanac of my local agent, and read the certificates, and if you have ever doubted you will

Doubt no more.

As a proof that the Blood Purifier and Pills are purely vegetable, I have the certificates of those eminent chemists, Professors Chilton of New York, and Locke of Cincinnati.

Read Dr. Roback's Special Notices and Certificates published in a conspicuous part of this Paper from time to time.

Price of the Scandinavian Vegetable Blood Purifier, $1 per bottle, or $5 per half dozen. Of the Scandinavian Vegetable Blood Pills, 25 cents per box, or 5 boxes for $1.

Principal Office and Salesroom, No. 6 East Fourth St., 2d Building from Main St., Cincinnati, O. Laboratory, No. 18 Hammond Street.

FOR SALE BY

A. M. Pett, Hastings, J. R. Tinkcom, Mankato, W. H. McCollom, Mankato, and by druggists and merchants generally throughout the United States, Canadas and Brazil.

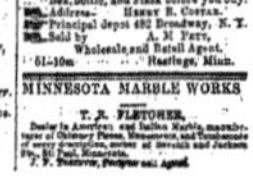

For Rats, Mice, Roaches, Ants, Bed Bugs, Moths in Furs, Woolens, etc., Insects on Plants, Fowls, Animals, etc. Put up in 25c, 50c, and $1 00 Boxes, Bottles, and Flasks. $3 and $5 sizes for Hotels, Public Institutions, etc.

"Only infallible remedies known."
"Free from Poisons."
"Not dangerous to the Human Family."
"Rats come out of their holes to die."

Sold wholesale in all large cities.
Sold by all druggists and retailers every where.
Beware! of all worthless imitations.
See that COSTAR's name is on each Box, Bottle, and Flask before you buy.
Address HENRY R. COSTAR.
Principal depot 482 Broadway, N. Y.
Sold by A. M. PETT,
Wholesale and Retail Agent,
51-10m Hastings, Minn.

MINNESOTA MARBLE WORKS

T. R. FLETCHER,

Dealer in American and Italian Marble, manufacturer of Chimney Pieces, Monuments, and Tombstones of every description, corner of Seventh and Jackson Sts., St. Paul, Minnesota.

T. P. [illegible], Proprietor and Agent.

Continued From First Page.

subscribers to some good educational journal. Instead of plodding along in the old ways they should take high grounds on the following, among other points:—

1. That teaching is a *profession* for which thorough qualifications are demanded, and that among them are accuracy in the use of language, conciseness in definitions, facility in illustration, an exact knowledge of all the sciences in which they are required by law to sustain an examination, a general understanding of those branches which will especially aid them in imparting instruction, a thorough knowledge of the details of the school room, and a discreet firmness in efforts to secure good order.

2. That the system of graded schools should be advocated for rural districts, as well as for our larger places, wherever the pupils are sufficient in number and qualifications for such schools, and that even where they are not some approximation to the plan should be made in the arrangement of classes in the same school room.

3. That school house architecture sustains an intimate relation to the intellectual and moral refinement of pupils, and that the people should be urged to make improvements in this respect.

4. And, in fine, that parents must be induced to co-operate with teachers in such measures as may be necessary to secure punctuality and regularity in the attendance of pupils and thoroughness in the order of the school.

Your committee recommend that the report of the executive committee, placed in our hands, be accepted and placed on file.

Gov. Holcombe, from nominating committee, made the following report, which was adopted:—

President,—Prof. T. F. Thickstun, of Hastings.

Vice President,—W. Holcombe, of Stillwater.

Secretary,—J. W. Stearns, of Winona.

Treasurer,—E. J. Thompson, of Chatfield.

Executive Committee,—Rev. D. Burt, of Winona, Prof. A. D. Williams, of Wasioja, Rev. J. Brooks, of Red Wing, I. Mattocks, of St. Paul, Mr. Risser, of Minneapolis.

Prof. Brooks, from executive committee, made the following report as to business of next meeting, which was adopted:

Paper on School Gymnastics,—J. W. Stearns, of Winona.

Educational Men Should be appointed to Educational Offices of every Description,—Prof. A. D. Williams, of Wasioja.

At What Age Should Scholars Begin the Study of Mathematics,—Prof. Thorp, of Red Wing.

The Application of the Graded System of Schools to Rural Districts,—V. J. Walker, of Winona.

Object Teaching,—Prof. Brooks, of Red Wing.

Course of Study for Graded Schools,—E. J. Thompson, of Chatfield.

School Room Practice,—B. F. Miller, of Monticello.

On motion of Prof. Brooks, Messrs. A. J. Meacham, Lewis, and C. C. Webster were appointed a local committee to make arrangements for the next meeting of convention.

Song by choir.

Mr. Dale, from music committee, reported in favor of the *Silver Lute* published by Messrs. Root & Cady, of Chicago. Adopted.

On motion of Mr. Shandrew, the secretary was directed to correspond with the publishers in reference to the introduction of the *Silver Lute* into the common schools of the state.

On motion of Rev. D. Burt, Dr. Ford, Prof. Brooks, Rev. Chas. S. Le Duc were appointed a committee to nominate six delegates to the national teachers' convention.

Dr. Ford, from the committee on qualifications of teachers, made a verbal report. Prof. W. T. Hatch, of same committee, reported the following resolution, which was adopted:

Resolved, That as an efficient means of elevating the character of the common schools of this state we urge upon school examiners to require a higher standard of qualifications in teachers and upon school boards more care in the employment of none but those who are well qualified and experienced teachers.

b t y t d

a committee on printing.

Rev. L. B. Tefft reported $28 15 already raised for the *School Friend*.

Committee on delegates to national convention reported Dr. Ford, Prof. Brooks, Prof Thickstun, Rev. J. G. Riheldaffer, Prof. Williams, Gov. Holcombe, with power to appoint substitutes. Adopted.

Adjourned till evening.

EVENING SESSION.

by b b by h
l by
of Winona.

Song by choir.

Lecture by Rev. L. B. Tefft, of Wenona; subject, The Active and Passive in Education.

The minutes of the second day's session were read and approved.

Song by the choir.

d b d
by

Our Ticket—Opinions of the Press.
From the Winona Republican:

Since the withdrawal of acting Governor Swift from the canvass, a few days ago, it became apparent that Col. Miller would be the nominee. He is well known in the state as a man of energy, ability, and honesty, and one whose patriotism has been well attested on the tented field, in battling with the enemies of our country. At the outset of our nation's troubles, he buckled on his armor and went forth as lieut. colonel of our glorious Minnesota First, and though he seemed to shun promotion, his patriotic services have been acknowledged on all hands wherever duty has called him. We believe he will make a competent and faithful governor, of which no Minnesotian need feel ashamed. Of Mr. Snerwood, of Fillmore county, the nominee for lieut. governor, who was the Speaker of the House at the last session of our Legislature, we have frequently before spoke in commendation. His constituents have amply indorsed him, and will indorse him for for a higher office on election day.

Mr. Blakely has discharged the duties of Secretary of State, since the resignation of Mr. Baker, with such entire acceptability that his renomination was conceded on all hands. He is a gentleman, and a faithful and competent officer.

The state is grateful for the service rendered by Messrs. Cole, Scheffer and McIlrath, and their re-nomination for the offices which they respectively hold, is the strongest of testimonials of their fitness for their several posts, and the esteem in which they are held by the union republican party of the state.

Mr. Potter, nominated for Clerk of the Supreme Court, has the esteem and confidence of the people of Houston, who have manifested their regard for him by unanimously asking for his nomination. That he will, by his acts, justify his neighbors' opinions of him, those who know him best will not doubt.

The ticket taken together embodies much personal merit. Let the loyal people of Minnesota go to work and elect it by such a majority as shall not leave a shadow of doubt as to the side on which our young state stands, in upholding the government in prosecuting the present war for the freedom and unity of our common country.

Elsewhere we publish the proceedings of the state convention, held on Wednesday of last week. Our readers will perceive that the convention was very harmonious in nominations, and the ticket nominated, in the main, is a very good one. We should, for some reasons, have preferred to see Mr. Baldwin in the place of Col. Miller. We believe he would make quite as good a governor as Col. Miller, but not as good a colonel, and we are decidedly opposed to taking a single man from the army, in the present condition of the country, for a civil officer, while civilians equally as competent can be found to occupy them. Col. Miller has been well liked as a colonel in the

d l l l

about it, but we should prefer being colonel of a good regiment to be governor of Minnesota, in the present crisis.

C. D. Sherwood, the nominee for Lieut. Governor, we think will be found one of the best nominations for that

th ld b v b d

long since named him as our candidate for that place. He is an active, energetic man, and as Speaker of the House last winter showed himself possessed of more than ordinary ability as a presiding officer.

Mr. McIlrath, the auditor, has made a very efficient officer, and his management of the school and state lands has been eminently satisfactory to the people

b l t
l t t h

capable and efficient officer, and we hope he will be elected by a large majority. Charley is an honor to the country of his nativity as well as the country of his adoption, and we haven't the least objection to Uncle Sam's adopting just as many such nephews as he pleases. Every loyal and true hearted German in the state will vote for Charley.

G. E. Cole, the candidate for Attorney General, has filled the office with credit to himself, and we believe advantageously to the state; at least the slight opposition made to his nomination is good evidence that a large majority of the convention believe him the most competent man for the place to be found.

Of course as the fellow citizen and neighbor of the attorney we are much obliged for the third compliment to the Rice County Bar.

D. Blakely, for Secretary of State was not our choice, but seems to have been that of the convention.

Considering the present condition of the country, what a national calamity it would be for any loyal state to pass in whole or part into the hands of copperheads, (self-styled democrats,) sympathizers with Jeff.'s rebellion. There is but one course for any loyal man to pursue, and that is to support the whole ticket.

From the Monticello Statesman.

The republican union ticket put in nomination as above, at the state convention held at St. Paul on Wednesday last, will recommend itself to the hearty support of all true and loyal friends of the government.

In times like these, the risk is too great to trust important national interests to those whose conversion to loyalty has not the assurance and guaranty of a reasonable probation.

We are personally acquainted with all the candidates except the lieut. governor. No one will question the integrity, patriotism, or energy of Col. Miller, and we are assured that whatever position he may occupy, the duties will be discharged with promptness and fidelity.

The nomination of Mr. Sherwood through the influence of those who know him, and his acceptable discharge of the duties of speaker of the house. Mr. Blakely is known to have been a very popular and efficient clerk in the legislature for several years past, and is every way a gentleman besides being good looking.

Mr. McIlrath, Mr. Scheffer, and Mr. Cole, are well known everywhere and

t d by l t
t ll
l d v b v

his position, he is industrious, indefatigable, accurate and reliable.

Let everybody support the ticket.

From the Mankato Record (dem.).

The republicans have certainly made an excellent nomination for governor. Col. Miller is, as we have before stated one of the very best men in the state. He is "honest, capable and true to his country," as he has demonstrated by the manner in which he has discharged every trust conferred upon him; and that, if elected, he will make a good executive officer, we sincerely believe, as his abilities are peculiarly suited for that position. In speaking thus of Col. Miller, we but do justice to a worthy man, though a political opponent; and should the democracy fail in the election of its standard-bearer, we have the satisfaction of knowing that the gubernatorial honors will fall upon a man in every respect worthy of them.

From the Mower Co. Register.

We are glad to place such a ticket at the head of our columns. The nominee for governor is perhaps the most popular man in the state, and we do not believe a better man could have been selected for the important position.

Charles D. Sherwood is known to the people of this community as a man who will do honor to the office to which he is nominated.

The remainder of the ticket consists of old officers, with the exception of Geo. F. Potter, nominee for Clerk of the Supreme Court, who have been tried and proved to be good men, and worth of their positions.

Mr. Potter will prove himself acceptable to the voters of Minnesota.

The republican union state convention was one of the most enthusiastic and harmonious ever convened in this state. The men placed in nomination for the different offices are all worthy the support of the people. Take the ticket entire, headed by the noble patriot, soldier, and statesman, Col. Stephen Miller, and we can with truth say that no better one was ever placed in the field in Minnesota. We invite a careful perusal of the platform. It is one that war democrats, as well as republicans, must approve in every particular.

The ticket nominated at the recent republican state convention, will be found at the head of our columns this

d d by v t t l t
th y l y l
t

ation be elected by an overwhelming majority as against any candidates running on a less loyal and patriotic platform.

b d t l

executive committee, which was appointed at the last national democratic convention, eleven are now open traitors.

MONETARY QUOTATIONS OF FOLLETT & RENICK.

New England, New York, New Jersey, Ohio, Canada, Philadelphia, Marine Bank, Minn., Bank of Chatfield, Peoples' Bank,

Bank State of Indiana, Iowa, Michigan, U. S. Demand Notes, Wisconsin, Bank of Minnesota, Winona Co. Bank, State Bank of Minn., Pittsburg.

Exchange.

FOR BANKABLE FUNDS.

	Buying.	Selling.
New York, Philadelphia, Boston, Chicago and Milwaukee,	½ prem. par.	½ prem. ½ prem.

PREMIUM FUNDS.

Gold,	[illegible]	25
Silver (large),	[illegible]	20
U. S. Demand Notes,	20	20
Canada,	[illegible]	20

RETAIL PRICES CURRENT.

FLOUR, per sack,	$2 50
WHEAT, per bushel,	60a65
CORN, do	40a45
OATS, do	40
POTATOES, do	40
BEANS, do	1 50
ONIONS, do	50
CRANBERRIES,	2 00
HAY, per ton,	4 00a5 00
WOOD, per cord,	3 00a4 00
SALT, per bbl	3 50
EGGS, per doz	15
BUTTER, per lb,	10a15
CHEESE, per lb	8a12
PORK, per cwt,	5a6
BEEF, per cwt,	3 00
HAMS, per cwt,	8a9
SHOULDERS, per cwt,	5a6
DRIED APPLES,	9
DRIED PEACHES,	18a20
SUGARS, per lb	12a17
MOLASSES, per gal.	70a1 00
COFFEE, Java,	40
do Rio,	35

WANTED.

Two Marble Workers, immediately. Apply at the Winona Marble Works, or at this office.

Hastings, Aug. 18, 1863. 19-tf

NEW ENGLAND HOTEL RE-OPENED.

CHAS. DAMEREL,

Having leased the above property, has thoroughly cleaned and refurnished the above old established hotel at Hastings, and is ready to do all in his power to conduce to the comfort and satisfaction of the travelling community, and solicits a share of public patronage.

In connection with the hotel I keep a livery and sale stable and feel confident I can please the majority with pleasant driving horses and steady and obliging drivers.

Teaming done at fair prices. Please call and see me at New England House.

CHAS. DAMEREL, Proprietor.

Hastings, Aug. 10, 1863. 18-6m

FARMING IMPLEMENTS.

U U

Hastings, - - Minnesota.

Indiana Fanning Mills,

We are now prepared to repair all kinds of agricultural implements in the best manner, and at short notice.

Thankful for the liberal encouragement we have received in the past we hope, by strict and prompt attention to business, to merit a continuation of it in the future.

Hastings, June 14, 1863. 10-tf.

COPARTNERSHIP NOTICE.

The undersigned, having formed a partnership connection under the firm name of Gardner & Meloy as dealers in all kinds of agricultural implements and the latest valuable and useful patents, to-wit:

J. H. Manny's Reaper and Mower.

The Ohio Reaper and Mower.

Header,

Warranted,

Mills.

The Model Clothes Dryer.
Linen Grain Bags.
Garden Rakes and Hoes.
Scythe Snaths and Stones.
Two, Three, and Four Tine Forks.

via Dunleith. Express passenger trains leave Dunleith morning and evening, making quick time and close connections to all points

EAST AND SOUTH.

No change of cars between Dunleith and Chicago. Elegant sleeping cars attached to night trains. Baggage checked through to all important points. Fare lower to southern points than any other railroad line, and as low to eastern cities as the lowest.

This is the only direct route to

St. Louis and Cairo,

and passengers will arrive at these points from eighteen to twenty-four hours quicker than by any route through Chicago.

Freight transported to Milwaukee, Chicago, or points South and East at as low rates and as quick time guaranteed as by any other route from the Mississippi River.

J. S. TILDESLY,
Gen. Western Agent.

Inquire for tickets by Illinois Central Railroad.

SAMUEL ROGERS, JR., Agent,
Cor. Vermillion and 2d Streets,
16-3m Hastings, Minn.

1863. PRAIRIE DU CHIEN ROUTE 1863.

For Milwaukee, Chicago, and all points East. The only direct route making sure connections, ample time being allowed on the river to insure the connection beyond any probable contingency.

The splendid first-class steamers

unequalled in elegance, speed, and comfort by any other line, leave Hastings daily about 10 P. M., making direct connection with express train leaving Prairie du Chien at 7.45 A. M., arriving at Milwaukee at 3.50 P. M., and Chicago 5.50 P. M., making direct connections at both points with trains for the East.

The change from steamers to cars being made at 7.45 A. M., passengers get a full night's rest and breakfast on board; advantages that cannot be secured by any other route. Magnificent palace cars with patent ventilators and dusters, rendering cars free from dust, and keeping the air pure and cool.

Through from Prairie du Chien to Milwaukee and Chicago without change of cars. Passengers by this route arrive at Chicago and all points East at the same time as via La Crosse, and twelve hours than via Dunleith. Fare as low as by any other route. VAN AUKEN & LANGLEY,
9-tf Agents, on Levee.

NEW YORK ADVERT'MENTS.

ENVELOPES AND WRITING PAPERS, AT WHOLESALE.

To Booksellers, Stationers, Druggists, Dealers in Fancy Goods, Merchants, and all others who purchase Envelopes and Writing Papers.

SAMUEL RAYNOR,

Begs leave to call the attention of dealers in Envelopes to the extensive assortment and superior quality of those manufactured by him. His machinery for manufacturing Envelopes is the latest and best—folding and gumming them in the most perfect manner. The assortment embraces over 700 kinds, including every size, style, color, and quality. The subscriber now has facilities for manufacturing half a million Envelopes per day, so that all orders can be filled promptly. Also the Irving and Harrison Mills Writing Papers, by the case, or in any quantity to suit the purchaser. All offered at the lowest possible prices, on the usual credit, or a discount off for cash.

Samples, with trade list of prices, furnished, when requested, and sent by mail free of postage. SAMUEL RAYNOR.

For sale in Hastings by W. D. Stanley, on Ramsey Street. 18-1m

y

Our Catalogue now embraces considerably over four thousand different subjects (to which additions are continually being made) of Portraits of Eminent Americans, etc., viz:

72 Major-Generals,	525 Statesmen,
190 Brig.-Generals,	127 Divines,
259 Colonels,	116 Authors,
84 Lieut.-Colonels,	30 Artists,
207 Other Officers,	112 Stage,
60 Navy Officers,	46 Prominent Women,

147 Prominent Foreign Portraits.

2,500 COPIES OF WORKS OF ART,

Including reproductions of the most celebrated Engravings, Paintings, Statutes, etc. Catalogues sent on receipt of stamp. An order for One Dozen Pictures from our catalogue will be filled on receipt of $1 80, and sent by mail *free*.

Photographic Albums.

Of these we manufacture a great variety, ranging in price from 50 cents to $50. Our Albums have the reputation of being superior to any others. The smaller kinds can be sent safely by mail at a postage of six cents per oz. The more expensive can be sent by express.

We also keep a large assortment of Stereoscopes & Stereoscopic Views. Our Catalogue of these will be sent to any address on receipt of stamp.

E. & H. T. ANTHONY,
Manufacturers of Photographic Materials,
501 Broadway, New York.

Friends or relatives of prominent military men will confer a favor by sending us their likenesses to copy. They will be kept carefully and returned uninjured.

Fine Albums made to order for congregations to present to their pastor, or for other purposes, with suitable inscriptions.

17-6mo

t t b

J

Importer, Wholesale Stationer,

And sole agent for Windsor and Clifton Mills Premium Papers, consisting of Commercial Notes, Letters, Bill, Legal, and Fools Caps, No. 18 Beekman Street, near Nassau, New York. Also proprietor and sole agent for the following new and useful articles:

Oliver's Patent Erasive Tips.

This Tip is different from any heretofore made, being easily fitted to any pencil. It is manufactured from vulcanized rubber of the best erasive quality, can be readily changed from one pencil to another, and is sold at an extremely low price. It is the most desirable article of the kind in the market.

Burnett's Patent Rubber Inkstand and Rack, an opaque inkstand, preserving ink from the decomposing effect of light.

Green's Patent Ink-Eraser & Paper-Cleaner, the best article made for rubbing out pencil-marks, accomplishing the work in one-half the time of ordinary rubber

The Patent Combination Paper-Cutter and Ruler,

l

Merritt & Brown's Pig Pen, a very superior steel pen, made and selected with the greatest care; put up two dozen in a box, six boxes enclosed in another neatly-finished box, the most convenient shape possible for retailing.

The National Portrait Chess and Checker Board, A neat, durable and cheap article for the million, comprising on the unused squares fine life-like photographic pictures of all our prominent generals and commanders, also the President, Secretary of State, etc. The pictures alone are worth at least double the cost of the board.

U

F. VAN AUKEN. S. H. LANGLEY

VAN AUKEN & LANGLEY,

MERCHANTS,

Dealers in Produce, and Agents for

Threshing Machines and Reapers,

U U

CASH CAPITAL,	$[illegible],000
NETT SURPLUS,	$125,000

Dividends on capital limited by its charter to seven per cent per annum—the entire profits go to the policy holders.

R. W. MONTGOMERY, Agent,
Hastings, Minn. Office on First Street in Gardner's new stone block. 42-1y

LEGAL NOTICES.

STATE OF MINNESOTA, SECOND Collection District,

is hereby given that the lists, valuations, and enumerations made and taken under the Excise Tax Law of the United States within division numbered three, comprising the county of Dakota, will be open for examination at the office of Eli Robinson, in the city of Hastings, in said county, on the 29th day of August, A. D. 1863, and will remain open for the space of fifteen days from said time.

Notice is also given that appeals will be received and determined relative to any erroneous or excessive valuations or enumerations by the assistant assessor of said division at the office of Eli Robinson, in said city of Hastings, in said county of Dakota, on the 8th day of September, A. D. 1863, and immediately thereafter until all appeals are disposed of.

H. G. O. MORRISON,
Assessor, 2d District.

Dated August, 21, 1863. 20-4w

MORTGAGE SALE.—WHEREAS DEfault has been made in the condition of a certain mortgage deed executed by Harvey Gillett and Georgie R. Gillett, his wife, of the county of Dakota, in the state of Minnesota to Allen E. Rich and Isaac B. Tozer, then and now partners in business under the firm name of Rich & Tozer, made, acknowledged, and delivered by said mortgagors to said firm of Rich & Tozer, mortgagees, and bearing date the 8th day of May, A. D. 1862, which said mortgage contains the usual power of sale to said Rich & Tozer and their assigns, and was duly filed for record with said mortgage in the office of the register of deeds of said county, on the 9th day of said May at four o'clock in the afternoon of that day, and was thereupon duly recorded in said office in book K of mortgages on pages 587, 588, and 589; which said mortgage was given to secure the payment of one hundred and twenty-three dollars and seventy-one cents with interest at ten per cent per annum according to the conditions of a certain promissory note made by said Harvey Gillett and bearing even date with said mortgage. And there is claimed to be due and is actually due and unpaid upon said note and mortgage at the date of this notice the sum of one hundred and thirty-four dollars and fifty cents. And no suit or proceeding at law has been instituted to recover the debt secured by said mortgage or any part thereof. The mortgaged premises are described as follows, viz: All that tract or parcel of land lying and being in Dakota County, state of Minnesota, and described as follows, to wit: Lot number fourteen (14) in block number three (3) in H. G. Bailly's addition to Hastings, as per recorded plat thereof now on record in the office of register of deeds in said county.

Now, therefore, notice is hereby given that by virtue of the power of sale in said mortgage contained and pursuant to the statute in such case made and provided the said mortgage will be foreclosed by a sale of said mortgaged premises at public auction to the highest bidder at the front door of the office of said register of deeds in Hastings, in said county, on the 3d day of October, A. D. 1863, at one o'clock in the afternoon of that day, to satisfy said mortgage debt and the expenses of said sale.

19-7t RICH & TOZER, Mortgagees.
A. M. Hayes, Att'y for said Mortgagees.
Dated Hastings, Minn., Aug. 18, 1863.

J. W. PRATT & CO.,
Dealers in
Cloths, Cassimeres, Vestings, and Tailor's Trimmings,
Also, Hats, Caps, and Gents'
FURNISHING GOODS.
Hastings, Minn., May 14, 1862. 1-tf

The subscriber would respectfully give notice to the people of Hastings and elsewhere that he has constantly on hand the largest stock of Foreign and American Marbles ever brought west of Lake Michigan, consisting of all kinds of

LARGE SPIRE MONUMENTS,
SKELETON MONUMENTS,
GRAVE STONES, MANTELS,
FURNITURE MARBLE, ETC.,

which he will finish to order in the most approved styles and for the lowest cash price. Parties wishing to purchase will do well to wait till my agent comes around or to write to me, before purchasing elsewhere. C. J. ALBRACH.

Shop opposite the court-house, Winona, Minn. 18-tf

WILKES' SPIRIT OF THE TIMES.

Office 201 William-st., New York,

George Wilkes, Ed. and Pro.

Four Dollars a Year in Advance.

To Clubs—5 Copies,	$17 00
" 9 "	30 00

No subscriptions received for less than three months.

Rates of Advertising.

15 cts per line	each single insertion.	
48 " " "	One month.	
$1 20 " "	Three months.	
$2 00 " "	Six months.	

Sinclair Tousey, No. 121 Nassau Street, New York, general wholesale agents for supplying dealers. T. R. Callender, agent for Philadelphia.

Postmasters are requested to act as agents, and retain 20 per cent for their trouble. This percentage is, however, not to be deducted from club rates.

SEWING MACHINES.

FINKLE & LYON'S

Sewing Machines.

These Machines make the lock-stitch alike on both sides, and use less than half the thread and silk that the single or double thread or loop-stitch machines do; will Hem, Fell, Gather, Cord, Braid, Bind, etc., and are better adapted than any other Sewing Machine in use to the frequent changes and great variety of sewing required in a family, for they will sew from one to twenty thicknesses of Marseilles without stopping, and make every stitch perfect, or from the finest gauze to the heaviest beaver cloth, or even the stoutest harness leather, without changing the feed, needle, or tension, or making any adjustment of Machine whatever!

They are simple in construction, and easily understood, and if any part is broken by accident it is readily replaced.

These are peculiar facts, and will go far to determine the choice of any intelligent buyer.

Please call and examine, or send for circular.

N. B. Local Agents wanted in sections not yet occupied. Address,

FINKLE & LYON S. M. Co.,
17-1y No. 538 Broadway,
New York.

U

1863. THE 1863.

MILWAUKEE WISCONSIN

Daily, Semi-Weekly, Weekly.

The proprietors of the *Wisconsin*, begs leave to announce that owing to increasing expenditures for Special Telegraphic and War Correspondence, together with various improvements in contemplation for the coming year, he has felt compelled to make some changes in the scale of prices at which it is furnished to subscribers. By comparison with the prices of other journals, it will be seen that the *Wisconsin* is still, as it ever has been, the cheapest paper in the North-West.

We shall continue to print the *Wisconsin* upon the plainest type and the finest paper that can be made, thus retaining the name of the "handsomest paper in the state."

The present proprietor has conducted the paper over fifteen years, and it is unnecessary for him to speak of his ability or enterprise as a Live Independent Newspaper. He will only say that his journal is faithfully pledged to the suppression of the rebellion and the destruction of the rebels in arms, by every means in the power of the Government, and to the most cordial and active support of the President in his Proclamation of Freedom.

Our list of correspondence embraces every regiment of Wisconsin soldiers, as well as the several grand divisions of the Union Army. The Local and Commercial Departments will receive the undivided attention of the most competent Editors and Reporters.

We call particular attention to the Semi-Weekly *Wisconsin*. It will be a large thirty-two column paper, without advertisements, made up expressly for country circulation. All matter of the Daily *Wisconsin* will appear in this sheet; thus the subscriber will receive all the news of a daily paper for the price of the semi-weekly.

DAILY WISCONSIN—BY MAIL.

Published every day (except Sundays,) at 9 A. M., 12 M., and 3 P. M., at the following rates:

1 copy 12 months, in advance	$8 00
1 copy 6 months, "	4 00
1 copy 3 months, "	2 00

SEMI-WEEKLY WISCONSIN.

Published every Tuesday and Thursday morning, as follows:

1 copy 1 year, in advance	$3 00
1 copy 6 months, "	1 50
4 copies 1 year (in one order)	10 00
10 copies 1 year " "	22 50

Additional copies at the rate of the club. Specimen numbers sent to any address.

WEEKLY WISCONSIN.

Published every Wednesday morning, and mailed every Tuesday evening.

1 copy 8 mos, in advance	$ 1 00
1 copy 1 year, "	1 50
10 copies 1 year, "	13 00
20 copies 1 year, "	25 00

Additional copies at the rate of the club.

An extra copy will be sent to persons getting up clubs of ten or more of the Weekly. Money in registered letters may be sent at our risk

38-tf

U

Critical Notices of the Press.

Its fresh leaves, its clear type, its entertaining variety, its severe but just criticisms upon the follies of the times, its elegantly written and instructive articles, and its able correspondence, all combine to make it the model newspaper of our country, and one that every family must prize. Its condensed weekly summary of foreign and domestic intelligence is altogether superior to that contained in any other journal. Being published, too, in a form for preservation and binding, if taken care of as it deserves to be, it will be found in future years as welcome a companion for the family and fireside as the day on which it was first perused.—N. Y. Evening Post.

We would not so often call attention to Harper's Weekly if we were not well satisfied that it is the best family paper published in the United states, and for that reason, and that alone, we desire to see it undermine and root out a certain kind of literature too prevalent, which blunts the morals of its readers, vitiates their taste for sensible reading, and is almost evil in its effects.—New London Advertiser.

Wherever we go—in rail cars and steamboats—we find it read with eagerness, because of its spirited sketches of passing events. We all like to look at the faces of men we have read of, and at ships and forts that have figured in the bloody scenes of war. [illegible] this paper furnishes the best illustrations. Our future historians will enrich themselves out of Harper's Weekly long after writers and painters and publishers are turned to dust.—N. Y. Evangelist.

TERMS.

One Copy for One Year,	$3 00
One Copy for Two Years,	5 00

An extra copy will be allowed for every club of ten subscribers, at $2 50 each, or 11 copies for $25.

Harper's Magazine and *Harper's Weekly* together, one year, $5 00. *Harper's Weekly* is electrotyped, and back numbers can be had at any time.

Vols. I., II., III., IV., V., and VI., for the years 1857 to 1862 inclusive, of Harper's Weekly, handsomely bound in cloth extra, price $4 38 each, are now ready. The postage upon *Harper's Weekly*, when paid in advance at the office where it is received, is twenty-six cents a year.

HARPER & BROTHERS,
48-tf Franklin Square, New York.

THE HASTINGS CONSERVER.

VOLUME III.---NO. 22. HASTINGS, DAKOTA COUNTY, MINNESOTA, TUESDAY, SEPTEMBER 8, 1863. $2 00 PER YEAR.

THE CONSERVER.

BY IRVING TODD.

TUESDAY, SEPTEMBER 8, 1863.

Single copies of the CONSERVER may be obtained at this office, or at the Bookstore. Price Five Cents.

Republican Union Ticket.

For Governor,
STEPHEN MILLER,
of Stearns County.

For Lieutenant Governor,
CHARLES D. SHERWOOD,
of Fillmore County.

For Secretary of State,
DAVID BLAKELY,
of Olmsted County.

For Auditor of State,
CHARLES McILRATH,
of Nicollet County.

For State Treasurer,
CHARLES SCHEFFER,
of Washington County.

For Attorney General,
GORDON E. COLE,
of Rice County.

For Clerk of the Supreme Court,
GEORGE F. POTTER,
of Houston County.

County Convention.

The republicans and all other unconditional union men of Dakota County, who are in favor of sustaining the administration in its efforts to suppress the rebellion, are invited to send delegates to a county convention to be holden at Teutonia Hall, in the city of Hastings, on Saturday, Sept. 12th, at 2 o'clock P. M., for the purpose of nominating the following county officers to be supported at the ensuing election:

State Senator,
Two Representatives,
Treasurer,
Sheriff,
Judge of Probate,
Register of Deeds,
Attorney,
Surveyor,
Coroner,
Commissioners in the 2d and 3d Districts,

The different townships will be allowed representation as follows:

Hastings 7; Ravenna 2; Nininger 3; Inver Grove 4; West St. Paul 2; Mendota 3; Eagan 3; [illegible] 3; [illegible] 3; Lakeville 2; Eureka 2; [illegible] 2; [illegible] 2; Waterford 2; Greenvale [illegible]; [illegible] 2; Lebanon 2; Marshan 2; Randolph 2; Douglass 1; Vermillion 2; Hampton 3.

It is recommended that the primary meetings be held on Thursday evening, Sept. [illegible], at such public places as may be most convenient.

By order of County Committee.
IRVING TODD, Chairman.
Hastings, Sept. 1st, 1863.

Town Caucus.

The unconditional union electors of Hastings are notified that there will be a caucus held at Teutonia Hall on Thursday evening, Sept. 10th, at 7½ o'clock to select seven delegates to the union county convention to be holden in this city on the 12th inst.

Per order of committee.
IRVING TODD, Chairman.
Hastings, Sept. 8th, 1863.

A Card.

To all union men of Dakota County:

In the present emergency of the country and to meet the very general desire of loyal men, the undersigned members of the Dakota County Republican Union Central Committee respectfully recommend that the delegates to be elected under the call issued by us to the county union republican convention to be holden in Hastings, Saturday the 12th inst., be elected in the manner indicated by the union mass convention holden at Hastings this day.

IRVING TODD,
H. G. O. MORRISON,
N. N. THOMPSON,
J. F. REMER,
I. M. RAY.

Hastings Sept. 5, 1863.

The Democratic Convention--Who Were Responsible, and the way to Rebuke.

The democratic party *de facto* of this state, in their late state convention, have very clearly and emphatically, as a fear of the penitentiary would permit, declared their opinions, sentiments, and convictions to be of a copperhead stripe. A majority of the men who composed the convention were of a doubtful character. The officers of the permanent organization were not above suspicion, and with one or two exceptions the members of the committee on resolutions were no better than the great unwashed Vallandigham.

These facts being true, it is not surprising that their platform should be a mixture of milk and water, and that their nominees should possess predominating copperhead proclivities.

That the premises we have stated are true is witnessed in two undeniable facts:—

1. That the *North-Western* dare not, even with all its vaunted Vallandighamism and copperhead tincture, place at the head of its columns the ticket which its democratic editor assisted to nominate.

2. That the ticket as presented is denounced by all democrats who have a desire to serve the people for a consideration, *i. e.* those who desire an office at the hands of the people. If other and more evidence of the copperhead virus of that convention was needed, it could be furnished in its own proceedings; but we have given enough to convince the most skeptical upon that point.

The members of that convention were selected by their constituents for their known assiduousness in democratic business and their love of the "time honored" etc.

They met in delegate convention and there solemnly declared in their platform that they were the representatives of the democracy of Minnesota, which they undoubtedly were, and then after attending to all the business their constituents required of them, besides appointing a democratic state central committee, they adjourned *sine die.*

While huddled together in convention and secret conclave, they felt strong and waxed bold and defiant; but the next day when they saw themselves in print, and heard the virtuous indignation of the people they slunk away to their holes, not so much ashamed of the child of their own begetting; but afraid of the loyal people whom they had outraged by their *nefarious* work.

The hue and cry now raised that the convention was led into this copperhead and semi-disloyal course by the intrigues of one or two wire pullers can not be crammed down the throats of the intelligent people of this state. There are stern and indisputable facts, to the contrary, that like Banquo's ghost "wont down" at their bidding. To show that there were more than "a few" with "ultra views" in that convention it will not be necessary to recapitulate their entire proceedings. In the first place then, A. D. La Due, a man whom even the *North-Western* classes with the indecent, was appointed chairman of the committee on resolutions.

The convention then, after a mature discussion, voted down the patriotic resolution of Col. Robertson proposing to move upon the enemy's works until we force an unconditional surrender," because it would pledge the democracy of this state to a support of the war for a restoration of the union.

Against this resolution Mr. La Due not only spoke, but introduced an antipodal resolution of his own. And there in face of evidence showing them that La Due was an unmitigated copperhead—they gave him the second highest nomination in their power. That La Due was fairly nominated and was clearly the choice of the convention is patent. He was nominated on the first ballot, which stood as follows:

A. D. La Due	71
J. K. Kidder	31
James S. Morris	9

Thus giving La Due a majority of 31 over all other competitors.

Taking all these facts together we are bound to believe that the members of that convention knew full well what they were about. And any statement to the contrary we believe to be a vile slander upon the democracy of this state.

This much shown up, the *North-Western* admits that it will be "a badly defeated ticket." And then consoles itself with the hope that the "candidates are wise enough to withdraw and allow a new ticket entirely to be nominated." But suppose they did withdraw, would that better matters any? What assurance have the people that the next ticket would be any better than the first?

True they might set up a ticket not so well known and composed of men who might act a little more judicially; but yet what right have we to suppose that they would not be away down in their hearts as treacherous as La Due and his followers? If you sow tares can you reasonably expect to gather a rich harvest of wheat? At this juncture the shameful fact obtrudes itself upon us that the democratic party of this state is rotten from center to circumference, and its leaders cannot be trusted in any position whatever.

The only chance now left for the war democrats and union men to serve their country at the ballot box is to come over and support the republican union state ticket.

Let them do so by all means and in that way effectually rebuke the copperheads.

The old party in this state rescued from the control of mutton heads and semi-traitors will once more take that manly stand that alone comports with the dignity of its past history.—*Faribault Statesman.*

We have often told these followers of latter-day democracy that their leaders were not one whit better than Wood and Vallandigham, and in return for this bit of information, given with the best of intention, we have been abused and persecuted with all the fiendishness of a Quantrell. We are glad to note, even at this late day, an inclination to return to loyalty and common sense. We are glad that they begin to see themselves as others see them.

This acknowledgement on the part of the *Statesman* is worthy of notice. And the people should bear in mind that the ticket Alexander Johnson refuses to support is pretty well tinctured with copperhead views.

We hope hereafter when we tell the democracy plain truths concerning their leaders that they will not again commit the suicidal act of heaping denunciations upon our head and accuse us of false intentions. We think too much of our democratic citizens to have them all politically damned at once. As matters now stand, we suggest that about the next best thing those democrats who are dissatisfied with the action of their convention can do is to come around to the polls and vote the republican union ticket. We give them a hearty welcome—and very poetically add that—

"While the lamp holds out to burn
The vilest sinner may return."

Mean.

We find the following choice bit of blackguardism in the correspondence of the La Crosse *Democrat.* The author of it is unknown, but, whoever he is, should be treated to a cold bath in the river. The assemblage referred to was above the average in point of appearance and deportment, and did nothing worthy of such wholesale slander. We attended the sessions of the association as reporter, and heard nothing of the kind referred to. The article is as false in statement as it is base in motive. We presume, however, a majority of the ladies present were *not* copperheads, they were too intelligent and refined for that, and it is the strongest recommendation in their favor. If the fellow has been snubbed by the girls, it is a poor way of taking revenge. It says:

The fascinating intellect of Minnesota is accumulated in this little city today. The school marms are gathering together, and holding a state teachers' convention. They constitute a charming picture. These fair flowers of humanity rival in beauty and simplicity the lilies of the field. Had I a poets eye or a painter's pencil I would give you sketches of these queenly belles that would stupefy in excessive bliss the most exemplary Fadladeen. When Byron described Lula as—

"Fat, languishing, and lazy,
Yet of a beauty that would almost drive you crazy,"

he but partly typefied those modest creatures in Minnesota whose pleasing duty it is to teach the young ideas how to shoot. Such a variegation of colors as tinge their cheeks, is only excelled by the hue of the rich and gaudy ribbons that surround and adorn their pretty faces. I have fears for the future of humanity, if the school-marms of the country are to be the sole educators of our youth; fears that a mingled multitude of modern Sampsons and Miltons will never again bless the earth; that is that a combination of physical strength and intellect will be a rarity. I notice that these school-marms are strongly wedded to negro sympathies, if not to negro sinners. At every mention of negro superiority, stamping and applause followed. One teacher advocated the commingling of blacks and whites—an amalgamation of races in schools and in society, which received the approbation of the audience. This shows you how deeply the views of abolitionism is seated in the weak and vacillating portion of the people; it shows you how dangerous is the influence that shall in future be brought to bear indelibly stamping these degrading teachings and doctrines upon our children. DR. ADONIS.

"The Flaunting Lie."

For the benefit of the democratic papers in the state which so often copy this phrase, we give the following paragraph from the New York *Tribune,* of the 20th ult. This would seem to settle the question:

"Mr. S. S. Cox, in his copperhead peregrinations through Ohio, has a habit of quoting a very spirited lyric evoked by the desecration of our National flag to the base uses of the slavehunters, beginning "All hail the flaunting lie!" and stating that they were written by Horace Greeley! The said Greeley would gladly be able to write so good a lyric as that, but never was, verse-writing being an achievement for which he has a very indifferent aptitude. The excellent stanzas which Mr. Cox falsely attributes to him were written by a young Irish democrat of this city, then and now a member of the Tammany Society, and a most ardent, effective coworker with Cox in the support for the Presidency of Buchanan in '56 and of Douglas in '60. And now if Cox will write as spirited and vigorous a poem on any subject—to be chosen by himself—its relative merits to be decided by three reputable judges of poetry chosen by himself—we will pay him $100 for it, and stipulate that he shall tell whatever falsehoods he pleases to our prejudice for the next six months without rebuke or exposure. We ask the Cincinnati *Enquirer, Ohio Statesman* and Cleveland *Plaindealer* to say whether this is not a fair offer."

The Lawrence Massacre.

The atrocious acts of Quantrell perpetrated upon the peaceable village of Lawrence and its industrious inhabitants are not equaled in their fiendishness by any of the crimes committed during this war in the interest of human bondage, and only find a parallel in the terrible descent of the Northmen upon the Romans.

Apropos of this question, the Chicago *Tribune* says:

QUANTRELL, THE COPPERHEAD.

The fact that the ruffian Quantrell, who burned Lawrence after massacreing one hundred and eighty of its men, women, and children, was at the copperhead convention at Springfield, on the 17th of June, seems to be well established; and the Springfield *Journal* asserts that he was accompanied by a few hundred of his followers, probably the very fellows who quenched their thirst for blood by butchering unarmed, unoffending, and sleeping citizens of a country village. That Quantrell and his associates were at home among the fire-in-the-rear gentry who go for the constitution-as-it-is by proposing to amend it for the advancement and enlargement of human slavery, there can be no doubt. "Birds of a feather," etc.

Honor to Whom Honor is Due.

We trust we are not violating the proprieties of journalism to express the hope that the county convention which meets next Saturday will re-nominate for the office of county commissioner for the district which he has represented during the past year, HENRY SPRAGUE, esq. We do no injustice to the other members of the board to say that Mr. Sprague has contributed in a very large degree towards producing that great change in county affairs which all our citizens must have noticed. Our county orders, under the judicious management of the board, have risen from seventy-five per cent discount almost to par; while a very large amount of taxes have been paid in, and an equally large amount of the rubbish of past years has been cleared up and settled advantageously to the county.

Where the people find a man fitted to discharge the duties of county commissioner, and possessing the experience of one term, they should by all means continue him in office. While the duties of that position attract but little public attention, they are of great importance to the citizens, and good or bad men in possession of them will produce an immediate fall or rise of our taxes.

"Judicial Blindness."

The *North-Western Democrat* has for a motto these words: "If we are not stuck with judicial blindness we shall cling," etc. Very appropriate since the action of the late democratic state convention, which was principally run by Judges Wilder, Chatfield, and Hamlin, three aspirants for the supreme bench. A pretty mess they made of it, and we don't blame the *Democrat* for wanting to haul off.

Mr. Stebbins refers to us, by way of reproach, as the little man." Were intellect always in keeping with size, the editor of the *Independent* would be a great man.

Vermont—"the star that never sets" —voted yesterday for governor and other state officers, three congressmen, and a state legislature. Counting upon the absence of many republicans who are in the army, the diminished interest always inseparable from large majorities, and the little capital they could make out of the draft, the democratic faction—a sort of mild copper article—were bold enough to undertake a *coup d'etat;* they canvassed the state with an energy worthy of a good cause, and left no stone unturned to make a strong fight. Now mark the result. Every state officer chosen is a republican, every congressman is a republican, every state senator is a republican, and of more than fifty members of the lower house heard from as we write, the coppers have got just two, and so far only two towns have given majorities on that side. Our congressmen have majorities of 6,000 to 8,000. The vote is lighter than in 1860, but the relative proportions are about the same. The democracy are entitled to credit for perseverence; they have been trying to elect somebody in Vermont for twenty years, and for twenty years they have regularly and hopelessly failed.—*New York Tribune, 3d inst.*

LOCAL AFFAIRS.

P. O. Notice.--Summer Arrangement.
Mail going East closes at 11 o'clock, A. M.
Way mail down closes at 8 o'clock, P. M.
Mail for St. Paul closes on the arrival of the boat from below in the afternoon.
Faribault mail leaves at 6 o'clock A. M., closes at 9 o'clock P. M.
Office hours from 8 A. M. to 8 P. M.
WM. H. SKINNER, Post-Master.

WILLSON is fitting up the room lately vacated by FRENCH, for dry goods, to which he will remove in a few days.

MAJ. O. T. HAYES, of the Mounted Infantry, has been in town for a day or two, looking remarkably well. He leaves to-day for St. Paul.

MARBLE WORKS.—Mr. ALDBACH has arrived in town with men and marble, and is now ready to fill all orders. Shop on Second Street, below Tyler.

FALL GOODS.—Call at PRATT'S and order a suit of fall clothing. You will need it, and you can't be better suited any where in the North-West. Try it and see.

NOTICE.—The next meeting of the Dakota County Agricultural Society will be held in Hampton on Thursday, Sept. 10th. Let there be a general attendance.

PILFERING.—Recently FOLLETT & RENICK have lost three gold pens from their bank, ROGERS one, and VAN KIRK one. Guess some one is preparing to act as secretary.

REMOVAL.—THOMAS is moving his large stock of hardware into his new building, near post-office, where he may hereafter be found ready to supply the wants of his customers.

There will be preaching at the University on Tuesday evening by some one of the ministering delegates to the Minnesota Baptist Association. The public are invited.

NEW SIGN.—We observe that ANDREWS has put out a large sign from the roof of his shop, to which all persons wishing any thing in his line should pay due attention. He has a fine display of jewelry in his cases, for sale at reasonable prices.

MOVED.—NEWMAN has moved his stock of dry goods in to his new building on Second Street, above the Bank of Hastings, where he will be pleased to see all those desirous of making good bargains. He has the finest room and one of the best stocks of goods in town.

TRY IT BY ALL MEANS.—If any of our readers have been troubled to make light and uniform biscuit, it is more than probably they do not use DeLand & Co.'s Chemical Saleratus. That is a pure article, not detrimental to health and sure in its effects. Try it by all means.

ANNIVERSARY.—The Twelfth Anniversary of the Minnesota Baptist Association occurs in this city on the 9th and 10th inst. The introductory sermon will be preached at the University at 10 o'clock, on the first day of the session. All the proceedings are public. A general attendance is desired.

THE COUNTY FAIR.—At the late meeting of the Agricultural Society it was voted to hold the annual fair at Hampton, on Thursday, Oct. 8th. A committee, consisting of WM. JONES, JAMES ARCHER, and Judge S. G. RENICK, was appointed to make all necessary arrangements. Due notice will be given to the public as to particulars.

SOLD.—We, in common with a number of others, were badly fooled last Friday night by attending what purported to be a Panorama of the War, by W. E. JAYNE. It was a very poor thing, and badly exhibited. We would inform the manager that every thing was not "as there represented!" It was a grand humbug on a small scale.

SAD ACCIDENT.—By the breakage of a plank in the tackling for hoisting stone in GARDNER'S new building, last Tuesday, two men named CALVIN DUTTON and THOMAS BENNETT, both well known citizens, were crushed beneath a large stone which was being elevated into the second story. The former was dangerously injured, having several ribs broken, and the latter receiving severe injuries in the head. Both are under the best of medical treatment, and are in a fair way to recover.

MASS CONVENTION.—Pursuant to a call for a union mass meeting, the citizens of Dakota County met at Teutonia Hall, in the city of Hastings, on Saturday the 5th inst. H. G. O. MORRISON was elected chairman, and R. W. MONTGOMERY chosen secretary. The following preamble and resolution was offered by Judge S. G. RENICK, and unanimously adopted:—

WHEREAS, The Republican Union Central Committee of this county have called a convention of unconditional union men to be holden in this city on the 12th inst. Therefore

Resolved, That the several towns and cities of this county be requested to send delegates to the said county convention irrespective of former party politics, and the said delegates be requested to nominate a union ticket and adopt the name and principles of the Union Party.

C. STEBBINS introduced the following resolution:—

Resolved, That this meeting will support none other than a union ticket for the several county offices, at the approaching election.

On motion of Hon. IGNATIUS DONNELLY the resolution was amended as to read as follows:—

Resolved, That this meeting will support none others than union men for the several county offices, at the approaching election.

The resolution as amended was then adopted unanimously.

On motion the convention adjourned *sine die.*

H. G. O. MORRISON, Chairman.
R. W. Montgomery, Secretary.

DIED.

In Cannon Falls, Minn., August 27, 1863, CHARLOTTE J. BARKER, wife of Horace A. Tabner, aged 34 years.

In this city, Aug. 21, of measels, MAMIE O., daughter of William E. and Aurelia F. MADDOCKS, aged two years and seven months.

Our little Mamie has gone to rest,
Where sickness, pain, nor death molest,
We cannot wish her back again,
In this cold world of grief and pain.
A. F. M.

On the 26th ult., at the residence of his daughter, Mrs. E. J. Harrison, in Vermillion, Mr. HUGH G. CALBRATH, in the 63d year of his age.

Mr. Calbrath was born in Tennessee, and emigrated to Illinois in an early day, where, by persevering industry, he accumulated enough of this world's goods to place him among the wealthiest farmers of the state. But the things of this world were not his God. For more than twenty years he lived a faithful and consistent member of the Cumberland Presbyterian Church, making himself useful and happy by his correct deportment and christian benefactions. His sufferings were protracted and severe, but borne with patience and christian resignation. His end was peaceful and happy; and he now rests—

Where sickness ne'er blasts,
Nor death devours.
T. M. GOSSARD.

Hastings, Sept. 1, 1863.

MONETARY QUOTATIONS OF FOLLETT & RENICK.
[CORRECTED WEEKLY.]

Bankable Funds.

New England,	Bank State of Indiana.
New York,	Iowa,
New Jersey,	Michigan,
Ohio,	U. S Demand Notes.
Canada,	Wisconsin,
Philadelphia,	Bank of Minnesota,
Marine Bank, Minn.,	Winona Co. Bank,
Bank of Clearfield,	State Bank of Minn.,
Peoples' Bank,	Pittsburg.

Exchange.
FOR BANKABLE FUNDS.

	Buying.	Selling
New York, Philadelphia, Boston,	½ prem.	½ prem.
Chicago and Milwaukee,	par.	½ prem.

PREMIUM FUNDS.

Gold,	25	30
Silver (large),	20	25
U. S. Demand Notes,	25	30
Canada,	20	25

RETAIL PRICES CURRENT.

CORRECTED WEEKLY BY C. F. BATCHELDER,
Hastings, Sept. 8, 1863.

FLOUR, per sack,	$2 50
WHEAT, per bushel,	60a65
CORN, do	40a45
OATS, do	40
POTATOES, do	[illegible]
BEANS, do	1 50
ONIONS, do	[illegible]
CRANBERRIES,	2 00
HAY, per ton,	6 00a8 00
WOOD, per cord,	3 00a4 00
SALT, per bbl	3 25
EGGS, per doz	12
BUTTER, per lb,	10a15
CHEESE, per lb	8a12
PORK, per cwt,	5a6
BEEF, per cwt,	5 00
HAMS, per cwt,	6a8
SHOULDERS, per cwt,	5a6
DRIED APPLES,	9
DRIED PEACHES,	16a20
SUGARS, per lb	12a17
MOLASSES, per gal	70a1 00
COFFEE, Java,	40
do Rio,	35

From the School Friend.

Educators and Their Habits.

One of the best recommendations in a teacher is correctness of habits. We have no patience with those who set themselves up as educators, and yet are as full of evil habits as humanity can well be. In no respect is it more necessary that a teacher be unexceptionable than in his every-day practice.

We appreciate clearness of demonstrations, conciseness in the use of language, fullness of knowledge, and copiousness of illustration in the instructor. They are all valuable—indispensably valuable. The teacher who should offer his services to a district, and yet be wanting in these characteristics, would be but a charlatan, and unworthy the patronage of a sensible community. But we can better do without intellectual endowments in the samplers, after whom our children are to copy for several hours of the day, than dispense with good habits. There is nothing so inveterate as habit. It sticks to its place in the soul like the seeds of mortality in the human frame.

The habits of a teacher are sure to be largely copied by his juvenile charge. They look to him for instruction, and they are bound to get it. If he is incapable of impressing them intellectually and righteously, he is sure of doing it through the force there is in the recurrence of some pernicious habit. They come to school for something, and something they will have, before the term passes. If there is no good, parents may rest assured that their children will go home freighted with evil.

We were pleased with those who assembled in this city as members of the State Teachers' Association. Their very appearance gave proof that they were not the slaves of the wicked but fashionable vices of the times. We do not believe that there was a tobacco smoker or chewer among the whole one hundred and thirty. The school room of such men, we vouch, will not exhibit any of the signs of excessive salivation which usually accompany the use of the meanest weed that ever cursed civilization. They are above the filthy business. A lady friend, remarkable for her correct taste, took notice of this fact; for we heard her descanting most eloquently to an equally sensible female upon the cleanliness and propriety of habit manifested among the various delegates. This is as it should be. No profession should be more pure than the teaching fraternity. And let all the people say amen.

The Wasioja school, or North-Western College, begins its fall term on the 27th of August; Hamline University on the 2d prox. Both schools are under the control of live, practical teachers. Both have become important educational centers. It should be the pride of the people of Minnesota to keep both full of students. We need these schools and a score beside to guide and cultivate the young geniuses that are growing up all around us.

The Stillwater, Chatfield, and Monticello graded schools also re-open soon. Each of these are under the management of competent and enthusiastic teachers. B. F. Miller, of Monticello, urges upon his patrons the paramount importance of classification among the pupils. Let his patrons look to it, and have the work accomplished at once.

We shall be glad to notice the schools of the different towns of the state, whenever an item shall be furnished us in reference to them. Will not the teachers and school commissioners take it upon them to send us any matters of educational interest that may transpire in their localities?—*Ib.*

Teachers are constantly writing to us for situations in the various schools of the state. We have now on hand one application from Pennsylvania, three from Illinois, one from Wisconsin, and one from Connecticut. Three of these are male and three female. Some desire positions in high schools; others in common schools. If a correct knowledge of them can be gained by letter, they would all be valuable acquisitions to our present corps of teachers. It seems to us that we need all the teachers in Minnesota that can honorably be induced to come here. No doubt many of the towns of the state would be glad to get a good teacher. We shall be happy to correspond with any individual or school committee that is in want of a teacher.—*Ib.*

The State Teachers' Association, we think, ought next year to continue at least, three days in its session. That will give a little time for normal instruction and gymnastic drill—two very necessary items to the teachers of the state just now. What think you, gentlemen of the executive committee?

THE CONSERVER.

BY IRVING TODD.

Office Over the Bank of Hastings, Exchange Block, Second Street.

Our Platform.

Resolved, That we, chosen to represent in convention the unconditional union men of Minnesota, grateful to Almighty God for the success which has hitherto crowned the arms of our country and for the prospect thus opened of a speedy, honorable, and lasting peace, do hereby, for ourselves and our constituents, reaffirm our determination to support our government by every means in our power in the vigorous prosecution of this war, —on our part, holy, just, and forced upon us by the criminal acts of others,—until not an enemy in arms shall be found within our borders. And to this we pledge our lives, our fortunes, and our sacred honor.

2. That we tender our grateful thanks to the survivors of our glorious armies, and our warm sympathy to the relatives of their gallant dead, who have won for the country so glorious victories, for themselves imperishable renown, and for us all an assurance of liberty and safety, for ourselves and our children, under our beloved and now well-tried government.

3. That with especial pride we point to the gallant achievements on many a hard-fought battle-field, of our Minnesota regiments. Their bravery, discipline, and patriotism have won for them a name that shall never die, and made forever honorable to a citizen of Minnesota.

4. That, without claiming for it exemption from error, we heartily endorse the general policy and conduct of our national administration; and we point to the recent magnificent triumph of our armies as its best vindication from the charge of incapacity so freely brought against it by those who prefer national ruin to success under the present administration. *Especially* do we approve the emancipation proclamation, and the raising of black troops, as being among the best possible measures to weaken the enemy and strengthen ourselves.

5. That our state administration and congressional delegation deserve our hearty approbation for the zealous and efficient co-operation they have afforded the national authorities in carrying on the war.

6. That we call upon those in authority to take such measures, by retaliation or otherwise, as shall effectually prevent brutal and barbarous treatment by the enemy of our soldiers, of whatever color.

7. That it is due to our shattered armies in the field, as well as to the sacred cause which they uphold, that their ranks should as speedily as possible be filled up by every means in our power. It is due to the country that the mobs raised to resist and prevent the draft, should not even seem to have succeeded a day longer than is necessary to enforce the laws.

8. That the way to peace is, and ever has been, open to the rebels; the only condition we have ever sought to impose is that they should lay down their arms and submit to the authority of the general government. We protest against the making of any terms with them in advance as to their *status* in communities, when they shall have returned to their allegiance. Having been declared "public enemies" by a recent unanimous decision of the Supreme Court of the United States, they must accept the consequences that legitimately flow from having placed themselves in that position.

A New York religious paper reports says: "Saratoga is full—full as never before. The gaiety is toned down. At the opening of the season, the display was great. Men and women suddenly rich, came here to show out. But the ton, who understand these matters, took the nonsense right out of all the snobs. Rich, and having their social position fixed, they need no outward display to defie their social status. They swung to the extreme of plainness, brought out muslin and calico dresses, locked up their jewelry, and put their coachmen and footmen in plain clothes. The effect was magical. The gaudy and gilded things stood alone as in a pillory, and soon disappeared. 'How plain Saratoga is,' is the general cry. 'I never saw so little dress and display,' runs from mouth to mouth. The ladies understand how to manage these matters."

At a meeting of the union men of Stetson, Maine, some days since, the following pithy resolutions were adopted:

1. That this rebellion is unconstitutional.
2. That it is constitutional to put it down.
3. That Mr. Lincoln is putting it down.
4. That we will support him while about it.
5. That Mr. Cony goes for the right.
6. That we will go for Mr. Cony.

The platform of the copperheads is thus succinctly set forth in a communication to the "Lounger's" column of *Harper's Weekly*:

"First. *Resolved*, That we are in favor of the war.

"Second. *Resolved*, That we are opposed to all measures for carrying it on."

By a rule of the Post Office Department, which is justified by the letter of the law, if the amount of the postage stamp upon a letter does not fully prepay it, double the amount of the deficiency is charged to the receiver. Formerly only the amount of the deficiency was charged. Thus a letter weighing the merest fraction over half an ounce, if prepaid with but a single stamp, is burdened with an additional postage of six cents which the receiver must pay.

We have no doubt it will be exceedingly satisfactory to our friends to be informed that on the 31st of March, 1863, the British national debt amounted in all to £798,832,137, three and a half times larger than was that of the United States on the 1st of July last.

An Editor's Life.

The following appeared originally in the Richmond *Whig*, some years ago, and went the rounds of the press. We think it is good enough to re-publish:

It does not require a master hand to sketch with fidelity that poor and abused class known as editors. As a cotemporary remarks, he may be the "responsible," the "foreign," the "literary," the "local," the "commercial," —in either department he is the subject of laudation, abuse, trials, and triumphs. He may have a ready pen, remarkable versatility of knowledge, a correct judgment, and a considerable nerve. If you intrude upon him, you discover him writing, reading, scissoring. He will talk, but his pen does not stop; he spatters the ink; he fumbles over books; he hunts among newspapers; he grows savage in a "leader," or learned in a "review" Politicians try to buy him; needy artists seek his favorable notice; inventors have models to show him. He is addressed on more subjects than it was ever intended a single mind should comprehend; and while his journal is called by some, influential, valuable, etc., there are others who bluntly pronounce it "scurrilous," and poor. Swimming upon floods of excitement, battling, chatting, arguing, consenting, exalting friends and crushing foes, thinking, working, is the sum and substance of an editor's career. At home, he writes with his wife at his elbow, and his child on his knee; in the street he weaves out those ideas, which, in a few hours will startle the men who now jostle and crowd him; in his sanctum he makes ready thunderbolts moulded with a pen, but more powerful than any ever hurled from above. He delivers lectures; he is a politician; he holds office; he is a traveler; he gives a verdict upon manuscripts which are more precious than the apple of their eye to aspiring authors; he pleads for the poor; he snubs the rich; he conciliates, he defies, he arouses nations, he dethrones kings; he is the guardian of liberty and omnipotent.

Up in the garrets, in out-of-way places—sometimes furnished like a parlor, sometimes worse than a pig-pen—in his *sanctum sanctorum*, the "holy of holies." Are you partial to frowns? Do you wish to hear a growl? Disregard the notices of "Editor's Room," "Private," "No Admittance," and *enter* the den; you observe the contracting brow; you do not know whether you are insulted or saluted; your tongue proposes to speak, and your legs incline you to run away; a head lifts itself; a worn pen and inked fingers point you to a seat which it takes you an instant to reach; but ere you have done so, the monster has his clutches so deeply in an idea that he has forgotten your existence. There you sit; you try to count the pyramids of newspapers, and wonder if to be an editor it is necessary to be a savage. You see books and maps; but you would as soon meddle with the cub of a bear as anything in which the wild animal before you has any interest. Delegations of devils, from the printing office, come for copy, and a great many things are going on, which are strange to you. Other gentry come in, who glance contemptuously at yourself. They seat themselves, and you hear nothing but scratch, scratch, with gold pens, steel pens, and goose quills; they clear their throats; they look up at the ceiling; they help each other when their ideas run aground; they write and re-write; they expunge and amend; they become cherful if their productions please them, and crusty if they do not.

Now remember that this mental toil must go on by day and night, when the head is dizzy by sickness, and the heart by sadness, that it entails study, research, and thought, that the themes are suggested and discussed within the hour; and you will understand why you are not wanted in an editor's sanctum. Presently, however, he will talk to you; he will cut short your long speeches; he will bring you at once to your business; he will dispatch it, and you will at once discover that necessity, if not inclination, urges him to resume his pen.

In the summer when the flowers are so tempting, at midnight, with the glare of artificial light pouring upon him, there he is a toiling slave. He writes of your pleasures, he adds to your joys. Do you ever think of his exhausted brain, his fading life, his premature death? Literature was, perhaps, a passion of his boyhood, and he has pursued the wicked phantom from year, to year, finding in the gratification of a refined taste, some small reward for his painful infatuation.

Teacher's Request of Parents.

1. Send your children to school seasonably and constantly.
2. Encourage them to respect and obey the rules and requirements of their school.
3. Encourage them to be orderly, etc.
4. Encourage them to be studious.
5. Visit them at school.
6. Have a regard to the character of the books your children read, and see that they read understandingly.
7. Aid me to check selfishness, and promote a spirit of kindness and forbearance.
8. Cultivate in your children habits of politeness and courtesy.

These duties, and others growing out of them, perform faithfully, and you will find a most abundant reward in the increased interest of your children, and their growth in knowledge and virtue.—*Northend's Teacher and Parent.*

No statue that the rich men places ostentatiously in his widow is to be compared to the little expectant face pressed against the window pane, watching for his father, when his day's labor is done.

Grammar and Composition.

This science, which the ancients made almost the foundation of knowledge, should receive, in many respects, more attention than has been yet accorded to it. Too much prominence, in my opinion, has been given to the mere technicalities of the science; too little to the practically useful portion.

The pupils in some schools have been required to commit and repeat, *verbatim*, melancholy pages of remarks, exceptions, and crude speculations—or, perhaps, in the opinion of some, abstruse philosophical commentaries on details of minor interest. These technicalities, theories, and abstractions, having, in most instances, only an incidental connection with the plain subject matter, and tending merely to confuse and dishearten the learner, who cannot distinguish the commentary from the principle, are "crammed," in common parlance, into the heads of pupils and shaken down, till their dizzy brains are in a maze of bewildering conjecture. They see sextuple-classed pronouns with unintelligible distinctions; "interrogatives," so styled, when there is no interrogation; and the same mode and tense admitting of indefinite variations in manner and time.

These distinctions, which belong rather to abstruse philolological treatises than to common school manuals, have linked themselves with the indispensable framework of the science. They are a necessity to the critical student of maturer years; but to the young learner, they seem to ornament the plain structure of grammar like the incomprehensible grotesque and arabesque of oriental design. In these labyrinthine mazes, in which science is complicated rather than symplified, the young martyr wanders for about two years in search of the missing clew; acquiring, perhaps, less knowledge of how to speak and write the English language correctly," unless much collateral training independent of any text-book is given—than he might gain in less than half the time by a method which reversed this order.

The training in some schools has been almost exclusively theoretical; limited to the definitions, illustrations, and elementary analysis. Conscious of the amount of these topics, and of the deficiency of their pupils in them, many of the teachers made parsing a subordinate exercise, and either ignored compositions and declamations altogether, or compressed them into a minimum of time, and devoted the hours thus wrested from their proper use, to extra drills in the technicalities referred to.

Composition writing is expected, not only from all the members of the grammar schools, but from the first class, at least, in the intermediate. The essays in some of the schools, in which the exercise is properly encouraged and assistance rendered to the pupils by giving them interesting topics, with plans and hints for procedure, would be creditable to more mature minds.

Several of the intermediate teachers have practiced descriptive writing in their schools with the most flattering success. Some who thought their pupils "too young to have any ideas," found on trial that the latter possessed more than had been "dreamed of in their philosophy."

In the high, and in a few of the grammar schools, a systematic plan of classification and arrangement, founded on the object method of teaching, has been adopted for all essay writing, that the subject may be treated in a natural and logical order. The development and expression of thought—the true object of education—must be secured by giving to composition writing much more time and attention than it has yet received.

A short composition daily on some interesting topic would promote habits of observation and thought, and impart, even to the young pupils, a command of language which few now possess. This, with colloquial and dictation exercises, in which all errors of expression should be corrected, would, I believe, impart more real knowledge of grammar, even as a science, and in less time, than close adherence to any text book in existence.

Each of our colleges is a camp, in which young soldiers are arming and drilling for mental and moral conflicts. They have victories to win in the barracks of their hearts, before they can go forth to the conquest of ignorance, worldliness, and sin. There is before them a long probationary term of apparent inaction, but of real industry in mustering their forces. They will be called to meet many open enemies, and to be on their guard against many a masked battery.

The scholar's office is especially honorable and important, in a time of great national agitation. War, whenever waged, has a tendency to make the national life feverish and superficial, and to give undue prominence to material forces. Shoulder straps will, for a generation, outshine the freshest laurels of scholarly merit. At such a time the influence of scholars, in leavening action with thought, and in giving calmness and depth to the national character, is invaluable.

In these exciting times, the country needs men of thorough education, who shall not only lead a retired life and man the strongholds of truth, but who shall enter every department of political activity, and make their training felt in the learned professions, in mercantile pursuits, and in political strifes. The country is aroused and thrilled as it has not been before. The changes which it is undergoing, and is destined to undergo, demand better ministers, editors, doctors, lawyers, merchants, and politicians. There will be enough to engage the heart and hand of every student who, by faithful study, and under the guidance of professors who are concerned to inspire him with a chivalrous love of truth and justice, shall have laid the foundation of a stable and honorable character.—*The Examiner.*

AGRICULTURAL.

State Fair—1863.

On Saturday, the 8th day of August, the executive committee of the state board of agriculture in session at the capitol, in St. Paul resolved to hold a state fair, at Fort Snelling, on the 30th day of September, and the 1st and 2d days of October, it having been ascertained that the necessary buildings and grounds could be procured there for that purpose, without charge to the society, through the beneficence of the proprietor, Hon. Franklin Steele, with the military approval of Maj. Gen. Pope, commanding the Department of the North-West. It was with considerable reluctance and feeling of doubt as to success that the committee finally came to this conclusion, owing to the unsettled condition of national affairs, as well as to the supposed failure in crops from the drouth; but, after consultation and correspondence with individuals in different parts of the state, the committee learned that in regard to the latter it seemed confined to certain localities, while in general crops were bountiful; while as to the former, the recent successes of the federal arms have buoyed the hopes of the people in the speedy and honorable close of the war with glorious results to the Union. With this changed aspect of affairs, the committee came to the conclusion as above. While sister state societies have kept up their annual exhibitions, or gatherings of farmers, manufacturers, and artizans, this society has for two years past abstained from them, only on account of the all-absorbing interest of the people in the struggle pending for self government and constitutional rights. Consequently the committee will expect the mutual aid and assistance of every well-disposed man and woman in the state. They call upon and earnestly appeal to all classes in the different pursuits of life, to meet them in a grand jubilee on the above named days. Let every one have some article for exhibition. Never mind the dry season. Let us show the world what we can produce in this state without rain. If you have not large vegetables, bring the largest you have, and so on; all contribute something. The society being on comparatively small outlay, will be able to pay good premiums. The vast improvements at Fort Snelling afford us every facility for the accommodation of both man and beast. Good stable for stock, good buildings for the exhibition of household goods, agricultural implements; in fact, everything. Forage will be furnished, with the exception of grain, for all stock on exhibition, and general security given for all articles. The season is a most delightful one; no better season for a three days holiday can be chosen than our beautiful Indian Summer. The far famed Minne-ha-ha, the twin cities Minneapolis and St. Anthony, the capital city, St. Paul, together with our beautiful lakes, are all within a radius of six miles. Good roads, fine conveyances, reasonable charges, all combine to make it attractive. Military in camp and garrison, bands of music, fire companies with "der machine" will be in attendance.

The committee will have some one of our most eminent agriculturists deliver the annual address. The material development of the state is their aim, the superiority and dignity of honest labor their motto.

All live stock for exhibition will be ferried across the river free of charge, the proprietor generously donating one-half, the society paying the other.

Ladies, if last, by no means least! You have always contributed largely and generously from the fruits of your labor to the success of our exhibitions, we feel full confidence in your assistance this year. Your handiwork, in all branches of industry, bears a wide reputation; we are sure of your ability to sustain it. Therefore, having exhorted the sterner sex, we have only to say we wish to make this "The Fair!"

W. L. AMES, President Board.
C. H. Clarke, Secretary.

Talent Appreciated by Talent.

The notion that genius will excite the deepest reverence in those by whom it is least understood is an ever-recurring and yet manifest delusion. Talent is best appreciated by talent, knowledge by knowledge; and the man who imagines that the higher he is removed above his judges the more they will admire him, might equally expect that he would look larger the farther he receded, or his voice sound louder the greater the distance from which he spoke. Excellence must be perceptible before it can be applauded, and for a cultivated understanding to display its stores to untutored ignorance is much like exhibiting colors to the blind. Thus Johnson was subjected to the complicated misery of conscious power, general neglect, and helpless poverty; and, with his expectations baffled, wretched in the present and without hope for the future, a less gloomy temperament than his would have sunk in despondency.—*Early Life of Johnson.*

BATCHELDER'S COLUMN.

GREAT ATTRACTIONS

AT THE

OLD STAND.

GEO. F. BATCHELDER,

(Successor to North & Carll)

WHOLESALE

AND

RETAIL

Dealer in

DRY GOODS,

GROCERIES,

Boots and Shoes,

HARDWARE, ETC.,

HASTINGS, MINN.

Having laid in an unusually heavy stock of staple wares, would invite the attention of the public to my large assortment of

GOODS,

Consisting of Imported and Domestic

SILKS, DELAINES,

LAWNS AND

CALICOES,

also to my stock of Foreign and Domestic

SHEETINGS,

These goods were purchased at exceedingly low rates, and am therefore enabled to sell at prices to suit the times.

A well assorted stock of

Hats and Caps,

for Men and Boys, of the latest styles.

READY-MADE

CLOTHING,

a fine assortment, custom made, from the best of cloths, bought expressly for this market, and will be sold at reasonable figures, for cash only.

A choice stock of pure and fresh

GROCERIES

Just received from the East, where especial attention was paid to their selection.

A fine lot of assorted

Boots and Shoes,

comprising Gent's, Ladies', Boy's, and Misses', of all varieties. The especial attention of farmers is invited to a large and complete stock of

HARDWARE.

The celebrated Moline Plow always on hand.

A long experience in and close supervision of the business, and personal attention to the buying of goods, gives confidence that entire satisfaction will be rendered to patrons. Customers will be waited on by experienced and accommodating salesmen, and their wishes promptly attended to. All goods warranted as represented.

GEO. F. BATCHELDER.

Hastings, June 9, 1863. 3-tf

THE CONSERVER.

Published every Tuesday Morning at HASTINGS, DAKOTA COUNTY, MINNESOTA.

Terms.

Single copy one year $2 00
" " six months, ... 1 00
" " three months, ... 50
Five copies, to one address, ... 8 75
Ten " " " 15 00
Twenty " " " and one to getter up of club, ... 30 00

Payment invariably in advance.

Address IRVING TODD, Publisher.

RATES OF ADVERTISING.

1 square 1 week	$1 00		2 squares 6 months	9 00
1 " 2 weeks	1 50		2 " 1 year	15 00
1 " 3 "	1 75		3 " 1 week	2 25
1 " 4 "	2 00		3 " 2 "	3 00
1 " 5 "	2 25		3 " 3 "	4 00
1 " 6 "	2 50		3 " 4 "	5 00
1 " 7 "	2 75		3 " 3 months	9 00
1 " 2 months	3 00		3 " 6 "	12 00
1 " 3 "	3 75		3 " 1 year	20 00
1 " 4 "	4 50		½ col 6 months	15 00
1 " 5 "	5 25		½ " 1 year	25 00
1 square 6 months	6 00		½ " 6 months	18 00
1 " 1 year	10 00		½ " 1 year	30 00
2 squares 1 week	1 75		1 " 6 months	25 00
2 " 2 "	2 50		1 " 1 year	40 00
2 " 3 "	3 00		1 " 1 year	50 00
2 " 4 "	4 00		1 " 1 year	70 00
2 " 2 months	5 00			

One inch in space will be counted as a square of solid matter.

Business cards on second page, not exceeding seven lines, seven dollars per year; each additional line one dollar.

Legal advertisements inserted at the rates prescribed by statute, and attorneys ordering such advertisements will be held responsible.

Special notices 15 cents per line for first insertion and ten cents for each subsequent insertion.

Transient advertisements must be paid in advance —all others quarterly.

Advertisements not otherwise ordered, will be continued until they are ordered out, and charged accordingly.

Patriotism.

Give me the death of those
Who for their country die;
And oh! be mine like their repose,
When cold and low they lie.
Their loveliest mother earth
Enshrines the fallen brave,
In her sweet lap who gave them birth,
They find their tranquil grave.
MONTGOMERY.

"WHAT A FIX."—At the late democratic convention, a fellow whom we will call A. was very anxious to be nominated for lieut. governor on the copperhead ticket. So he went around to his next friend, B., when the following conversation took place:

"Now B., I've got a d—n good show for the nomination of lieut. governor, and I want all my old friends to go in for me. I hope you'll do your best."

"I did not know that you were a candidate," said B., scratching his head and looking amazed.

"Yes, I am," said A. "now go in big." Here B.'s eyes were fixed on vacancy, and he looked very solemn. At length A. aroused him from his reverie by inquiring what he was thinking about. Scratching his head and speaking very moderately, B. replied:

"I was just thinking that if you are nominated for lieut. governor, and our ticket is elected, and the governor should die, *what a h—l of a fix the state would be in!*"—*Milwaukee Sentinel.*

SYMPATHY.—A story is told of a man, in Pittsburg, in search of a lost child, a few days since, being hailed by a ponderous Hibernian, who thrust his half-naked frame through the window of a dilapidated three-story wooden building.

"Is it a child ye want?"
"Yes."
"About three years old?"
"Yes."
"Has he fair hair?"
"Yes."
"Blue eyes?"
"Yes."
"Red stockins, an' smoked colored gaiters?"
"Yes."
"Had he a plain dress and a white straw hat on 'im?"
"Yes! Yes! Have you got him up there with you?"
"Ah, no, sir; but I saw his mother a while ago looking for the darlin."

The Master and Fellows of Trinity College, Cambridge, have at length decided the greatly vexed question, as to whether Homer did or did not wear wooden legs. They now confidently assert that he did not, as, though it may be painful to say it, they have come across the Poet's Feet in the *Iliad;* and, in the same work, a subject calling for peculiar remark, has been the constant use of his little to.

The handsome young ladies who recently attended the tables at crystal palace fair, near London, sold choice cigars to their admirers and obtained an enormous advance on the common price, by simply biting off, first, the end to be placed in the smoker's mouth.

IMPUDENT.—What part of a soldier's duty would the ladies take the most delight in? We wrote "present arms," but a snarly old Benedict at our elbow suggests "dress parade." We wouldn't like to be in his shoes if his wife should find him out.

It is stated that there is a Spanish girl seventeen years old, Lyons, France, who can lift a weight of three hundred pounds with her hair. We have seen many a young girl, who, having beautiful hair, could draw a regiment of men with it.

An item for hen-pecked husbands, occured in the Lowell police court. On Wednesday a woman named McOsker was sentenced to the house of correction for being a common scold.

Jones complained of a bad smell about the post-office, and asked Brown what it could be. Brown didn't know, but suggested that it might be caused by the "dead letters."

It is a popular delusion that powder on a lady's face has the same effect as in the barrel of a musket—assists her to go off.

Mr. and Mrs. Brewer, of Wayne County, Ky., have twenty-two children. This is perhaps the most extensive Brewery in the West.

HARDWARE.

PRINTING.

FURNITURE.

MISCELLANEOUS.

BOOKS AND STATIONERY.

PUBLICATIONS.

PATENT MEDICINES.

THE CONSERVER.

EDUCATIONAL.

BY PROF. T. F. THICKSTUN.

The State Teachers' Association.

We were more than gratified with the size and doings of this body which closed its third annual session in this city a few days ago. There were *one hundred and thirty* delegates in attendance, representing a large part of the eastern and southern portions of the state. The high school and the common school were both represented. The graded schools of the larger towns were, we believe, without an exception present by their delegates to teach the people the superior efficiency of this form of school organization. The rural districts also had a very liberal representation in the transactions of the occasion. There is, perhaps, no grade of school in the state, worthy of the name, that was left out of the assemblage. We regard this meeting, therefore, as a fair representative of the educational sentiments of the whole state. Were all the educators of Minnesota assembled, they would not materially alter what was done by the late meeting of the teachers and friends of schools.

The results reached by the association were such as every really educational state in the country has arrived at long years ago. There was not a dissenting voice on the subject of the state superintendency, not one on normal schools, on teachers' institutes, on town, county, and district supervision. These were all deemed a necessity, pressing, and absolute. They must be elements in our common school system, or it will fall into self-ruin not many years hence. It can no more live without these than the body can live without head, lungs, and heart. The whole association stands pledged to work with all its might for these improvements during the year upon which we have entered.

There was an evident increase of power in the association. The influence emanating from so many different sources, embracing as it did so great a diversity of talent and of profession—all thrown together into one channel, must inevitably make itself felt. It was palpably felt during the meeting; it must also be felt during the session of the legislature this winter, if it be rightly managed. We are satisfied that there is not an intelligent legislator in the state, had he been present, who could have demurred from an iota of the proceedings in reference to the great cardinal school principles advocated by the association. The tide was irresistable, it swept right onward to the results above indicated.

The contrast between the past and the present is most encouraging. This increase of power in the deliberations of the association means something. The state is awaking. Schools are found to be a necessity. Free schools and all the accompaniments thereof can no longer be kept from the people. They will have them. Will the legislature make a note of the fact?

In the name of the teachers and friends of schools in the state we demand of our county and state representatives, who, in a few months, will assemble at St. Paul, a distinct recognition of these matters. We demand it also in the name of the fifty or sixty thousand children of the state. We demand it in consideration of the general interests of the state. Farmers, mechanics, merchants, and professional men all prefer an enlightened citizenship and good school facilities rather than the reverse. They will settle among us, if we have good free schools; they will stay away, if we have them not.

The fourth anniversary of the association meets by invitation with the people of Red Wing in August next.

In a short time all the political officers of state and county will be nominated. The governor, lieutenant-governor, and secretary of state, among the state officers, and the senators and representatives, among the county officers, ought to stand pledged to the re-establishment of the superintendency of public instruction and the inauguration of a permanent system of normal schools. If the teachers and friends of schools would address letters to the various candidates for these offices, a great work would be accomplished. Especially let the senators and representatives be written to, and their views obtained on these two important measures. Let such correspondence be published, and it will open the eyes of hundreds in every county. It will be seen that those interested in schools are awake. It will show the aspirants after public position that they must be school men, if they would get the votes of the people. Will not the teachers take this matter in hand?

NEW ADVERTISEMENTS.

SEWING MACHINES.

FARMING IMPLEMENTS.

RAILROADS.

NEW YORK ADVERT'MENTS.

LEGAL NOTICES.

STATE OF MINNESOTA, SECOND Collection District,
Assessor's Office, St. Paul, August, 1863.

Public Notice

is hereby given that the lists, valuations, and enumerations made and taken under the Excise Tax Law of the United States within division numbered three, comprising the county of Dakota, will be open for examination at the office of Eli Robinson, in the city of Hastings, in said county, on the 29th day of August, A. D. 1863, and will remain open for the space of fifteen days from said time.

Notice is also given that appeals will be received and determined relative to any erroneous or excessive valuations or enumerations by the assistant assessor of said division at the office of Eli Robinson, in said city of Hastings, in said county of Dakota, on the 8th day of September, A. D. 1863, and immediately thereafter until all appeals are disposed of.

H. G. O. MORRISON,
Assessor, 2d District.
Dated August, 21, 1863. 20-4w

MORTGAGE SALE.—WHEREAS DEfault has been made in the condition of a certain mortgage deed executed by Harvey Gillett and Georgie R. Gillett, his wife, of the county of Dakota, in the state of Minnesota to Allen E. Rich and Isaac B. Tozer, then and now partners in business under the firm name of Rich & Tozer, made, acknowledged, and delivered by said mortgagors to said firm of Rich & Tozer, mortgagees, and bearing date the 8th day of May, A. D. 1862, which said mortgage contains the usual power of sale to said Rich & Tozer and their assigns, and was duly filed for record with said mortgage in the office of the register of deeds of said county, on the 9th day of said May at four o'clock in the afternoon of that day, and was thereupon duly recorded in said office in book K of mortgages on pages 587, 588, and 589; which said mortgage was given to secure the payment of one hundred and twenty-three dollars and seventy-one cents with interest at ten per cent per annum according to the conditions of a certain promissory note made by said Harvey Gillett and bearing even date with said mortgage. And there is claimed to be due and is actually due and unpaid upon said note and mortgage at the date of this notice the sum of one hundred and thirty-four dollars and fifty cents. And no suit or proceeding at law has been instituted to recover the debt secured by said mortgage or any part thereof. The mortgaged premises are described as follows, viz: All that tract or parcel of land lying and being in Dakota County, state of Minnesota, and described as follows, to wit, Lot number fourteen (14) in block number three (3) in H. G. Baily's addition to Hastings, as per recorded plat thereof now on record in the office of register of deeds in said county.

Now, therefore, notice is hereby given that by virtue of the power of sale in said mortgage contained and pursuant to the statute in such case made and provided the said mortgage will be foreclosed by a sale of said mortgaged premises at public auction to the highest bidder at the front door of the office of said register of deeds in Hastings, in said county, on the 3d day of October, A. D. 1863, at one o'clock in the afternoon of that day, to satisfy said mortgage debt and the expenses of said sale.

19-7t RICH & TOZER, Mortgagees.
A. M. Hayes, Att'y for said Mortgagees.
Dated Hastings, Minn., Aug. 18, 1863.

PUBLICATIONS.

THE HASTINGS CONSERVER.

VOLUME III.---NO. 23. HASTINGS, DAKOTA COUNTY, MINNESOTA, TUESDAY, SEPTEMBER 15, 1863. $2 00 PER YEAR.

THE CONSERVER.

BY IRVING TODD.

TUESDAY, SEPTEMBER 15, 1863.

Single copies of the CONSERVER may be obtained at this office, or at the Bookstore. Price Five Cents.

Republican Union Ticket.

For Governor,
STEPHEN MILLER,
of Stearns County.

For Lieutenant Governor,
CHARLES D. SHERWOOD,
of Fillmore County.

For Secretary of State,
DAVID BLAKELY,
of Olmsted County.

For Auditor of State,
CHARLES McILRATH,
of Nicollet County.

For State Treasurer,
CHARLES SCHEFFER,
of Washington County.

For Attorney General,
GORDON E. COLE,
of Rice County.

For Clerk of the Supreme Court.
GEORGE F. POTTER,
of Houston County.

County Ticket.

For Senator,
N. N. THOMPSON.

For Representatives,
J. F. REHSE,
S. C. HOWELL.

For Treasurer,
D. B. TRUAX.

For Sheriff,
H. J. TAYLOR.

For Judge of Probate,
I. M. RAY.

For Register of Deeds,
H. A. MONSER.

For District Attorney,
R. W. MONTGOMERY.

For Surveyor,
C. B. LOWELL.

For Coroner,
P. HARTSHORN.

For Commissioner—2d District,
HENRY SPRAGUE.

For Commissioner—3d District.
JOSIAH BURWELL.

Our Ticket.

We have the pleasure of presenting to our readers this week the ticket nominated by the union convention last Saturday, for their support at the ensuing election. We had intended to give an extended notice of the candidates, but the pressure of other matter and the prolonged absence of the editor prevents us from so doing in this issue. The ticket is a good one, and we heartily endorse it, predicting that it will receive a generous support from the people at the polls and be triumphantly elected.

Coming Round.

Not long since the democratic press was very busy in its denunciations of the republican statement that there is but one way to establish a peace worthy of the name, and *that way is by force of arms.*

This was a fixed philosophical fact, which those who had taken pains to study the nature of this contest at once admitted; but the leading democratic journals came out boldly and planted themselves plump against it.

Thus the Chicago *Times* said:

"Support of this war and hostility to it shows the dividing line between the enemies and friends of the union. He who supports the war is against the union, because the war is the most terrible engine for the destruction of the union which Beelzebub himself could have invented.

The professed element, therefore, who has his senses about him and is deliberately for the war, is not a democrat in fact, but an abolitionist of the most radical, violent, and destructive kind."

But the very language which they then used, showed plain enough that they were not so sure of the tenableness of the ground on which they stood. They sought to frighten the people into an opposition to the war by dubbing all those who supported it as "abolitionists" etc.

The recent victories all along the line from the Atlantic to the Mississippi have wrought great changes in the minds of some men, and we are now happy to chronicle that fact that very many democrats, if we may believe their words, are coming over to the support of the war and all of its attendant necessaries.

The Shakopee *Argus*, in speaking of the copperhead action of the recent state convention, says that the true democracy "are at this time in favor of sustaining the government in the prosecution of the war—of pushing unhesitatingly forward against the insolent and boastful foe until the last echo of rebel cannon shall have died away, and our flag, unstained by dishonorable compromise with rebels in arms against us, shall float in triumph throughout all rebeldom—a terror to traitors as it has ever been to tyrants."

Again it patriotically adds in language as truly and certainly republican as any that can be found:

"There is put one way for peace—honorable peace—and that is by force of arms. The rebels have told us upon all occasions, and at all times, that they would not compromise. War to the bitter end is their only terms. To talk of compromise, while they believe in the final success of their arms, or until they fully abandon the idea of success, is wrong, and can result in no good to us."

How long is it since such language used by a republican was denounced as fiendish and the speaker as an abolitionist?

If the *Argus* is sincere in its convictions, we are happy to welcome it to the true fold.

The Crippled Soldier.

We see a cripple pass our window; a poor, forlorn fellow, stumping on a crutch. The right sleeve of the blue coat flutters uselessly in the breeze, as does also the right leg of his pantaloons. Slowly and sadly he moves along, and the children stop their play to look. "So funny," they say. Once he was a boy, as blithe and active as the little curly-headed lad yonder leaning on his bat, the ball half protruding from his pocket. No one could excel him at running and wrestling, while at marbles and tag he was the acknowledged chief. He grew up. The manly limbs expanded and developed. The muscles became hard and firm by constant exercise. He was a man, justly proud of his strength and endurance. The war broke out. He saw the efforts of the enemies of our country to subvert this government reared by our forefathers and consecrated by their blood. He saw, and the proud spirit boiled with indignation. Leaving home and friends and all that was dear to him, he rushed to the field, with thousand of others,—

"To fight,
In a just cause, and for our country's glory."

He escaped with his life, but doomed through the period of his natural existence to humiliation and dependence.

Those empty folds are wonderfully suggestive—they speak volumes. They tell of privations, forced marches, hardships, and dangers endured. We see the conflict, the carnage, the mighty rush of battle; hear the whistling of the pitiless bullets, the shouts of the victors, and the groans of the dying. Then comes the weary days and nights in the hospital, roughly cared for, and half starved. No loved one near to smooth the hardened pillow, or beguile the lingering hours of their unvarying tediousness. The long days of intense pain and suffering—the convulsive efforts of nature to effect a restoration of the system. The discharge, the return home, a burden to self and friends, unfit for employment, an incumbrance to society, and dependent on government for a pittance as support—like an old, worn out horse: turned-out to grass because of no further service.

This is not an isolated case—the land is full of such. Would to God that it were otherwise. Woe to the authors of this unholy rebellion which has fallen so crushing and heavily on many a now desolate and cheerless hearthstone, and has weighed down many a tender and confiding heart to the earth. Great is their sin—terrible will be their punishment. The blood be upon their heads and their children forever.

Strong Testimony.

Gen. Grant, the conqueror of larger armies, and the captor of more prisoners and artillery than any commander of modern times, is warmly in favor of enlisting negroes in the federal army, and is lending all his aid and influence to that important work. Let the miserable cavillers of the copperheads be dumb.—*Nashville Union.*

Such is the testimony of all the fighting generals in this war. The negro can and will fight, if he has half a chance. It is not likely that any man would enlist in the army unless there was some inducement. As the white man enlisted to save his country and government from ruin, so let the negro for his liberty. But whew! wont the democrats hereabouts be down on Grant?

Shooting Affair at New Lisbon, Wis.

A terrible affray occurred at this place on Thursday night, 10th inst., in which two men lost their lives, and three others were seriously injured. It happened in this wise, as we learned on the spot from Capt. Arnold, commanding post:—

Peter Bellinger, of Milwaukee, got into a political discussion with one of the citizens, in which he energetically expressed what is termed copperhead principles. The conversation became general, and quite warm on both sides. Finally a soldier of Company C, 30th Regiment, took offence at some of his remarks, and threatened violence. Mr. B. stepped out, loaded his revolver, and returned, stating that he was prepared to continue the argument and defend himself. After roll call a party of soldiers came back and threatened to arrest him for disloyal sentiments and carrying concealed weapons. A squabble then ensued in which Mr. B. shot four of the soldiers, killing one instantly, Ebret Oleson, and severely wounded E. Wilson and J. B. Elgin; also C. Cummings slightly. All of these are of Company C, and from Trempeleau. The two former are not expected to live. Mr. B. was pursued by the now infuriated crowd, dragged out of the Georgia House, into which he had fled, and his head literally pounded into a jelly. He was a stout, robust man, was slightly in liquor at the time, and it seems to be the general opinion that he met with his deserts.

The Campaign Conserver.

To meet the growing great demand this fall for political documents, the publisher of the CONSERVER has concluded to issue a campaign paper for the term of eight weeks, commencing with Sept. 22d and ending with Nov. 10th, the latter number containing the complete election returns. To place it within the reach of all, it will be afforded at the following low rates, barely paying for the white paper:

5 copies to one address,	$1 50
10 copies to one address,	2 50

And any larger number in same proportion. No clubs smaller than five can be received. Send in your orders accompanied with the cash, as speedily as possible. Postmasters and others friendly to the cause are invited to act as agents in securing names. Address

IRVING TODD,
23-2w Hastings, Minn.

A Card.

Editor of Conserver:

Permit me through your columns to return my sincere thanks and kindest regards to the members of the union county convention in tendering to me the honorable position as their candidate for state senator, and would certainly have yielded to their urgent solicitations could I have done so in justice to my private business which may call me from the state the coming winter. No better ticket could have been selected. The interest of every part of the county was consulted. Every man honest and capable of discharging the duties assigned him with honor to himself and credit to the county. I shall ever hold in grateful recollection the members of that convention for their estimation of my humble self in the honor conferred on me.

S. G. RENICK.

Hastings, Sept. 15, 1863.

Editor of Conserver:

I see according to the proceedings of the union convention of last Saturday I received the nomination for representative. I informed one of the delegates of the convention, prior to my nomination, that I was not a candidate for office, also that I would not be able to attend the convention. While I am thankful to my friends for the honor they wished to confer on me, I cannot accept the nomination on account of my business. Respectfully yours,

J. F. REHSE.

Hastings, Sept. 15, 1863.

COLLEGE EDUCATION.—Do you call it education to put a boy into a hole and work out of him a certain amount of mathematics and work into him a certain number of languages? Is a man dressed because one arm has a spotless wristband, unquestionable sleeve buttons, a handsome sleeve, and a well-fitting glove at the end, while the man is out at the other elbow, patched on both knees, and down at the heels? Should we consider nature a success if she concerned herself with carrying nutriment to the stomach, and left the lungs, and the liver, and the nerves, to shift for themselves? Yet so do we, educating boys in these dens called colleges. We educate the mind, the memory, the intellectual faculties; but the manners, the courtesies, the social tastes, the greater part of what goes to make life happy and genial, not to any good, we leave out of view.—*Gail Hamilton.*

LOCAL AFFAIRS.

P. O. Notice.—Summer Arrangement.
Mail going East closes at 11 o'clock, A. M.
Way mail down closes at 6 o'clock, P. M.
Mail for St. Paul closes on the arrival of the boat from below in the afternoon.
Faribault mail leaves at 6 o'clock A. M., closes at 9 o'clock P. M.
Office hours from 8 A. M. to 8 P. M.
WM. H. SKINNER, Post-Master.

FOR SALE.—See notice of lands for sale, in advertising column.

REPRESENTATIVE.—We are told that R. W. HENRY, of Point Douglas, has been nominated for the legislature in Washington County.

COMING.—The Black Swan will appear before the public next Thursday evening, 17th inst., at Teutonia Hall. Turn out.

COURT.—The September term of the district court is in session at Teutonia Hall. Full proceedings will be given in our next.

RETURNED.—We notice that Mayor THORNE and Mr. BALLARD have arrived home from lengthy visits at the East. Also Jo. BARKER, of the 4th Minn. Regiment.

OPENED.—The Central University commenced its fall term yesterday very auspiciously. The attendance was quite good, and prospects favorable.

NEWMAN.—Of all the dry good establishments in this city NEWMAN's is undoubtedly the best. If you do not believe it just step around and examine his extensive stock.

NOTICE.—The Synod of Minnesota will hold its annual meeting in the Presbyterian Church at Hastings, commencing at 7½ o'clock on the last Thursday of September.

CHAS. S. LADUC, Stated Clerk.

ALWAYS GET THE BEST.—Especially in getting saleratus—as the best costs but a trifle more than the poor. The best goes farther than the poor, and is much more healthy. We can recommend the chemical saleratus to be the best.

NEW FRONT.—ANDREWS, the great jewelry man, has put in a new glass front to his establishment. This improvement is a benefit to ANDREWS as plenty of light is admitted, and people can see for themselves that he keeps good articles.

DAILY LINE.—The favorite light-draught boat, *Jeannettiee Roberts*, makes daily trips from St. Paul, connecting with the Prarie du Chien packets below Prescott. O. S. HUTCHINSON, formerly of Prescott, is clerk, and a very clever, obliging officer.

GOOD HOTEL.—Sojourners at La Crosse will find the Harrington House an excellent place to stop, and we can safely recommend it to the traveling public. Mr. BRADLEY is a capital landlord, and spares no pains to entertain his guests.

MINUTES.—The Twelfth Annual Session of the Minnesota Baptist Association took place in this city last week. The attendance, though not large, was tolerable, and it passed off very harmoniously. Full proceedings are given elsewhere.

GROCERIES.—Mr. FRENCH returned from the East last week, having purchased a large and choice stock of groceries which he offers for sale at wholesale and retail. His store-room is not excelled in the city, being entirely new and built expressly for his business. Call and see him.

CURIOUS.—On Saturday, near Beef Slough, our attention was called to numerous cakes of ice floating in the river. It appeared hard and firm as in mid-winter, and was quite a rarity in September. Perhaps we should say that it came from several barges that were aground, and had been thrown overboard to lighten ship.

TEACHERS' INSTITUTE.—Prof. W. T. HATCH, County Superintendent of Pierce County, will hold a teachers' institute at Prescott three days, commencing to-day, 15th inst. A cordial invitation is extended to the friends of education in this vicinity to be present and take part in the exercises. An opportunity of which we hope they will avail themselves.

MILITARY.—Our town abounds in military, and shoulder straps are quite plenty. We have noticed Maj. DOWNIE, of the 1st, Lieut. COLLINS, of the 7th, and several others. We are indebted to Col. DONALDSON, formerly of the 4th, and now of the army of the Mississippi, for a copy of the Vicksburg Daily *Citizen*, printed on wall paper, and other relics.

REMOVED.—WILLSON has removed into Exchange Block, on Second Street, where he has fitted up one of the best store-rooms in town. He leaves for New York to purchase his fall stock, and intends to bring on one of the finest assortments of goods ever exhibited in Hastings.

PERSONAL.—While returning from Milwaukee we had the company of THOS. W. KNOX esq., of the New York *Herald*, now on a tour of observation in Minnesota and North-Western Wisconsin. Mr. KNOX, it will be remembered, was the war correspondent court-martialed by Gen. SHERMAN for publishing "contraband" intelligence. He is a genial, whole-souled fellow, and wields a ready pen.

NEW PAPER.—We have been receiving for some time past the *Mower County Register* which we have heretofore failed to notice. It is a six column sheet, neatly printed, and edited by H. R. DAVIDSON. It is a good local paper, and the way it gives the copperhead ticket of that place "fits" is n't slow. The citizens of Austin should give the *Register* a hearty support for there is nothing like supporting a home paper. Success to you, Bro. DAVIDSON, is our best wish.

YE DEVIL RETURNETH THANKS.—MARK WILLSON, ye man who keeps the best and cheapest (so the ladies say) stock of dry and fancy goods in town, has the thanks of "ye devil" and sundry other "personages" for something less than a dozen water and muskmelons, received one day last week. "Ye devil" made an impromptu speech upon the occasion; but as the sundry other "personages" were boisterously moving upon the melons, the reporter was only able to catch the last grand ortorical flourish of ye satanic majesty: "*Bully for Willson!*"

GRAPES.—This kind of wild fruit grows in abundance in the bottoms and on the side hills. We understand that there is literally no end to them in the bottom below the city. Baskets and sacks full of them are toted out every day. Bushels of grapes are offered for sale in this market. The grape is an excellent fruit for many purposes, and in this new country comes in good play to a certain extent the want of apples. Grape wine and jelly are not bad luxuries and our readers will find that as Mrs. Toodles says "it will be so handy to have them in the house," about Christmas time.

DEMOCRATIC TICKET.—At a convention held at South Branch Inn yesterday, the following ticket was put in nomination:

Senator,—D. F. Langley, of Hastings.
Representatives,—K. N. Guiteau, of West St. Paul, G. F. Ackly, of Lakeville.
Treasurer,—Michael Comer, of Eagan.
Sheriff,—Stephen Newell, of Burnsville.
District Attorney,—T. R. Huddleston, of Hastings.
Judge of Probate,—Seagrave Smith, of Hastings.
Register of Deeds,—Edmond Eichhorn, of Hastings.
Surveyor,—W. C. Cowler, of Hastings.
Coroner,—William Felton, of Nininger.
Commissioners,—2d district Geo. Egbert, of Ravenna; 3d dist.,—Geo. Bohrer, of Inver Grove.

FRUIT.—Under the head of State News we have collected several items respecting fruit in this state. We have, for a long time, been of the opinion that nearly all the different varieties of fruit could be grown in Minnesota, and the evidences we have there presented are sufficient proof of the fact. It is always the case in new countries that the first two or three efforts at fruit raising are failures; but as population gathers in and the land is brought under vigorous cultivation the prospects are enhanced. We think that we hazard no truth in saying that in a few years Minnesota will raise fruit enough to supply home consumption. Young orchards are being planted in many places, and the prospects are as fair as they were at an earlier day in the older states for large orchards and plenty of fruit. Perhaps it would be well for those who intend to raise fruit to get their trees near home as possible. Trees taken from a distance are not so liable to live and bear as those acclimated.

COUNTY CONVENTION.—At a meeting of the delegates chosen by the several towns to represent them in county convention, on motion of Mr. Morrison, of Inver Grove, Isaac Heslet was chosen chairman, and, on motion of Mr. White, of Hastings, Wm. Lee was elected secretary.

On motion of Moses Bixler, a committee on credentials was appointed, consisting of John White, Moses Bixler, and H. G. O. Morrison. Said committee reported as follows, which was adopted:

Hastings—C. N Wilson, H. Montgomery, John White, L. L. Twichell, Wm. Lee, D. W. Truax, T. M. Smith.
Vermillion—John McKay, Andrew Warsup.
Marshan—Wm. Lyon, George Panchott.
Rosemont—J. P. Abraham, T. Clark, B. Verrill.
Empire City—Isaac Heslet, F. G. Ray.
Castle Rock—Ditus Day, Dr. W. E. Potts.
Mendota—H. E. Descaries, N. J. March, C. D. Pierce.
Hampton—L. N. Holden, C. S. Barton, G. McKay.
West St. Paul—Moses Bixler, Horace Browly, Jacob Stulzman, N. N. Thompson, William North.
Randolph—D. B. Hurlbut, D. H. Morrill.
Waterford—J. P. Nagley, J. W. Roath.
Lebanon—C. S. Verrill, John Gilman.
Nininger—P. F. Countryman, Virgil Dyer, William Hanna.
Inver Grove—Isaac VanBuskirk, H. G. O. Morrison.
Sciota—Walter Hunter, Murry Huntress.
Greenvale—S. C. Howell.
Douglass—Reuben Cecil.
Eureka—G. B. Mallory, S. Livingston.

On motion of H. Montgomery, the following resolutions were adopted:

Resolved, That this organization be known and styled the Dakota County Union Organization.

Resolved, That we will strengthen the arms of the present administration, encourage the soldiers in the field, and pledge our lives, our fortunes, and our sacred honor, to aid in crushing out this gigantic and wicked rebellion, for the restoration of the union, the maintainance of the constitution, and the supremacy of the laws.

Resolved, That on this platform alone recognizing and sustaining the loyal and condemning the disloyal do we enter this campaign, and we hereby invite all, of whatever political faith who endorse the above ideas to unite and co-operate with us for their fulfillment.

On motion, the convention proceeded to the nomination of candidates, and Messrs. Montgomery and Morrison were chosen tellers.

On motion, delegates were authorized to cast the entire vote of their towns.

First ballot for senator was as follows:

S. G. Renick,	11
H. G. O. Morrison,	4
Eli Robinson,	6
A. M. Hayes,	1
C. W. Lange,	5
D. B. Truax,	4
N. N. Thompson,	12
J. F. Rehse,	3
Blank,	1

Mr. Thompson here, in conference with Judge Renick, offered to withdraw in his favor, and the delegates tendered him the unanimous nomination if he would accept, but the Judge positively declined a place on the ticket, and with this understanding a second ballot was taken with the following results:

N. N. Thompson,	24
S. G. Renick,	14
E. Robinson,	8

On motion, N. N. Thompson was declared the unanimous choice of the convention.

The ballot for first representative was then taken:

J. F. Rehse,	38
D. B. Truax,	1

J. F. Rehse was declared the nominee.

For second representative L. C. Howell had 38 votes, and was nominated unanimously.

D. B. Truax was nominated for treasurer by acclamation.

Ballot for sheriff resulted thus:

O. S. Taylor,	10
H. J. Taylor,	20
Wm Jones,	2
I. M. Ray,	1

H. J. Taylor was announced as the nominee.

For judge of probate, I. M. Ray was chosen by acclamation.

For register of deeds;

H. A. Monser,	21
W. H. McCollum,	21

Result of second ballot;

H. A. Monser,	27
W. H. McCollum,	12

H. A. Monser was declared the nominee.

R. W. Montgomery was nominated for district attorney, C. B. Lowell for surveyor, and P. Hartshorn for coroner, by acclamation.

Josiah Burwell, of Inver Grove, was nominated for commissioner in the 3d district and Henry Sprague, of Nininger, for the 2d district.

A central committee, consisting of D. E. Eyre, C. Stebbins, Irving Todd, H. G. O. Morrison, and H. Caskey was appointed by the chair.

On motion, the committee was empowered to appoint town committees.

It was resolved that the [illegible] of this convention shall be [illegible].

Adjourned *sine die.*

ISAAC HESLET, President.
William Lee, Secretary.

THE CONSERVER.

BY IRVING TODD.

Office Over the Bank of Hastings, Exchange Block, Second Street.

Our Platform.

Resolved, That we, chosen to represent in convention the unconditional union men of Minnesota, grateful to Almighty God for the success which has hitherto crowned the arms of our country and for the prospect thus opened of a speedy, honorable, and lasting peace, do hereby, for ourselves and our constituents, reaffirm our determination to support our government by every means in our power in the vigorous prosecution of this war,—on our part, holy, just, and forced upon us by the criminal acts of others,—until not an enemy in arms shall be found within our borders. And to this we pledge our lives, our fortunes, and our sacred honor.

2. That we tender our grateful thanks to the survivors of our glorious armies, and our warm sympathy to the relatives of their gallant dead, who have won for the country so glorious victories, for themselves imperishable renown, and for us all an assurance of liberty and safety, for ourselves and our children, under our beloved and now well-tried government.

3. That with especial pride we point to the gallant achievements on many a hard-fought battle-field, of our Minnesota regiments. Their bravery, discipline, and patriotism have won for them a name that shall never die, and made forever honorable to a citizen of Minnesota.

4. That, without claiming for it exemption from error, we heartily endorse the general policy and conduct of our national administration; and we point to the recent magnificent triumph of our armies as its best vindication from the charge of incapacity so freely brought against it by those who prefer national ruin to success under the present administration. *Especially* do we approve the emancipation proclamation, and the raising of black troops, as being among the best possible measures to weaken the enemy and strengthen ourselves.

5. That our state administration and congressional delegation deserve our hearty approbation for the zealous and efficient co-operation they have afforded the national authorities in carrying on the war.

6. That we call upon those in authority to take such measures, by retaliation or otherwise, as shall effectually prevent brutal and barbarous treatment by the enemy of our soldiers, of whatever color.

7. That it is due to our shattered armies in the field, as well as to the sacred cause which they uphold, that their ranks should as speedily as possible be filled up by every means in our power. It is due to the country that the mobs raised to resist and prevent the draft, should not even seem to have succeeded a day longer than is necessary to enforce the laws.

8. That the way to peace is, and ever has been, open to the rebels; the only condition we have ever sought to impose is that they should lay down their arms and submit to the authority of the general government. We protest against the making of any terms with them in advance as to their *status* in communities, when they shall have returned to their allegiance. Having been declared "public enemies" by a recent unanimous decision of the Supreme Court of the United States, they must accept the consequences that legitimately flow from having placed themselves in that position.

The True Cause.

The true reason why the army of the West has always been victorious is found in the fact that it has been properly educated. It has fought for correct principles. The Chicago *Tribune* of the 3d inst. says:

The telegraph announces that Gen. Grant has written a letter to the President relative to the mission of Gen. Thomas for organizing negro regiments in the south-west. In that letter the general pledges his hearty support in the movement, and takes occasion to endorse the emancipation proclamation, and promises most valuable results from the use of negro troops. This announcement will give joy to every loyal man, and fire the copperhead heart. With the exception of McClellan, Buell, and Fitz John Porter, every general in the army now endorses the proclamation, and stands by its author. The secesh concern in this city having disposed of Garibaldi, will now set up its howl of abolitionist at the hero of the Mississippi, and devote columns of where hitherto it has found only subjects of laudation. Let but a man promise to stand by the government, and he is doomed instanter to copper head wrath. Gen. Grant has placed himself in that category.

SIMMERING DOWN.—Three of the seven nominees of the democratic state convention have declined, on account of the disloyalty of the platform. Every democratic paper in the state which has come to hand, with one exception, repudiates the ticket. That exception is the St. Cloud *Union*; and we congratulate the remaining nominees on its adherence to their fortunes. It cannot be said that the great copperhead party of Minnesota is without an organ. And, it is an organ of which La Due, McKenny & Co. ought to be proud. It is n't issued oftener than about once a month, but when it comes out it tells. It sustains the copperhead candidates and their platform right up to the hilt, without question or evasion. In its own language:—

"We endorse convention, nominations, and platform—that is our opinion, *simmered down!*"

The *Union's* party, in November, will be precisely like its "opinion."—*Pioneer.*

The slanders of the copperhead papers against the patriotism of the negro are receiving frequent refutations. A negro in Rhode Island was enrolled in two towns, and drafted in both. Instead of taking advantage of this informality, he goes for one town, and sends a substitute for the other. What white man could do more? Out of fifty-three men drafted in Enfield, Conn., fifty-two paid their $300. The remaining gentleman was a darkey, who expressed his determination to go and represent the town!

Children's Temper.

"My child has such a dreadful temper," sighs many a woman, "I really cannot tell what to do with him. It is over like a flash, and he is sorry for it, but on some new provocation it breaks out again as strong as ever. I lose all my own patience in trying to make him more patient."

Very likely the tendency you so much deplore in your child arises from qualities very valuable in themselves. He is full of a hundred eager purposes which a sluggish "good-natured" child knows nothing of. He has an active, restless temperament, which, *if* rightly directed, will make him an earnest worker when he grows up; and, of course, he will meet with a great many rubs and jars in carrying out his child plans. People do not respect little children enough, or they would not interfere needlessly with their "work." It is quite as important to them as yours is to you, and it is quite as irritating to have it all spoiled. If you repress your child's anger by angry words, you have only turned the quick flash into sullenness, which will nurse the evil temper for hours. You may rest assured you have done a great deal more harm than good. Bright, cheerful words, and a firm, restraining hand, will have far more weight. If he has been wronged, teach him to bear it bravely; give him a little anecdote to illustrate your point—every child will stop for a story—and when it is over, he may have "forgotten what he was crying about." But the best way is to prevent the irritating causes, when you can. Never be afraid of making your child too happy. Oh! it is this blessed sunshine of our childhood that makes the heart grow rich in precious treasures of love and gentleness. It is in the bright atmosphere of happiness that we learn our choicest lessons, which we must teach and practice all our lives. And the earlier you begin to teach your little one his obligation to God for all his conduct, the more abundant will be your success in repressing the evil of the natural heart. Go away with him and pray for his forgiveness, after an act of disobedience or an outbreak of passion. Teach him to pray, also, not for forgiveness only, but also for help to keep from doing so again. Tell him Jesus will easily help him, if he will only stop and pray when Satan tempts him to get angry. They will believe you a great deal more readily than older people. There is no disposition better fitted than a little child's to receive the kingdom of heaven.

Never do too much at a Time.

One great secret of success in life is to know when to expend and when to husband strength. Those who accomplish most are not those who work the longest, but those who work at the right time, and under the most favorable circumstances. Sir Edward Bulwer Lytton has been one of the most prolific authors of the age, but he has given only a few hours each day to literary labor. He says of himself, in a recent lecture:

"Many persons, seeing me so much engaged in active life, and as much about the world as if I had never been a student, have said to me, When do you get time to write all your books? How on earth do you contrive to do so much work? I shall surprise you by the answer I make. The answer is this: I contrive to do so much by never doing too much at a time. A man, to get through work well, must not overwork himself; for if he do too much to-day, the reaction of fatigue will come, and he will be obliged to do too little to-morrow.

"Now, since I began really and earnestly to study, which was not till I had left college, and was actually in the world, I may, perhaps, say that I have gone through as large a course of general reading as most men of my time. I have traveled much, and I have seen much; I have mixed much in politics, and the various business of life; and in addition to all this, I have published somewhere about sixty volumes, some upon subjects requiring much research. And what time do you think, as a general rule, I have devoted to study—to reading and writing? Not more than three hours a day, and when Parliament is sitting, not always that. But then, during those hours, I have given my whole attention to what I was about."

Wonders of the Microscope.

There are several species of minute creatures, which, from their extreme smallness and some resemblance in form, are called by the general name of mites. Place under the glass of a microscope one of the mites found in cheese, in a crawling posture, with the back part uppermost. The shape will be seen to be a kind of oval, but more obtuse at the tail end. It has three regions, or parts, as in the larger insects. The hinder part seems covered with one entire shell, so curiously polished that, as in a convex mirror, it shows the picture of all the objects round about. The middle, or crest, seems divided and covered with two shells, which, running one within the other, the mite is able to draw in or thrust out, as it finds occasion; and it can do the same with its snout.

The whole body is of a pearl-color, and transparent, so that different motions of the intestines may be discerned. Several long white hairs grow in different places; some of which are longer than the whole animal; They all appear straight and pliable, excepting two that issue from the head, which seem to be the horns.

CHILDHOOD.—There is a magic charm in its winning ways—honesty and truthfulness in its expressions of affection; there is something grand and lofty in that young, untainted soul, which should pass through life uncorrupted by the deception and sensuality of the world.

A Letter From Edward Everett.

BOSTON, Aug. 24, 1863.

James C. Conkling, Esq., Chairman, etc.:

My Dear Sir:—I received, a few days ago, your letter of the 12th, inviting me to attend the Grand Mass Meeting of the unconditional union men of the state of Illinois, to be held on the 2d of September, in Springfield.

It will not be in my power to attend the meeting, but its objects as explained by you, have my cordial sympathy.

The elections soon to be held will be of more than usual importance. They will throw light on the great question, how far it is possible for a free government, constituted in its legislative and executive branches by popular choice, to prosecute with vigor a war of considerable duration, and which entails heavy burdens on the community. As a representative government is mainly carried on by party organizations, the great interests of the community, both in peace and war, are too apt to become the arena in which the opposite parties strive for the mastery. Questions, in themselves of secondary importance to the general welfare, are often contested with vehemence and passion, and that by men of ability and patriotism, working themselves up to the belief that they are contending for matters of vital importance. Within my experience, the policies of the country have successively turned from four or five questions, regarded at the time as of the greatest moment, but now utterly obsolete and forgotten.

These unprofitable contest, while they last, are the source of great embarassment to the administration of the general government for the time being, which finds itself thwarted in all its measures, however patriotic and beneficial their tendency by indiscriminate opposition, aiming only at an electioneering triumph. This is a very serious evil even in time of peace, greatly enhancing the difficulties and burdens of public life, and highly detrimental to the public interest.

In time of war the evil becomes one of tremendous magnitude. The questions that then present themselves are naturally more important than ordinary political issues in time of peace, while every blow struck at the measures of the government, though designed only to affect a change of administration, really affords aid and comfort to the enemy.

This will be the case when the opposition to the government measures is sincerely dictated by honest difference of opinion. Nay, it will ever be the case when the opposition is directed against measures palpably mistaken either on grounds of principle or policy. No administration is free from error, and if party spirit is allowed to prevail, its errors will be severely criticised, usually exaggerated, and often fiercely denounced, till the attention of the country, instead of being fixed on the great and main questions on which all good patriots are agreed, is turned to side issues of minor, or often factitious importance. In this way the administration of the government is weakened and embarassed, and the vigorous prosecution of the war, which every patriotic citizen admits to be the paramount object is in some degree parallized.

I have doubted the policy of some measures of the administration, and strongly disapproved others; but regarding the persons in power for the time being as the constitutional agents of the people for carrying on the government—considering the war, which has been forced upon us by the ambitious demagogues of the South, as a question of national life or death—that to have the doctrine of secession established at the mouth of the rebel cannon is simply to consign the country to a future of eternal border war, and to lay its dishonored fragments at the feet of foreign powers—I cannot but think it unpatriotic to attempt, for the sake of a party triumph, to make political capital out of the difficulties, or, if you please, the errors, unavoidably incident to the conduct of a war of such gigantic dimensions.

It is a pretty safe test, in cases of this kind, to ask how the views and measures of a party ar regarded by the common enemy. Applying this test in the present case, nothing is more certain than that the triumph, at the approaching election, of any party organized and operating for the prostration of the administration, would be regarded with unmingled satisfaction by the leaders of the rebellion and their sympathyzers abroad. Indeed, their last hope is in our divisions.

Candor requires me to add, that if it is the duty of good citizens to abstain from factious opposition, it is, in time of war, not less the duty of an administration, as well in civil as military and naval affairs, to assume a position wholly independent of party. I am afraid it is impossible in time of peace, to carry on representative government except on a party basis.

During the existence of war, especially of war which taxes to the utmost, the energies and resources of the country, party support, in proportion as it is relied upon, is an element not of strength but of weakness.

If all good men and good patriots in the loyal states, whether in office or out of office, sacrificing when necessary, a little pride of personal feeling and of party association, would cordially unite for the attainment of the objects which they all approve, viz: The vigorous prosecution and successful termination of the war, the next New Year's day would witness the prostration of the rebellion and its leaders; the return of peace and the restoration of the union.

With the best wishes that the meeting at Springfield may promote these ends, I remain, dear sir, very respectfully,

Your friend and fellow-citizen,

EDWARD EVERETT.

AGRICULTURAL.

Interesting to Farmer's Wives.

As a general rule, it is most economical to buy the best articles. The price is, of course, always a little higher, but good articles spend best. It is a sacrifice of money to buy poor flour, meal, sugar, mollasses, butter, cheese, lard, etc to say nothing of the injurious effect upon the health.

Of West-India sugar and molasses the Santa Cruis and Porto Rico are considered the best. The Havana is seldom clean. White sugar from Brazil is sometimes very good. Refined sugars usually contain most of the saccharine substances, therefore there is probably more economy in using loaf, crushed, and granulated sugars than we should at first suppose.

Butter made in September and October, is best for winter use. Lard should be hard and white, and that which is taken from a hog not over a year old is best.

Rich Cheese feels soft under the presure of the fingure. That which is very strong is neither good nor healthy. To keep one that is cut, tie it up in a bag that will not admit flies, and hang it up in a cool dry place. If mold appears on it wipe it off with a dry cloth.

Flour and meal of all kinds, should be kept in a cool, dry place.

The best rice is large, and has a clear, fresh look. Old rice sometimes has little black insects inside the kernels.

The small white sago, called pearl sago, is the best. The large brown kind has an earthly taste. These articles, and tapioca, ground rice, etc., should be kept covered.

The cracked cocoa is the best, but that which is put up in pound papers is often very good.

To select nutmegs, prick them with a pin. If they are good the oil will instantly spread around the puncture.

Keep coffee by itself, as its oder affects other articles. Keep tea in a close chest or canister.

Oranges and lemons keep best wrapt close in soft paper and laid in a drawer of linen.

When a cask of molasses is bought draw off a few quarts, else the farmentation produced by moving it will burst the cask.

Bread and cake should be kept in a tin box or stone jar.

Salt cod should be kept in a dry place where the oder of it will not effect the air of the house. The best kind is that which is called dun, from its peculiar odor. Fish skin for clearing coffee should be washed, dried, cut small, and kept in a box or paper bag.

Soft soap should be kept in a dry place in the cellar, and should not be used till three months old.

Bar soap should be cut into pieces of a convenient size, and laid where it will become dry. It is well to keep it several weeks before using it, as it spends fast when it is new.

Hazel Nuts.

Hazel nuts are the fruit of the wild bush of Corylus Avellana, unchanged or unimproved by cultivation. The fruit differs from that of the domesticated varieties only in being smaller, while the tree is more hardy. This plant, which is a native of all the cooler parts of Europe, Northern Asia, and North America, is the parent of the many varieties of nuts and filberts now cultivated for their fruit. The filbert is the fruit of the tubulosa variety of the Corylus Avellana. The term was originally applied to those kinds of nuts which have very long husks but owing to the number of varieties that have of late years been obtained, this distinction, which was never scientific, appears to be nearly disregarded, and nuts and filberts are almost synonymous terms, excepting that the wild uncultivated fruit and those varieties which most nearly approach it are never called filberts. In order to preserve filberts in a fresh and plump state, it is only necessary to prevent their parting with their moisture by evaporation. Burying them in heaps in the earth, or jars in a cellar, and covering them with dry sand are all excellent planes. The hazel nut of America is smaller than that of Spain, but it possesses a more pleasant taste, and might be gathered in large quantities in many places. It is however, never gathered like chestnuts for the market, all the filberts and hazel nuts sold are imported. About 182,000 bushels are exported from Spain annually.—*Sic. American.*

BLACK INK.—One quart of soft water, four ounces nut-gall, one and a half ounces gum arabic, one and a half ounces copperas. Soak the nut-gall in three-fourths of the water, the gum arabic in one-half the remainder, warmed, and the copperas in the other half. Let them stand in separate vessels forty-eight hours, then mix ready for use. This ink will not spoil by freezing.—*Rural New Yorker.*

The *Country Gentleman* hints that the quality of cheese is too frequently spoiled by want of knowledge and care in its manufacture, and says: "Too muce rennet makes the cheese smell rank. Too much salt makes it hard, tastless, and liable to crack. Too little salt, and it becomes rancid, and spoils entirely."

TO DESTROY ANTS.—Ants that frequent houses or gardens may be distroyed by taking flour of brimstone half a pound, and potash four ounces; set them in an iron or earthen pan over the fire till dissolved and united; afterwards beat them to a powder in water, and wherever you sprinkle it, the ants will die or fly the place.

TO TAKE RUST OUT OF STEEL.—Rub well with sweet oil, and let the oil remain upon them for forty-eight hours. Then rub with leather sprinkled with unslacked lime, finely powered, until all the rust disappears.

BATCHELDER'S COLUMN.

GREAT ATTRACTIONS

AT THE

OLD STAND.

GEO. F. BATCHELDER,

(Successor to North & Carll)

WHOLESALE

AND

RETAIL

Dealer in

DRY GOODS,

GROCERIES,

Boots and Shoes,

HARDWARE, ETC.,

HASTINGS, MINN.

Having laid in an unusually heavy stock of staple wares, would invite the attention of the public to my large assortment of

GOODS,

Consisting of Imported and Domestic

SILKS, DELAINES,

LAWNS AND

CALICOES,

also to my stock of Foreign and Domestic

SHEETINGS,

These goods were purchased at exceedingly low rates, and am therefore enabled to sell at prices to suit the times.

A well assorted stock of

Hats and Caps,

for Men and Boys, of the latest styles.

READY-MADE

CLOTHING,

a fine assortment, custom made, from the best of cloths, bought expressly for this market, and will be sold at reasonable figures, for cash only.

A choice stock of pure and fresh

GROCERIES

Just received from the East, where especial attention was paid to their selection.

A fine lot of assorted

Boots and Shoes,

comprising Gent's, Ladies', Boy's, and Misses', of all varieties. The especial attention of farmers is invited to a large and complete stock of

HARDWARE.

The celebrated Moline Plow always on hand.

A long experience in and close supervision of the business, and personal attention to the buying of goods, gives confidence that entire satisfaction will be rendered to patrons. Customers will be waited on by experienced and accommodating salesmen, and their wishes promptly attended to. All goods warranted as represented.

Geo. F. Batchelder.

Hastings, June 5, 1863. 5tf

THE CONSERVER.

Published every Tuesday Morning at
HASTINGS, DAKOTA COUNTY, MINNESOTA.

Terms.

Single copy one year	$2 00
" " six months	1 00
" " three months	60
Five copies, to one address	8 75
Ten " " "	15 00
Twenty " " " and one to getter up of club	30 00

Payment invariably in advance.

Address Irving Todd, Publisher.

RATES OF ADVERTISING.

1 square 1 week	$1 00	2 squares 6 months	9 00
[illegible]	[illegible]	[illegible]	[illegible]

One inch in space will be counted as a square of solid matter.

Business cards on second page, not exceeding seven lines, seven dollars per year; each additional line one dollar.

Legal advertisements inserted at the rates prescribed by statute, and attorneys ordering such advertisements will be held responsible.

Special notices 12 cents per line for first insertion and ten cents for each subsequent insertion.

Transient advertisements must be paid in advance —all others quarterly.

Advertisements not otherwise ordered, will be continued until they are ordered out, and charged accordingly.

God Bless the Little Children.

God bless the little children,
We meet them everywhere;
We hear their voices round our hearth,
Their footsteps on our stair;
Their kindly hearts are swelling o'er
With mirthfulness and glee;
God bless the little children,
Wherever they may be.

We meet them 'neath the gipsy tent,
With visage swart and dun,
And eyes that sparkle as they glance
With roguery and fun;
We find them fishing in the brook
For minnows, with a pin;
Or creeping through the hazel bush,
The linnet's nest to win.

We meet them in the lordly hall,
Their stately father's pride,
We meet them in the poor man's cot—
He hath no wealth beside.
Along the city's crowded street
They hurl the hoop or ball;
We find them 'neath the pauper's roof—
The saddest sight of all.

For there they win no father's love,
No mother's tender care—
Their only friend the God above,
Who hears the orphan's prayer.
But dressed in silk, or draped in rags,
In childish grief or glee,
God bless the little children,
Wherever they may be.

A French Trick.—A dandy was walking under the arcades of the Rue de Rivoli, in Paris, holding in his hand a gold headed cane of splendid workmanship. A man supported by two crutches came up, and asked for alms in a pitiful tone. The dandy, moved to pity, gave the beggar a small silver coin. At the same moment a person near him suddenly exclaimed, "How can you, sir, allow this rogue to deceive you? Please to lend me your cane, and I will show you that the rascal runs better than I can." The dandy, without reflecting, lent his cane; the beggar, the moment he perceived it in his detractor's hand, threw away his crutches and took to his heels, and was followed by the man with the cane, whilst the spectators, and the dandy particularly, remained in convulsions of laughter at the sight, and exclaiming alternately, "O, he will be caught." "No, he will not be caught." But both the racing heroes disappeared at the next turning in the street, and their victim remained waiting for his splendid cane, which cost five hundred francs.

A bevy of children were telling their father what they got at school. The eldest got reading, and spelling, and definitions. "And what do you get, little one?" said the father to a rosy cheeked little fellow, who, at the time was slily driving a ten penny nail into the door panel.

"Me! oh, I gets readin', spellin', and spankings."

A dutchman was relating his marvelous escape from drowning when thirteen of his companions were lost by the upsetting of a boat, and he alone was saved.

"And how did you escape their fate?" asked one of his hearers.

"I tid not go in te pote," was the dutchman's placid answer.

Fun is the most conservative element of society, and ought to be cherished and encouraged by all lawful means. People never plot mischief when they are merry. Laughter is an enemy to malice, a foe to scandal, and a friend to every virtue. It promotes good temper, enlivens the heart, and brightens the intellect. Let us laugh when we can.

"Now, papa, tell me what is a humbug?" "It is," replied papa, "when mamma pretends to be very fond of me, and puts no buttons on my shirts till I remind her of it a dozen times." Queer definition that, still there's some truth in it.

"Jimmy, what is the meaning of a shepard?" "A man who watches sheep." "Then a man who watches cows must be a coward, of course," said Samuel, with a broad grin.

If you relish your food, labor for it; if you would enjoy your raiment, pay for it before you wear it; if you would sleep soundly, take a clear conscience to bed with you.

Women have more strength in their looks than we have in our laws, and more power in their tears than we have in our arguments.

A sour old bachelor says he always looks under the marriage head or the news of the week.

HARDWARE.

ATTENTION EVERY BODY!

Buy Where You Can Buy Cheapest and get Good Articles.

If you want good hoes and forks, go to Thomas' Hardware Store.

If you want good scythes and snaths cheap, go to Thomas'.

HARDWARE.

If you want fine table and pocket cutlery, go to Thomas' Cheap Store.

If you want nails or iron cheap, go straight to Thomas', and no where else.

If you want any kind of tools cheap and good, go to Thomas.

If you want hatchets or axes of the best quality, go to Thomas' Cheap Store.

If you want kerosene oil cheap and good go to Thomas.

HARDWARE.

If you want stoves and tinware of the best quality and cheap as the cheapest, go to the cheap hardware store of John Thomas.

If you want locks, latches, butts and screws, or any kind of house trimmings, Thomas' is the place to buy.

If you want sheep shears, gopher traps, smooth irons, iron bench screws, augurs, auger bitts, hand bells, cow bells, or any article kept in a hardware store, go to Thomas' and get it cheap and of the best quality.

HARDWARE.

Try it and see if you cannot make money at it.

John Thomas.

Hastings, May 14, 1863. 5-tf

HARDWARE.

M. MC HUGH,

Dealer in

HARDWARE,
TINWARE,
STOVES, ETC.,

Corner of Second and Vermillion Streets, Hastings, Minnesota,

has on hand and is constantly receiving a general assortment and a full supply of

Iron,
Nails,
Tinware,
Glass,
Sash,
And
Putty,

Also the best stock of

CUTLERY

ever before exhibited in this market. These goods have been bought expressly for this trade, and will be sold on the most reasonable terms for cash.

I am also agent for, and have on hand, the celebrated

STEWART COOKING STOVE,

known to be the best cooking stove manufactured.

Hastings, May 14, 1863. 5-tf

H. H. PRINGLE,

Wholesale and Retail Dealer in

HARDWARE, IRON, NAILS,

STOVES AND TINWARE,

Mechanics' Tools,

Building Materials,

AGRICULTURAL IMPLEMENTS,

PAINTS, OILS, GLASS,

SASH, DOORS, BLINDS, ETC

HASTINGS, MIN,

TIN,

SHEET IRON & COPPER W'K

ON HAND OR MADE TO ORDER.

BRICK DRUG STORE,

R. J. MARVIN.

Dealer in

DRUGS,
MEDICINES,
CHEMICALS,
ETC., ETC.

On hand a large stock of

PAINTS,
OILS,
COLORS,
GLASS, AND
PAINTERS'
STOCK GENERALLY.

Also

Garden and Field

SEEDS.

Please give me a call before purchasing. Try my goods and prices, which is a better test than blowing.

May 1, 1863. 5-tf

PRINTING.

ALL KINDS OF

PRINTING

Neatly and Cheaply Executed

AT THE

CONSERVER OFFICE.

Cards,
Programmes,
Bill-Heads,
Circulars,
Posters,
Etc.,

Printed to Order and at

SHORT NOTICE.

Having received a choice supply of

NEW MATERIAL

from the East, am prepared to do

PLAIN AND FANCY WORK,

in styles to defy competition.

Orders from the country promptly attended to.

IRVING TODD.

FURNITURE.

H. BUTTURFF,

Manufacturer and Dealer in

FURNITURE, UPHOLSTERY,
DOMESTIC WILLOW WARE,
CRIBS, HOBBY HORSES,
PROPELLERS, BABY-JUMPERS,
FEATHERS, PILLOWS, MATRESSES
COMFORTERS, WINDOW SHADES,
TABLE and FLOOR OIL CLOTH,
CARPETS, CURLED HAIR, etc. etc.

PARLOR FURNITURE,

Cane Seat and Common Chairs, Extention, Dining and Centre Tables, Rocking Chairs, Bedsteads, Wardrobes, Bureaus, Tin Safes, Picture Frames and Looking glasses.

I keep employed the best of workmen, and manufacture to order, with neatness and dispatch.

N. B. Coffins on hand and made to order.

Hastings, Nov. 20, 1862. 32-tf

THE LIVING AND THE DEAD CAN be supplied at

Herzog & Corson's

with all kinds of

Sash, Doors,
Blinds, Chairs,
Cabinet Ware,
Planing, Matching,
Sawing, Turning
Etc., Etc.

Coffins of all kinds and styles, a large lot always on hand. Sole agents for

THE METALLIC BURIAL CASES.

Come and buy a good article cheap for cash or produce. Wood, Lumber, Pork, etc. taken in exchange for work.

Sale Rooms and Factory corner of Second and Eddy Streets, west of S. Roger's store.

Herzog & Corson.

Hastings, Jan. 1, 1863. 28-tf

F. VAN AUKEN. W. H. LANGLEY

VAN AUKEN & LANGLEY,

STORAGE,

FORWARDING & COMMISS'N MERCHANTS,

Dealers in Produce, and Agents for

Threshing Machines and Reapers,

RAILROAD & STEAMBOAT

TICKET AGENTS.

EQUITABLE LIFE ASSURANCE SOCIETY,

OF NEW YORK.

CASH CAPITAL,	$100,000
NETT SURPLUS,	$130,000

Dividends on capital limited by its charter to seven per cent per annum—the entire profits go to the policy holders.

H. W. Montgomery, Agent.

Hastings, Minn. Office on First Street in Gardner's new stone block. 42-1y

MISCELLANEOUS.

BLACKSMITH SHOP.

PLOWS! PLOWS!! PLOWS!!

I have just established myself in the above business on Second Street, above Herzog & Corson's Furniture Factory, and am prepared to do all kinds of Blacksmithing.

Also, constantly on hand all kinds of plows of the most approved patterns and made of the best material. I shall be obliged for a share of public patronage, and shall always warrant my work to be of the best quality.

John Bateman.

Hastings, Nov. 25, 1862. 36-tf

BOOKS AND STATIONERY.

W. P. STANLEY,

DEALER IN

Books and Stationery,

Paper Hangings, Curtains, Fixtures, Cord, and Tassels; buff and green Holland, oil green cloth for shades; Photographs of our generals and other distinguished individuals and albums to put them in; Yankee Notions, all the leading Magazines and Newspapers, Eastern and Western, St. Paul Dailies; agent for Prince & Sons Melodeons. 41-tf

CAPITAL NEW BOOKS,

JUST PUBLISHED BY

JOHN BRADBURN,

(Successor to M. Doolady,)

Bookseller, Publisher, and Wholesale Book Jobber,

49 WALKER STREET,

(near Broadway,)

NEW YORK CITY.

Leaves from the Diary of an Army Surgeon.
By Doctor Thos. T. Ellis,
Late Post Surgeon at New York, and acting Medical Director at White House, Va.
Cloth. 350 pages. 12mo. Price $1.
A Liberal Discount to the Trade.
Each copy contains an autograph letter from Gen. McClellan.

DR. CUMMING'S REPLY TO BISHOP COLENSO.
Bishop Colenso Fully Answered.
His Errors refuted, and the Mosaic authorship of the Pentateuch clearly established, by the Rev. John Cumming, D. D., in a series of lectures.
Cloth. 271 pp. Price $1.

The Actress in High Life.
AN EPISODE IN WINTER QUARTERS.
By a lady of South Carolina.
Cloth. 461 pp. 12mo. $1 25.

Adventures by Sea and Land of the Count de Ganay;
OR, THE DEVOTION AND FIDELITY OF WOMAN
An Episode of the Colonization of Canada.
By H. Emile Chevalier.
Cloth. 312 pp. 12mo. $1.

Les Miserables.
By Victor Hugo.
Five Volumes in One.
Fantine, Marius, St. Denis,
Cosette, Valjean.
Cloth. 476 pp. 8vo. $1 50.

Hans of Iceland;
THE DEMON OF THE NORTH.
A Romance.
By Victor Hugo.
Cloth. 187 pp. 8vo. 50c.

Arbitrary Arrests in the South.
SCENES IN THE EXPERIENCE OF AN ALABAMA UNIONIST.
By R. S. Tharin, A. M.
Native of Charleston; for thirty years a resident of the Cotton States; and commonly known in the West as "the Alabama Refugee."
Cloth. 245 pp. 12mo. $1.

Lives and Letters of Abelard and Heloise.
By O. W. Wight.
Cloth. 319 pp. 12mo. $1.

Three Years in Chili.
Cloth. 156 pp. 12mo. 75c.

Woods and Waters.
THE SARANACS AND RACKET.
By Alfred B. Street.
Cloth. 341 pp. 12mo. $1 25.

Stories of Frontier Adventure in the South and West.
By W. T. Coggeshall,
Author of Home Hits and Hints, Poets and Poetry of the West, etc.
Cloth. 313 pp. 12mo. $1.

The Battle of Waterloo.
By Victor Hugo.
Paper Covers. 75 pp. 16mo. 15c.

Trips in the Life of a Locomotive Engineer.
Paper Covers. 224 pp. 12mo. 50c.
Cloth, $1.

Our Farm of Four Acres,
AND THE MONEY WE MADE BY IT.
From the 12th London Ed. by Harriet Martineau.
Paper Covers. 148 pp. 12mo. 25c. Cloth 38c.

These Books may be obtained at Retail, in this town, from the store of W. D. Stanley, on Ramsey Street. 16-1m

THE ATLANTIC MONTHLY.—BEGINning of a new volume. The number for January, 1863, begins the eleventh volume of the *Atlantic Monthly*. From the commencement, in 1860, the *Atlantic* has rapidly increased in circulation, and it now has the largest class of readers since its beginning, five years ago. Its prosperity steadily augments, and it continues, amid all the fluctuations and dangers incident to our national crisis, to gain ground in the estimation of the public. At a time so pregnant with events which touch the future destinies of America in every vital particular, the publishers and editors do not deem it necessary to promise that its pages will never swerve from the honest paths of loyal patriotism and universal freedom. It opinions have always been on the side of Liberty, Progress, and Right, and the course it first adopted in its early career will ever be faithfully maintained.

The staff of writers regularly contributing to the *Atlantic Monthly* embraces many of the best known authors in American literature, and warrants the publishers in promising to its readers the best essays, the best stories, the best poems, which American talent can furnish.

LIST OF REGULAR CONTRIBUTORS.

In prose and poetry the *Atlantic* staff of writers is unequaled. The following authors are still among the regular contributors: James Russell Lowell, Henry W. Longfellow, Louis Agassiz, Ralph Waldo Emerson, Nathaniel Hawthorne, T. W. Higginson, Author "Margret Howth," Oliver W. Holmes, John G. Whittier, E. P. Whipple, Bayard Taylor, George S. Hillard, Mrs. H. B. Stowe, "The Country Parson," Rhee Terry, Harriet E. Prescott. The *Atlantic's* list of contributors includes many of the leading writers of America.

Terms.—The *Atlantic* is for sale by all book and periodical dealers. Price 25 cts a number. Subscriptions for the year $3, postage paid. Yearly subscriptions received or single numbers supplied by any dealer, or by the publishers. Specimen numbers sent gratis on application to the publishers. Inducements for subscribing, list of premiums, etc., furnished on application to the publishers.

Ticknor & Fields, Publishers,
135 Washington Street,
44-tf Boston, Mass.

PUBLICATIONS.

THE CONTINENTAL MONTHLY.—The readers of the *Continental* are aware of the important position it has assumed, of the influence which it exerts, and of the brilliant array of political and literary talent of the highest order which supports it. No publication of the kind has, in this country, so successfully combined the energy and freedom of the daily newspaper with the higher literary tone of the first-class monthly; and it is very certain that the magazine has given wider range to its contributors, or preserved itself so completely from the narrow influences of party or faction. In times like the present, such a journal is either a power in the land or it is nothing. That the *Continental* is not the latter is abundantly evinced by what it has done—by the reflection of its counsels in many important public events, and in the character and power of those who are its staunchest supporters.

Though but little more than a year has elapsed since the *Continental* was first established, it has during that time acquired a strength and a political significance elevating it to a position far above that previously occupied by any publication of the kind in America. In proof of which assertion we call attention to the following facts:

1. Of its political articles republished in pamphlet form, a single one has had, thus far, a circulation of one hundred and six thousand copies.

2. From its literary department, a single serial novel, Among the Pines, has, within a very few months, sold nearly thirty-five thousand copies. Two other series of its literary articles have also been republished in book form, while the first portion of a third is already in press.

No more conclusive facts need to be alleged to prove the excellence of the contributions to the *Continental*, or their extraordinary popularity; and its conductors are determined that it shall not fall behind. Preserving all "the boldness, vigor, and ability" which a thousand journals have attributed to it, it will greatly enlarge its circle of action, and discuss, fearlessly and frankly, every principle involved in the great questions of the day. The first minds of the country, embracing the men most familiar with its diplomacy and most distinguished for ability, are among its contributors; and it is no mere flattering promise of a prospectus to say that this magazine for the times will employ the first intellect in America, under auspices which no publication ever enjoyed before in this country.

While the *Continental* will express decided opinions on the great questions of the day, it will not be a mere political journal: much the larger portion of its columns will be enlivened, as heretofore, by tales, poetry, and humor. In a word, the *Continental* will be found, under its new staff of editors, occupying a position and presenting attractions never before found in a magazine.

TERMS TO CLUBS.

Two copies for one year,	$5 00
Three copies for one year,	6 00
Six copies for one year,	11 00
Eleven copies for one year,	20 00
Twenty copies for one year,	36 00

Paid in advance. Postage 36 cents a year, to be paid by the subscriber. Single copies $3 a year, in advance. Postage paid by the publisher. 12-tf

John F. Trow, 50 Greene St., N.Y.,
Publisher for the Proprietors.

ONLY $1 25 A YEAR IN CLUBS OF 4.

Arthur's Home Magazine,

For 1863. Vols. XXI. and XXII. Edited by T. S. Arthur and Virginia F. Townsend. Contains novelets, stories, poetry, fashions, steel and wood engravings, needlework patterns in great variety, a mother's department, children's department, housekeeper's and health departments, with literary reviews, and all the accessories of a first-class magazine.

The Lady's Book bears this flattering testimony to the character of *Arthur's Home Magazine*:

"As we have often before said, it is, without controversy, the best $2 magazine published in the country; and this is the strongly outspoken testimony everywhere given by the press. We know of no periodical that so well deserves the praise bestowed. The editors never tire in their endeavors to give each month a rich and varied literary repast to their readers. Their work is kept fully up to the standard of their promise, is never dull, yet always full of instruction. We have often said, and repeat it again, that it should make a part of the reading of every household. We know of no better educator of the people, young and old. Of the editors we need not speak; their names are household words all over the country. In their hands no periodical can fail to reach the highest point of excellence."

A new serial by T. S. Arthur will be commenced in the January number entitled Out in the World.

Rare and elegant premiums are sent to all who make up clubs: 1. A large photographic copy of that splendid engraving Shakspeare and his Cotemporaries. 2. A large photographic copy from an engraving of Huntington's celebrated picture Mercy's Dream. 3. A similar copy of Herring's Glimpse of an English Homestead.

Terms.—$2 a year in advance and one premium plate. Two copies $3. Three for $4. Four for $5. Eight and one to getter up of club for $10. One of the premium plates is sent to every getter up of a club, small or large. Three red stamps must be sent to pay the postage on each premium. Address

T. S. Arthur & Co.,
323 Walnut Street, Philadelphia.

THE INDEPENDENT, EDITED BY *Henry Ward Beecher*, is a religious newspaper, and a real newspaper. It affords its readers fair and thoughtful editorial discussions of the most important facts and occurrences and interests of this nation and of the world. A comprehensive record of facts, men and movements of the religious world. A full and careful weekly history of the progress of the rebellion. Ample chronicles of the important general news; home and foreign. Fair and careful accounts of new books; made on the express principle of serving as a safe guide to buyers. Interesting correspondence from Washington; from the West; from the army; from abroad. Six columns a week of carefully selected matter for *family reading*; being prose and poetry, suited to interest both the old people and the young people. A full chronicle of the progress of business and of the current prices of merchandise, produce and live stock in New York City

ONE SERMON EVERY WEEK

By Rev. Henry Ward Beecher. The following eminent writers are special contributors to its columns:—

Mrs. Harriet Beecher Stowe,
Rev. Theodore L. Cuyler,
Rev. Robert M. Hatfield,
Rev. George B. Cheever,
Horace Greely,
Bayard Taylor,
John G. Whittier.

Terms.—$2 per annum, paid in advance. Specimen numbers sent gratis.

Joseph H. Richards, Publisher,
No. 5 Beekman Street, New York.

For sale by news agents.

PATENT MEDICINES.

DR. ROBACK'S

STOMACH

BITTERS

ARE NOT

TO BE EXCELLED

AS A

STOMACHIC

AND

Regulator

OF THE

DIGESTIVE ORGANS.

These Bitters

are not offered to the public as a medicine which will cure all the "ills which flesh is heir to," but as a remedial agent —a great regulator of the system.

In the Bilious districts of the West and South there has, for a long time, been much needed an article of Stomach Bitters, which, if taken in proper quantities, and at the proper time, are a sure preventive of

Bilious Fever,
Fever and Ague,
Liver Complaint,
Dyspepsia,
Indigestion,
Jaundice,
Kidney Complaints,

and all diseases of a similar nature.

These Bitters

are composed of rare and powerful roots and herbs, which make them

Highly Tonic.

Dr. Roback's
Stomach Bitters
are the poor man's friend.

Dr. Roback's
Stomach Bitters
save the poor man many Doctor's Bills.

Dr. Roback's
Stomach Bitters
are the rich man's Solace and Comfort.

Dr. Roback's
Stomach Bitters
invigorate the weak and debilitated.

Dr. Roback's
Stomach Bitters
drive away melancholy and make Life enjoyable.

Dr. Roback's
Stomach Bitters
are the Soldier's Friend, by preventing Diarrhea, Dysentery, Rheumatism, etc.

These Bitters are put up in quart bottles, of which the above is a facsimile. The label is finely engraved, and is provided with a safe-guard from counterfeiters. Price $1 per bottle, or six for $5.

C. W. Roback, Proprietor, No. 4 East Fourth Street, Cincinnati, to whom all orders should be addressed.

FOR SALE BY

A. M. Pett, Hastings, J. R. Tinkcom, Mankato, W. H. McCollum, Mankato, and by druggists and merchants generally throughout the United States, Canadas and Brazil.

For Rats, Mice, Roaches, Ants, Bed Bugs, Moths in Furs, Woolens, etc., Insects on Plants, Fowls, Animals, etc. Put up in 25c, 50c, and $1 00 Boxes, Bottles, and Flasks. $3 and $5 sizes for Hotels, Public Institutions, etc.

"Only infallible remedies known."
"Free from Poisons."
"Not dangerous to the Human Family."
"Rats come out of their holes to die."

Sold wholesale in all large cities.
Sold by all druggists and retailers every where.
Beware! of all worthless Imitations.
See that Costar's name is on each Box, Bottle, and Flask before you buy.
Address Henry R. Costar.
Principal depot 482 Broadway, N. Y.
Sold by A. M. Pett,
Wholesale and Retail Agent.
51-10m Hastings, Minn.

FRED. B. CURTISS. W. C. COWLES.

CURTISS & COWLES,

DEALERS IN

Shoe and Harness Leather,

saddlery hardware, shoe findings, etc. Ramsey Street, near Levee, and lumber of all descriptions at corner of Second and Eddy Streets.

Hastings, Feb. 19, 1863. 46-tf

THE CONSERVER.

Minnesota Baptist Association—Twelfth Session.

FIRST DAY.

1. The Association met at the University in Hastings at 10 o'clock A. M.

2. The introductionary sermon was preached by Prof. T. F. Thickstun, from Deut. 1: 12, assisted in the exercises by Rev. M. Heath.

3. A collection for the widows and orphans' fund was then taken, amounting to $6 30.

4. The officers of the association were chosen by ballot, brethren Herzog and Tozer acting as tellers. Rev. J. F. Wilcox was selected moderator; D. D. Merill Cor. Secretary; T. F. Thickstun Clerk; and A. H. Cavender, Treasurer.

5. Prayer was offered by Rev. A. S. Lyon, afterwhich the moderator read the rules of order.

6. A committee of arrangements was appointed consisting of brethren Humphry, Cavender, and Herzog.

7. Visiting brethren accepted the invitation to take seats in the association as follows: Rev. E. T. Sedgwick of Zumbro Association; Rev. D. N. Mason, of the Southern Association; Rev. J. Arnold and W. C. Shepard of the Central Association; Rev. A. Gale, General Itinerant of the American Baptist Home Mission Society; Rev. S. T. Catlin, *Osceola, Wis.*; Rev. T. B. Rogers and brethren H. C. Marshall, H. Pope, and P. Felt of the St. Croix Valley Baptist Association; and Rev. J. R. Baumes of New London, Conn.

The invitation was extended to other denominations also.

8. The letter of the Hastings church was read, welcoming the association.

9. The committee of arrangements reported in part: 1. That we adjourn to meet at two o'clock P. M. 2. That the first business be reading of the letters of the churches. 3. That we meet in the evening for preaching.

10. Adjourned with prayer by Bro. Gale.

AFTERNOON SESSION.

1. Prayer by Bro. Pease.

2. The standing committees were then filled by the moderator as follows:

On Resolutions—Rev. J. D. Pope, and Deas. Herzog and Allen.

On Obituaries,—Rev. M. Heath, and Dea. Cavender.

On Circular Letter,—Rev. J. R. Baumes, W. A. Stone, and the Author.

On Next Anniversary,—Revs. Gale, Weedon, and Catlin.

On Application of Churches,—Bros. Tozer and Mason.

On Missions,—Revs. Pease, Sedgwick, and Shepard.

On Auditing Accounts,—Dr. Keith.

On Central University,—Revs. Thickstun, Gale, and Humphry.

3. Bro. Pease was then appointed to preach the home mission sermon in place of Bro. Heath who declined on account of ill health.

4. The letters from the churches were then read; showing an increase in the association by baptism of 22, and by letter and experience, 52.

5. Bro. Pease preached, using Heb. 2:10, after which a collection for home mission was taken amounting to $10 71.

6. The committee of arrangements reported that the association spend from 9 o'clock to 10 o'clock of the morning session in prayer and conference, and that the remnant of the forenoon be spent in miscellaneous business.

7. Bro. Mason from committee on applications reported, That an application for dismission from the Red Wing church to unite with Zumbro Association had been laid before them, and the committee recommended that the request be granted.

I. B. Tozer,
D. N. Mason.

The report was adopted.

8. Adjourned with prayer by Bro. Mason.

EVENING SESSION.

1. Usual introductory services.

2. Bro. Baumes of New London, Conn., preached from Mark 10: 17.

3. After remarks by Bro. Pope on missions a collection for foreign mission was taken, amounting to $14 56.

4. Adjourned with prayer by Rev. C. S. La Due.

SECOND DAY.

1. Association met at 9 A. M. and spent a delightful and encouraging hour in prayer and conference.

2. Opened the business of the asso. with prayer by Dea. Cavender.

4. The circular letter was read as per recommendation of the committee by the author Bro. Lyon, and adopted.

5. The following report on obituaries was read by Bro. Heath and adopted:

Your committee on obituaries beg to report that, it becomes their painful duty to record the names of a number from the membership of our churches who have passed away from earth during the past year. The sadness of their loss, however, is palliated by the fact that they have fallen asleep in Jesus. Their piety renders it fitting that we offer a tribute to the memory of exalted christian worth. Dr. Wm. H. Davol, who had come to our state for the benefit of his health, after a year's residence in St. Paul, returned in May last to his home in Rhode Island to die. The letter from the church at St. Paul, of which he was a member, at his death says: "Although but five years a christian, Dr. Davol had made rare attainments in discipleship, and was remarkable for devotion and humility. In the prayer and covenant meetings his gentle, loving, earnest tones went to every heart. As a man of superior abilities and education his gifts were all directed to Christ. He has left a legacy of wise counsels and by his holy example he being dead, yet speaketh.

Sister Theodosia Harris, an active member of Castle Rock Church, departed this life calmly trusting in Christ. Sister White, of Northfield, after years of affliction, which was borne with christian fortitude, passed away strong in the hopes and consolations of the Gospel. Bro. Cole, of the same church, in the vigor of manhood, with resignation and peace has gone home. A youthful sister also of the same church but about two months a member, peacefully and joyfully received the summons and entered into rest. Of the Hastings Church Sister Van Duzee passed happily to the better land. Also Sister Lizzie Hesketh, 10 years old, died of consumption, ripe in her early youth in spiritual attainments and rich experience. Thus youth, middle age and age pass away bidding us "be ye also ready."

Also Sister Kane, a colored sister, faithful to the last, amid much suffering, died in the full hope and confidence of going home to be with the loved Jesus.

M. Heath.
A. M. Cowder.

6. Bro. Pope offered prayer that these bereavements be sanctified to the good of the churches.

7. Bro. Pope, from the committee on resolutions, reported the following which were adopted separately after considerable and spirited discussion:

Your committee on resolutions would offer the following as the sense of this body:

1. That we deem it of prime importance and vital to the welfare of the churches that they recognize the command, "Go ye into all the world and preach the gospel to every creature" as a perpetual binding obligation, and that the spirit of missions be cherished and cultivated until it shall be the prevailing spirit of all the members, official and privates, old and young, male and female, rich and poor.

2. That we cordially approve the plan adopted by our missionary societies of dispensing with collecting agents, leaving this work to pastors and members of the churches, and we accept the responsibility which it involves.

3. That we earnestly recommend and urge upon all our churches the immediate adoption of a systematic method of religious and charitable contributions which shall be regular and reach all the membership, requesting the pastors to take the lead in this matter by repeated preaching on the subject and by personal effort, and the churches to make full reports to the association of the results.

4. That the time has come for the churches of Minnesota to make much larger payments on the debt of gratitude which we owe to the American Baptist Home Missionary Society to whose liberal aid is due in a great degree our present existence and standing.

5. That we heartily respond to the call of the American Baptist Missionary Union for special efforts during this its Jubilee year, pledging ourselves to make it a year of liberal giving to replenish its treasury, praying that it may be a year of signal blessings in the conversion of the heathen to Christ.

6. That as intelligence is a first condition in right action and successful effort we urge the members of the churches to keep themselves informed on all the benevolent movements of the times, and for this purpose we recommend the *Christian Times, Missionary Magazine, Macedonian, Home Evangelist*, and *Young Reaper*; that it is our special desire that the publication society place in this field as many colportours as possible, thus furnishing us at an early day with our best denominational and religious literature.

7. That at this time in the sore trials of our beloved country we express our gratitude to the God of nations for the recent victories which he has given to our arms and for the prospects of a speedily conquered peace; that we utterly detest the spirit of opposition manifested in some portions of the North against the draft and a vigorous prosecution of the war, as mean and despicable beyond all endurance; that we extend our deepest sympathies to the bereaved whose loved ones have fallen in battle or by disease, and to the thousands of our brethren who have been disabled or maimed by wounds, and also to the soldiers still in our service; and that to the support of our government, the maintenance of its honor, the effectual suppression of all rebellion against its authority, we pledge our moral influence, and whereever needed, the service of our lives, praying that God, whom we know to be just, will through this struggle break the accursed yoke of American slavery, and sanctify the whole country to the glory of the Redeemer's kingdom.

In behalf of the committee,
J. D. Pope, Chairman.

8. After the adoption of the third resolution the remainder of the report was laid upon the table, preparatory to an adjournment.

9. Adjourned with prayer by Bro. Gale.

THURSDAY AFTERNOON.

1. Met at 2 o'clock, and opened with prayer by Bro. Baumes.

2. The appointment of an advisory committee was referred to the committee on next anniversary.

3. The committee on next anniversary reported the place of our next meeting be left with the officers of this body; that Bro. M. Heath be the preacher; that Bro. Pope be his alternate; that Bro. Wm. Humphrey preach the missionary sermon; and that Bro. G. H. Keith write the circular letter. We also nominate for the missionary committee Brethren A. H. Cavender, G. H. Keith, and D. D. Merill.

A. Gale.
L. Waldron.
C. T. Catlin.

The report was accepted.

4. Bro. Thickstun was appointed to represent the association in the state convention.

5. The committee on Central University reported:

1. That culture, moral and intellectual, being a necessity in every religious organization, we are bound as a denomination so to shape our plans that high schools shall spring up for the education of the young people of the state.

2. That to this end we recommend to the Baptist Churches of the state to assume the liabilities and general management of the Central University under such an organization as shall be deemed expedient at a meeting called for the purpose.

3. That the arrangements for such an organization be consummated as far as possible during the coming session of the convention at Faribault.

T. F. Thickstun,
A. Gale,
W. H. Humphrey.

The report was unanimously adopted.

6. The treasurer and auditor submitted the following:—

Money left over from last year.	$100 73
Interest on same at 7 per cent,	9 15
Collection this session for Widow and Orphans' Fund,	6 30
Collection this session for Home Missions,	10 71
Collection this session for Foreign Missions,	14 56
Total	171 45

A. H. Cavender, Treas.

I have audited the above account and find it correct.

G. H. Keith.

7. The report of the committee on resolutions was then taken from the table, and the discussion upon them resumed and completed. The fifth was passed by a rising vote, each one thereby pledging himself to do something for its proper execution. The seventh was adopted by *every person in the house* rising and singing the hymn beginning, "My Country, 'tis of thee," to America.

8. T. F. Thickstun led in thanksgiving worship for the recent brilliant victories that had been visited upon our union arms.

9. The missionary committee reported that they find from the reading of the letters and an extended intercourse with Bro. Gale, our indefatigable missionary, that there is a large portion of our association in great need of missionary effort, and of pastors to gather the scattered sheep into the folds already formed, and those that should be formed.

The following districts urgently demand the attention of good, earnest, faithful preachers to break unto them the bread of life, and muster recruits into the army of the Lord. Dakota County with a population of 9,152 is without a baptist pastor save Bro. Humphrey at Hastings. The Minnesota Valley from Fort Snelling to Mankato is an extensive field with Bro. Heath as the only settled American pastor, and where, two years ago, we had six pastors.

The following churches are without pastors:—

St. Anthony, Shakopee, Red Wing, Richfield, English Church at Chasca, and Carver, Stillwater, and Chisago.

This situation of things has been brought about in a great measure by the Indian troubles, which have driven some of our preachers away from their fields. Some others have gone into the army as chaplains.

We recommend that our pastors, and preachers who are not pastors, go out two and two on Saturdays and remain over the Sabbath or longer, visiting, preaching, and holding meetings as the wants of the people may require.

We respectfully recommend these facts to the attention of our Home Mission Society, and to the preachers in our associational limits. We find that there has not been as much attention paid to missions, either foreign home or domestic, in our field as there should have been, and we hope, therefore, that larger contributions may be made during the coming year.

10. A resolution was here offered in reference to a fast day, but no copy of it having been left with the clerk, it cannot appear.

11. Dr. Keith offered the following resolution which was adopted:—

Resolved, That the thanks of this association are due, and are hereby tendered to the Baptist Church and citizens of Hastings for their kind and christian hospitality exhibited to the delegates during its session.

12. Minutes were read and corrected.

13. The moderator dismissed the association with a few appropriate remarks and with prayer.

MONETARY QUOTATIONS OF FOLLETT & RENICK,

[CORRECTED WEEKLY.]

Bankable Funds.

New England,	Bank State of Indiana.
New York,	Iowa,
New Jersey,	Michigan,
Ohio,	U. S. Demand Notes.
Canada,	Wisconsin,
Philadelphia,	Bank of Minnesota,
Marine Bank, Minn.,	Winona Co. Bank,
Bank of Chatfield,	State Bank of Minn.,
Peoples' Bank,	Pittsburg.

Exchange.

FOR BANKABLE FUNDS.

	Buying.	Selling.
New York, Philadelphia, Boston, Chicago and Milwaukee,	½ prem. par.	½ prem. ¼ prem.

PREMIUM FUNDS.

Gold,	[illegible]	[illegible]
Silver (large),	[illegible]	[illegible]
U. S. Demand Notes,	[illegible]	[illegible]
Canada,	[illegible]	[illegible]

RETAIL PRICES CURRENT.

CORRECTED WEEKLY BY G. F. BATCHELDER,

Hastings, Sept. 15, 1863.

FLOUR, per sack,	$2 50
WHEAT, per bushel,	[illegible]
CORN, do	[illegible]
OATS, do	40
POTATOES, do	50
BEANS, do	1 50
ONIONS, do	[illegible]
CRANBERRIES,	2 00
HAY, per ton,	[illegible]
WOOD, per cord,	[illegible]
SALT, per bbl	[illegible]
EGGS, per doz.	[illegible]
BUTTER, per lb.	[illegible]
CHEESE, per lb	[illegible]
PORK, per cwt.	[illegible]
BEEF, per cwt.	5 00
HAMS, per cwt.	[illegible]
SHOULDERS, per cwt.	[illegible]
DRIED APPLES,	[illegible]
DRIED PEACHES,	[illegible]
SUGARS, per lb	[illegible]
MOLASSES, per gal.	70a1 00
COFFEE, Java,	[illegible]
do Rio,	[illegible]

LEGAL NOTICES.

STATE OF MINNESOTA.

Sale of School Lands.

In accordance with an act entitled "an act to establish the State Land Office and for other purposes," approved March 10th, 1862, the following parcels or tracts of land will be sold at public auction, at the office of County Treasurer, in the town of Hastings, on Wednesday, the fourth day of November, 1863, at 10 o'clock A. M.:

Lands on which Fifteen per cent of the Purchase Money must be paid down.

Part of Sec.	Sec.	Town.	Range.	App. val. per acre.	App. val. of improv'ts.
DOUGLASS.					
ne qr of ne qr	16	113	17	$5 00	$25 00
[illegible]	[illegible]	[illegible]	[illegible]	[illegible]	[illegible]
MARSHAN.					
[illegible]	[illegible]	[illegible]	[illegible]	[illegible]	[illegible]
RANDOLPH—HAMPTON.					
[illegible]	[illegible]	[illegible]	[illegible]	[illegible]	[illegible]
INVER GROVE.					
[illegible]	[illegible]	[illegible]	[illegible]	[illegible]	[illegible]
VERMILLION.					
sw qr of sw qr	16	114	18	5 00	
WATERFORD.					
se qr of se qr	16	112	19	5 00	
CASTLE ROCK.					
[illegible]	[illegible]	[illegible]	[illegible]	[illegible]	[illegible]
EMPIRE CITY.					
[illegible]	[illegible]	[illegible]	[illegible]	[illegible]	[illegible]
ROSEMOUNT.					
[illegible]	[illegible]	[illegible]	[illegible]	[illegible]	[illegible]
EUREKA.					
[illegible]	[illegible]	[illegible]	[illegible]	[illegible]	[illegible]
LAKEVILLE.					
[illegible]	[illegible]	[illegible]	[illegible]	[illegible]	[illegible]
LEBANON.					
[illegible]	[illegible]	[illegible]	[illegible]	[illegible]	[illegible]
LAKEVILLE.					
[illegible]	[illegible]	[illegible]	[illegible]	[illegible]	[illegible]
EAGAN.					
[illegible]	[illegible]	[illegible]	[illegible]	[illegible]	[illegible]
MENDOTA.					
[illegible]	[illegible]	[illegible]	[illegible]	[illegible]	[illegible]

Lands on which Seventy-Five per cent of the Purchase Money must be paid down.

Part of Sec.	Sec.	Town.	Range.	App. val. per acre.	App. val. of improv'ts.
[illegible]	[illegible]	[illegible]	[illegible]	[illegible]	[illegible]
HASTINGS.					
[illegible]	[illegible]	[illegible]	[illegible]	[illegible]	[illegible]
INVER GROVE.					
[illegible]	[illegible]	[illegible]	[illegible]	[illegible]	[illegible]
WEST ST. PAUL.					
[illegible]	[illegible]	[illegible]	[illegible]	[illegible]	[illegible]

The balance of the purchase money is payable any time within twenty years, at the option of the purchaser, if interest at seven per cent per annum is annually paid in advance.

Interest to the first day of June, 1864, must be paid at the time of purchase.

Persons purchasing land upon which other parties have made improvements will be required to pay the owner of the same the appraised value of his improvements, one half to be paid at the time of the sale and the balance six months thereafter, with interest at seven per cent per annum.

In case the person occupying or improving the land has damaged the same, the appraised amount of damage will be deducted from his improvements, and when the occupant is the purchaser the damage will be added to the price of the land.

No lands will be sold for less than the appraised value.

Purchase money payable in specie and legal tender notes.

CHAS. McILRATH,
22-6 Commissioner of State Land Office.

MORTGAGE SALE.—WHEREAS DEfault has been made in the condition of a certain mortgage deed executed by Harvey Gillett and Georgie R. Gillett, his wife, of the county of Dakota, in the state of Minnesota to Allen R. Rich and Isaac B. Tozer, then and now partners in business under the firm name of Rich & Tozer, made, acknowledged, and delivered by said mortgagors to said firm of Rich & Tozer, mortgagees, and bearing date the 9th day of May, A. D. 1862, which said mortgage contains the usual power of sale to said Rich & Tozer and their assigns, and was duly filed for record with said mortgage in the office of the register of deeds of said county, on the 9th day of said May at four o'clock in the afternoon of that day, and was thereupon duly recorded in said office in book K of mortgagees on pages 587, 588, and 589; which said mortgage was given to secure the payment of one hundred and twenty-three dollars and seventy-one cents with interest at ten per cent per annum according to the conditions of a certain promissory note made by said Harvey Gillett and bearing even date with said mortgage. And there is claimed to be due and is actually due and unpaid upon said note and mortgage at the date of this notice the sum of one hundred and thirty-four dollars and fifty cents. And no suit or proceeding at law has been instituted to recover the debt secured by said mortgage or any part thereof. The mortgaged premises are described as follows, viz: All that tract or parcel of land lying and being in Dakota County, state of Minnesota, and described as follows, to wit: Lot number fourteen (14) in block number three (3) in H. G. Bailly's addition to Hastings, as per recorded plat thereof now on record in the office of register of deeds in said county.

Now, therefore, notice is hereby given that by virtue of the power of sale in said mortgage contained and pursuant to the statute in such case made and provided the said mortgage will be foreclosed by a sale of said mortgaged premises at public auction to the highest bidder at the front door of the office of said register of deeds in Hastings, in said county, on the 3d day of October, A. D. 1863, at one o'clock in the afternoon of that day, to satisfy said mortgage debt and the expenses of said sale.

19-7t Rich & Tozer, Mortgagees.
A. M. Hayes, Att'y for said Mortgagees.
Dated Hastings, Minn., Aug. 18, 1863.

STATE OF MINNESOTA, SECOND Collection District,

Assessor's Office, St. Paul, August, 1863.

Public Notice

is hereby given that the lists, valuations, and enumerations made and taken under the Excise Tax Law of the United States within division numbered three, comprising the county of Dakota, will be open for examination at the office of Eli Robinson, in the city of Hastings, in said county, on the 29th day of August, A. D. 1863, and will remain open for the space of fifteen days from said time.

Notice is also given that appeals will be received and determined relative to any erroneous or excessive valuations or enumerations by the assistant assessor of said division at the office of Eli Robinson, in said city of Hastings, in said county of Dakota, on the 8th day of September, A. D. 1863, and immediately thereafter until all appeals are disposed of.

H. G. O. Morrison,
Assessor, 2d District.
Dated August, 21, 1863. 20-4w

THE HASTINGS CONSERVER.

VOLUME III.---NO. 24. HASTINGS, DAKOTA COUNTY, MINNESOTA, TUESDAY, SEPTEMBER 22, 1863. $2 00 PER YEAR.

THE CONSERVER.

BY IRVING TODD.

TUESDAY, SEPTEMBER 22, 1863.

Single copies of the CONSERVER may be obtained at this office, or at the Bookstore. Price Five Cents.

Republican Union Ticket.

For Governor,
STEPHEN MILLER,
of Stearns County.

For Lieutenant Governor,
CHARLES D. SHERWOOD,
of Fillmore County.

For Secretary of State,
DAVID BLAKELY,
of Olmsted County.

For Auditor of State,
CHARLES McILRATH,
of Nicollet County.

For State Treasurer,
CHARLES SCHEFFER,
of Washington County.

For Attorney General,
GORDON E. COLE,
of Rice County.

For Clerk of the Supreme Court.
GEORGE F. POTTER,
of Houston County.

Union County Ticket.

For Senator,
N. N. THOMPSON.

For Representatives,
P. VAN AUKEN.
S. C. HOWELL.

For Treasurer,
D. B. TRUAX.

For Sheriff,
H. J. TAYLOR.

For Judge of Probate,
I. M. RAY.

For Register of Deeds,
H. A. MONSER.

For District Attorney,
R. W. MONTGOMERY.

For Surveyor,
C. B. LOWELL.

For Coroner,
P. HARTSHORN.

For Commissioner—2d District,
HENRY SPRAGUE.

For Commissioner—3d District.
JOSIAH BURWELL.

The County Ticket.

Never before has it been our good fortune to place at the head of our columns a ticket which we could support with better grace or have more confidence in a triumphant election.

N. N. THOMPSON, the candidate for state senator, is a farmer residing in the township of West St. Paul, and is well known throughout the county for his integrity and zealous interest in public affairs. He is, moreover, a thorough loyal man, and will use all his influence for the prosecution of the war. We are confident that the best interests of the county demand for him a seat in the next senate, and we believe that the people will see to it that he gets it.

For representatives we have P. VAN AUKEN, of Hastings, and S. C. HOWELL, of Greenvale, both practical, industrious men, and both abundantly qualified to look after our affairs in the house. The former was the honored mayor of our city last year, and no one can deny that public matters were not as well, if not better, attended to during his administration as in any previous one. The latter is a solid, substantial farmer, one that men can look up to, and who will discharge all duties, public or private, great or small, in an acceptable and straight-forward manner.

D. B. TRUAX, of Nininger, is the candidate for treasurer, and a better one could not have been found in the county. A thorough accountant, scrupulous and above reproach, he is capable of conducting the affairs of that responsible office as to give complete and general satisfaction. He is well known throughout the county, and nothing that we can say is needed to give him esteem and popularity among the people.

For sheriff we have H. J. TAYLOR, of Randolph, a plain, practical man, and possessing all the requisites for the office. Although comparatively little known in the county, we can safely recommend him as a candidate for the position, and trust that he will be elected.

I. M. RAY, the present sheriff, who has faithfully and satisfactorily conducted the business of that arduous office for two terms, is the nominee for judge of probate. He is undoubtedly well qualified for the position, and is morally certain of an election.

H. A. MONSER, formerly an active democrat, is the candidate for register of deeds. He is an industrious, hard working man, and deserves the suffrages of the electors of the county. Since the breaking out of the war he has been an ardent supporter of the administration, and loud in denunciation of traitors and copperheads.

The candidate for district attorney is R. W. MONTGOMERY, a young man recently from Illinois and engaged in the practice of law in our city within the past year. He is possessed of a remarkably clear and active mind, very attentive to his business, and in general favor among his acquaintances. Of his qualifications for the office we have no doubts, neither of his election.

C. B. LOWELL, the present able deputy, is the nominee for surveyor, the business of which office he has been conducting for the past two years, and with very great success. He has also been largely engaged in the state survey of school lands, and his labors have been highly approved by the auditor. He is one of the oldest surveyors in the county and state, and is abundantly qualified for the office, besides being thoroughly acquainted with the surveys of the vicinity. An item of great importance and worthy of consideration by the voters. Give us men of experience in all departments of trust, and much of the expense and inconvenience of conducting public affairs will be obviated.

P. HARTSHORN, for coroner, is a life-long democrat, having until recently acted with that party. He has had ample experience in public affairs, and is at present police justice of our city. He will fill that, or any other office, with credit to himself and constituents.

HENRY SPRAGUE and JOSIAH BURWELL are the candidates for commissioners in the 2d and 3d districts. Mr. Sprague is a present member of the board, and one of the most active and attentive to business. The county is largely indebted to him for its present prosperous condition, and should consult its interests by retaining him in the position. Mr. Burwell, of Inver Grove, is also a well-to-do farmer, and will make a faithful and competent manager of affairs. Such men should not be overlooked at the polls, and we trust will not be.

Such is the ticket presented to you for your support and suffrages. The candidates are, without exception, capable and unexceptionable, and worthy of the highest confidence of the people. Contrast them with the other ticket, given elsewhere, and decide to cast your ballot for the right, and let the copperheads plainly understand that their traitorous and malevolent schemes meets not with your sanction and approval. Let the voice of the people be distinctly heard, and evil and designing men will tremble and bow their heads with shame.

Falseness of Democratic Argument.

Just now the democratic press is very zealous in clamoring for the rights of the states which pretend (and democrats concide with the pretension) to have seceded from or rebelled against the federal government of the United States.

As if the government did or intended to infringe upon the rights of the southern states, the Chicago *Times* says:

"The administration refuses the insurgent states permission to return unless they submit to a destruction of their *rights*."

Now all such arguments and all such statements are false, and have no foundation whatever upon which to rest.

1. The states referred to have not seceded, and they never can. It is an utter impossibility for one or more states to secede from the union. Consequently the states not having seceded the "administration" cannot "refuse permission" for them to return.

2. Even if the states could and had seceded "the administration" has no desire, on its part, to interfere with the constitutional rights of the states, either north or south.

If we understand matters and things rightly "the administration" in settling up this war difficulty has nothing to do with the states, but deals directly with the people of the several states. The government or administration is the offspring or child of the people and not of the states; hence all the power, life, vitality, and strength of the government is derived from the people,—the source of legitimate authority.

The fact is apparent that all this wrangling among democrats was gotten up by them as an election scheme. The government has no right to meddle with the rights of the states. And therefore has no desire to do so.

A portion of the people of the states have rebelled against the government, and it is using its constitutional right to compel that portion of the people to obey the laws which all assisted to make. Whenever they shall signify their willingness to lay down their arms, return to their allegiance, and obey all the constitutional laws of the land, the government or "the administration" and its friends will be happy and willing to receive them and protect them in all their lawful rights and see that justice is done them in all things. What more can they ask?

All these truths being well known, and the democratic press, having no cause whatever, sought by falsehood and deception to create a disruption of sentiment between the government and the loyal people. The attempt has been discovered, and will be nipped in the bud. The people are too intelligent to be hoodwinked in that style. All this democratic *hocus pocus* argument that the states will not be protected in their rights is a dodge that wont win. The party in power gained its present position because it contended for the constitution as it is, declaring that:—

"The citizens of each state shall be entitled to all privileges and immunities of citizens in the several states."

Having always respected the rights of the states and the liberties of the people, the republican union party will always continue so to do, democratic precept to the contrary notwithstanding.

The Copperhead Ticket.

We give below the ticket made, composed of, and supported by the copperhead elements of this county. We should have said of this town, for Hastings has five out of nine of the principal offices on the list. There should have been one more invented so that Hastings could have another chance. Here they are—are n't we proud of them!:—

Senator,—D. F. Langley, of Hastings.
Representatives,—K. N. Guiteau, of West St. Paul, G. F. Ackley, of Lakeville.
Treasurer,—Michael Comer, of Eagan.
Sheriff,—Stephen Newell, of Burnsville.
District Attorney,—T. R. Huddleston, of Hastings.
Judge of Probate,—Seagrave Smith, of Hastings.
Register of Deeds,—Elmond Eichhorn, of Hastings.
Surveyor,—W. C. Cowles, of Hastings.
Coroner,—William Felton, of Nininger.
Commissioners,—2d district Geo. Egbert, of Ravenna; 3d dist.,—Geo. Bohrer, of Inver Grove.

The Campaign Conserver.

To meet the seeming great demand this fall for political documents, the publisher of the CONSERVER has concluded to issue a campaign paper for the term of eight weeks, commencing with Sept. 22d and ending with Nov. 10th, the latter number containing the complete election returns. To place it within the reach of all, it will be afforded at the following low rates, barely paying for the white paper:

5 copies to one address,	$1 50
10 copies to one address,	2 50

And any larger number in same proportion. No clubs smaller than five can be received. Send in your orders accompanied with the cash, as speedily as possible. Postmasters and others friendly to the cause are invited to act as agents in securing names. Address

IRVING TODD,
Hastings, Minn.
23-3w

The Fall Elections.

Encouraging to the heart of every loyal man are the results of the several state elections which have already taken place. California has cast overwhelming majorities for the union, and now the voice from Maine comes rushing through the nation. Returns from 187 towns give Corey 43,455, Bradbury 29,439. Union majority 14,016, showing a net gain over last year of 9,535. The union ticket has probably caried every county of the state. The senate will be unanimously union, while the house will have a majority of at least 80. Good for Maine.

Let not the people be deceived by the loyal professions of the democratic leaders now, in the hour of victory. Let them remember that they did all in their power to embarass the government in the hour of defeat.

Little Rock, Ark., has been peaceably captured by our troops, and the cavalry of Gen. Davidson is pursuing the retreating enemy.

The 7th, 9th, and 10th Minnesota regiments are being concentrated at Fort Snelling, previous to going South.

Too Bad.

We had apprehended a warm contest the coming campaign on state officers, and had thought of a number of good things to say for the ticket and especially for Col. Miller. These are rendered thunder lost by the complete smash-up of the democratic ticket, and having nobody to fight, must put on our coat again and keep mum. It is really too bad, but it can't be helped.

For Representative.

Mr. Rohse having declined to become a candidate for representative, the committee, after consultation with a number of our citizens, have substituted instead P. VanAuken, of Hastings, a good man and one who will be elected.

Henry L. Moss, esq., of Cannon Falls has been appointed United States District Attorney for the district of Minnesota in the place of George A. Nourse, resigned. Mr. Moss held the same office in territorial days, and performed the duties acceptably.

Destruction of Charleston.

Escaped union prisoners bring the report to Fort Moultrie that Charleston was shelled three days and completely destroyed. If this be true, good enough.

A CONTENTED MAN.—A druggist was aroused by the ringing of his night bell, went down stairs, and had to serve a customer with a dose of salts. On his return his wife grumbled out, "what profit do you get out of that penny?" "A ha'penny," replied the assiduous druggist. "And for that ha'penny you will keep both me and yourself awake for a long time," rejoined the wife. "Never mind," added the placid druggist, "the dose of salts will keep him awake much longer, let us thank Heaven that we have the profit and not the pain of the transaction."

NEW ADVERTISEMENTS.

LOCAL AFFAIRS.

P. O. Notice.—Summer Arrangement.
Mail going East closes at 11 o'clock, A. M.
Way mail down closes at 8 o'clock, P. M.
Mail for St. Paul closes on the arrival of the boat from below in the afternoon.
Faribault mail leaves at 6 o'clock A. M., closes at 9 o'clock P. M.
Office hours from 8 A. M. to 8 P. M.
WM. H. SKINNER, Post-Master.

THANKS.—We are indebted to Hon. CYRUS ALDRICH for a number of valuable public documents.

NOTICE.—We are requested to notify the young people not to forget their prayer meeting at Methodist Church on Sunday afternoon at 4 o'clock.

CLOTHING.—PRATT has gone to Chicago to purchase a new supply of goods, and will return soon with a tip-top assortment. Call in and leave your orders before the rush.

TO OUR READERS.—Call at NEWMANS, on Second Street, and examine his large stock of dry goods, to which he is constantly making additions. If you do n't wish to purchase, 't will do no harm to look it over.

DEPARTED.—Mr. JOHN LOWELL, who has been in the mercantile business for some time on Second Street, has returned to Stillwater, his former residence, taking his stock of goods with him.

JEWELRY.—Call at ANDREWS' and examine his beautiful assortment of watches, clocks, and jewelry. It is good for weak eyes, and don't cost anything. Engraving done to order, in the best of style.

COUNTY FAIR.—The Annual Fair of the Pierce County (Wis.) Agricultural Society will be held at Prescott on Friday and Saturday of this week, Sept. 25th and 26th. Hon. H. L. HUMPHREY, of Hudson, delivers the address.

PICTURES.—E. A. BEACH, of Taylor Falls, has taken the rooms over THORNE & NORRISH'S store, where he is prepared to take all sorts of pictures in good style and at reasonable rates. Drop in and see.

COURT.—By reason of the detention of Judge MCMILLAN on Beef Slough Bar, and his consequent absence the sheriff adjourned the court on the second day thereof, at 9 o'clock, until the March term, agreeably to the statute in such case made and provided.

WORTH CONSIDERING.—Good diet makes healthy children and adults. Good saleratus helps to make nutritious, healthy diet. Hence use De Land & Co.'s chemical saleratus as it is perfectly pure and better than soda for all purposes.

ON FURLOUGH.—Most of the returned companies at Fort Snelling have been paid off and furloughed until the 30th, and our town is full of blue coats. They seem pleased to be among their friends again, and we are certainly glad to have them.

PERSONAL.—S. S. FIFIELD, of the Polk County *Press* dropped in a few moments last week. He has been on a trip down the river, and, from the odor of night caps, etc., we conclude he has been and done it. Whether it be so or not, SAMUEL, here's to you.

Rev. W. H. HUMPHREY, formerly of Halifax, Nova Scotia, has been settled as the pastor of the Baptist Church of this city. We hear him well spoken of as a faithful minister of the Word of Life. He commences his labors with the church on the first Sunday in October.

NEW GOODS.—Macomber has just received the handsomest lot of silver ware ever brought into this market, comprising pie and butter knives, goblets, cake baskets, napkin rings, etc., all of the best quality and latest styles. Also many other articles in his line, neat and pretty. Call in.

FOR THE SOLDIERS.—We have before us a letter from the corresponding secretary of the Chicago Sanitary Commission, acknowledging the receipt of $11 00, a collection taken in the Presbyterian Church of this place for the benefit of the soldiers, for which many thanks were returned.

S. M. BOOTH, of Milwaukee, delivered a very able and patriotic lecture at Prescott recently, we are sorry to say to a very small audience. Although not endorsing his private habits and ways of thinking, as a public lecturer he has few equals, and should command attention wherever he goes. His paper, the *Daily Life*, is an excellent family journal, and well worth the small sum ($2 00) required for a year's subscription. Send for a specimen copy.

PREACHING.—The Synod of Minnesota meets in the Presbyterian Church, of this place, on Thursday. Rev. Mr. MATTOCKS, of St. Paul, will preach in the evening, at the usual hour.

CHILLY.—The weather for the past few days has come off cold, and on Saturday morning we had a most severe frost. Most too early in the season yet for such an atmosphere.

FIREMEN'S BALL.—Hope Company No. 1 propose to give a grand ball on Monday Evening, Oct. 5th, for the purpose of raising money towards a fire engine. See advertisement.

SOCIABLE.—The Ladies' Sociable will meet at the University on Friday evening of this week. Oysters will be served on the occasion. Let every body attend, and bring his wife or—cousin with him.

ARRIVALS.—JOHN H. MUZZ, of Red Wing, has taken possession of the store vacated by THOMAS, and is fitting up with a first rate stock of goods.

Z. B. FLINT, of River Falls, Wis., has moved into WILLSON'S old stand where he is prepared to attend to customers. They are both good men and will prove great additions to the business of the town.

THE BLACK SWAN visited our town last week, and sang to well-filled houses on Thursday and Friday evenings. She has the most remarkable voice we ever heard, combining the fullness of the basso, the shrillness of the tenor, the richness of contralto, and the clearness of the soprano. This, added to thorough cultivation and good taste in execution, renders her a singer of no mean merit. She will draw wherever she goes.

BANKS OF ISSUE.—We are pleased to announce to the public that two banks of issue are, or soon will be, in operation in Hastings, a need which we are particularly glad to see filled. They are as follows:

Thorne's Bank—capital $25,000 secured entirely by United States bonds. The bills are of the denomination of $1's, $2's, and $5's. J. L. THORNE president, and SIDNEY MILLS, jr cashier.

Bank of Hastings—capital $25,000, secured wholy by United States 5.20's. Denomination of bill are $1's, $2's, $3's, and 5's. S. G. RENICK president, and L. S. FOLLETT cashier.

THE COUNTY FAIR.—At a late meeting of the agricultural society, at Hampton, a committee, consisting of Messrs. DAMPHIER, GEO. HAMSTON, and GILBERT MCKAY, was appointed to prepare grounds for the approaching fair, and CHAS. LEWIS was chosen as marshal for the occasion. Judges were also selected, but we have not been furnished with the list, as should have been done by the secretary. The fair comes off two weeks from next Thursday, Oct. 8th, and we hope the farmers and others will take interest enough to make it the best ever held in the county. Bring on youre large vegetables, produce, manufactures, etc., and let us have a fair what is a fair.

EDUCATIONAL.

BY PROF. T. F. THICKSTUN.

Discipline.

There is no part of the duties of the school room so difficult and yet so thankless as the exercise of an effective discipline. A teacher may demonstrate well or rather indifferently, and still the majority of the employers will be quite well satisfied. A teacher may be exact in his personal habits or somewhat slack, and yet meet with no censure from the district—the people will in either case be very well pleased. A teacher may have a fine education, or he may be a perfect loggerhead in knowledge, and still keeps the smiles of both his pupils and his parents to the end of his quarters. It is not difficult to please those about him in all these respects, if he be in possession of a reasonable amount of tact in his intercourse with the school and the district.

But it tests the man when he attempts to govern. Every atom of wit which he possesses will be be tasked to its utmost. Those who are indifferent to the amount of knowledge stowed away in the pedagoguers cranium or to the methods which his employers in imparting instruction; at exceedingly exacting and imperious when the government of thier children is concerned. Every man expects that every pupil shall have just the regulations upon him that bind him when he is at home. The teacher being *in loco parentis*, he must by some magnetic impulse be transmuted into the very being of each parent in the district the moment one of their children steps across the threshold of the school-house door. To the child who has a parent soft and sugary the teacher must be soft and sugary. To the boy that rules his mother, father, and Athens, the teacher must submit with the sweetest and most unresisting disposition. To the child who is the subject of wholesome and steady discipline, the teacher must be a wholesome and steady disciplinarian. To the child who is hauled and slashed about from morning till night, the lord of the school room must be a sledge-hammer, dealing his iron blows on every side with a power and inconsiderateness equally surprising. Now how shall the teacher suit all these. It is plainly an impossibility. He will inevitably cross the track of some of the good people of his district. He may do the best thing possible—just what an angel would have done—and yet some will be displeased. Their grief is that he does not do as they do at home. The question of right never once enters their mind.

Here is the origin of three fourths of the failures in school teaching; it lies in the domain of the discipline instituted. Some catering, flimsy system is adopted in the hope of pleasing every body, which in the end pleases nobody.

There is no safer policy in the world than to adopt a firm, rigid, and intelligent system of government, and then steadily adhere to it through thick and thin. Of course extreme parents will fall out with you. Vengeance will be in their eye and upon their lips, whenever they meet you or speak of you. But that is no consideration of yours, stand by your disciplinary plans.

A teacher can please as a demonstrator for years, when in part of government he would fail in a month. We do not study the art and science of school discipline as much as we should. We invite the attention of teachers to this subject.

The Pierce County, Wis., Teachers' Institute commenced at Prescott last week under the able management of Prof. W. T. Hatch. We have heard nothing of the proceedings, but we presume that the teachers had a good and profitable time. The teachers' of both town and county are wide awake to the improvement of the schools.

Miss Jennie Buell has opened a select school for small children on Ramsey Street, nearly opposite Stanley's book store. Miss B. has established herself as a good and faithful student; as a disciplinarian she has all to win, but we have strong faith. We commend her warmly to the educated public.

Of all the vanities and fopperies, the vanity of high birth is the greatest. True nobility is derived from virtue, not from birth. Titles, indeed, may be purchased; but virtue is the only coin that can make the bargain valid.

"Why is a secesh house occupied by union forces like the copyright of a book? Because it is 'entered according to the act of Congress.'"

THE CONSERVER.

BY IRVING TODD.

Office Over the Bank of Hastings, Exchange Block, Second Street.

Our Platform.

Resolved, That we, chosen to represent in convention the unconditional union men of Minnesota, grateful to Almighty God for the success which has hitherto crowned the arms of our country and for the prospect thus opened of a speedy, honorable, and lasting peace, do hereby, for ourselves and our constituents, reaffirm our determination to support our government by every means in our power in the vigorous prosecution of this war, —on our part, holy, just, and forced upon us by the criminal acts of others,—until not an enemy in arms shall be found within our borders. And to this we pledge our lives, our fortunes, and our sacred honor.

2. That we tender our grateful thanks to the survivors of our glorious armies, and our warm sympathy to the relatives of their gallant dead, who have won for the country so glorious victories, for themselves imperishable renown, and for us all an assurance of liberty and safety, for ourselves and our children, under our beloved and now well-tried government.

3. That with especial pride we point to the gallant achievements on many a hard-fought battle-field, of our Minnesota regiments. Their bravery, discipline, and patriotism have won for them a name that shall never die, and made forever honorable to a citizen of Minnesota.

4. That, without claiming for it exemption from error, we heartily endorse the general policy and conduct of our national administration; and we point to the recent magnificent triumph of our armies as its best vindication from the charge of incapacity so freely brought against it by those who prefer national ruin to success under the present administration. *Especially* do we approve the emancipation proclamation, and the raising of black troops, as being among the best possible measures to weaken the enemy and strengthen ourselves.

5. That our state administration and congressional delegation deserve our hearty approbation for the zealous and efficient co-operation they have afforded the national authorities in carrying on the war.

6. That we call upon those in authority to take such measures, by retaliation or otherwise, as shall effectually prevent brutal and barbarous treatment by the enemy of our soldiers, of whatever color.

7. That it is due to our shattered armies in the field, as well as to the sacred cause which they uphold, that their ranks should as speedily as possible be filled up by every means in our power. It is due to the country that the mobs raised to resist and prevent the draft, should not even seem to have succeeded a day longer than is necessary to enforce the laws.

8. That the way to peace is, and ever has been, open to the rebels; the only condition we have ever sought to impose is that they should lay down their arms and submit to the authority of the general government. We protest against the making of any terms with them in advance as to their *status* in communities, when they shall have returned to their allegiance. Having been declared "public enemics" by a recent unanimous decision of the Supreme Court of the United States, they must accept the consequences that legitimately flow from having placed themselves in that position.

Brownlow's Knoxville Whig and Rebel Ventilator.

I propose to publish a weekly and tri-weekly journal, bearing the above title, at Knoxville, in East Tennessee; and the weekly paper, made up from the contents of the tri-weeklies, I propose to send out to distant subscribers, for two dollars per annum, invariably in advance. Subscriptions and remittances will be forwarded to me at Cincinnati, from which point I expect to ship my paper and materials. I expect to issue the first number in October, as it was in that month, two years ago, my paper was crushed out by the God forsaken mob at Knoxville, called the confederate authorities. I will commence with this hell born and hell-bound rebellion where the traitors forced me to leave off, and all who wish the paper would do well to begin with the first issue, as I intend that single paper shall be worth the subscription price to any unconditional union man.

In the role of my editorial conduct, I shall abjure that servility which destroys the independence of the press, and cast from me that factious opposition which gives to the party what is due to the country. And whilst the name of my journal indicates, in unmistakable terms, its politics, I shall, as a faithful sentinel, forget whigs, democrats, know nothings, and republicans, and remember only my government, and the preservation of the federal union—as richly worth all the sacrifices of blood and treasure their preservation may cost—even to the extermination of the present race of men, and the consumption of all the means of the present age.

Publishers inserting this prospectus once, prominently, and sending me the paper to Cincinnati, will be favored with an exchange. W. G. BROWNLOW.

September 7, 1863.

Gen. Grant announces that his reason for extending Gen. Logan's furlough is, that he (Logan) is engaged in an effective service fighting copperheads at home as rebels in the South. It is the same here, and while our brave boys are conquering the rebels in the field, let it not be said that we lack the spirit to conquer the copperheads at home.—*Press.*

The Boston *Post* chronicles a scarcity of clergymen in that city, and says that a funeral was recently postponed for two days on account of the impossibility of obtaining a clergyman to officiate.

Mrs. Harriet N. Austin, of Dansville, New York, has come out in favor of ladies riding on horseback astride. The present style of riding, she says, is unsafe, ungraceful, unhealthy, and unnatural.

A good many men are in the best health when they are out of spirits.

Rules for Teachers and Pupils.

The following rules are those adopted for the public schools of Madison, Wis., and may be suggestive elsewhere:

TEACHERS.

1. Teachers shall observe and carry into effect all the regulations of the superintendent and board of education, in relation to their respective schools, and attend punctually and regularly the weekly meetings of teachers, under the direction of the superintendent.

2. The salaries paid entitle the board to the services of the teachers for five and one half days each week, except legal holidays.

3. Teachers shall be present at their respective school-houses, both morning and afternoon, at least thirty minutes before the time prescribed for the opening of the school. They shall require their scholars to be in their seats punctually at the appointed time; and shall commence their schools, without allowing any time for scholars to assemble, after school hours. They shall also close their schools precisely at the hour appointed.

4. All teachers shall keep their school registers, neatly and accurately, according to the forms prescribed therein, and fill out the blank reports of the condition and progress of their respective schools, according to the direction of the superintendent.

5. It shall be their duty to exercise a vigilant watchfulness over the general conduct of their pupils, and, on suitable occasions to encourage and instruct them in correct manners, habits, and principles.

6. They shall be entrusted with the immediate care of their respective school-rooms, and the furniture, apparatus, or other school furniture belonging therein; and shall be held personally responsible for any damage done during school hours, or while the building is under their control.

7. Teachers may have power to suspend from school such pupils as have been guilty of gross misconduct or insubordination to school regulations; immediate notice of which shall be given to the superintendent and to the parents or guardian of the pupils.

8. Teachers are expected to practice such discipline in their respective schools as would be exercised by a judicious parent in his family; to resort to corporeal punishment only in cases of extreme necessity, when other measures have failed, and to make record of the same, and the reason why it was inflicted.

9. All teachers shall be examined by the superintendent and the examining committee of the board, at least once in each year; and the result of such examination shall be reported to the board, with some recommendations for its action.

10. Such examinations shall take place within one week after the close of a school term.

11. The annual examination shall take place during the first week succeeding the summer term.

12. Every new applicant for a teacher's situation shall, before being employed, pass an examination satisfactory to the board; which examination shall be separate from the examination of those who have been previously engaged in teaching in the schools of the city; and such examination shall take place as soon as practicable after the close of a school term.

13. All teachers passing a satisfactory examination before the examining committee will receive a certificate of qualification from the superintendent and board of education.

PUPILS.

1. No child shall be admitted as a pupil in a primary school who has not attained the age of five years. Nor into the intermediate or grammar schools unless regularly transferred or found upon examination qualified to enter the lowest class therein, except by permit of the superintendent.

2. All pupils are required to be in their respective school rooms before the time of begining school, and to be regular in their daily attendance.

3. Scholars who shall accidentally or otherwise injure any school property, whether school furniture, apparatus, or buildings, fences, trees, shrubs, or any property whatever belonging to the school estate, shall be liable to pay in full for all damages.

4. Every pupil who shall be absent from school shall bring to his teacher a written excuse from his parent or guardian for such absence.

5. A scholar absenting himself from his seat for one entire week shall forfeit all right thereto, and can be re-admitted only as a new pupil.

6. Whenever any pupil shall be tardy or absent four times during two successive weeks, his seat in the school may be declared vacant, and he can be re-admitted only by the written consent of the superintendent or by direction of the board.

7. Any scholar who shall absent himself from any regular examination, or who fails to render a sufficient excuse for such absence, shall not be allowed to return to the school without the consent of the board of education.

8. For open disobedience or insubordination a pupil may be suspended by a teacher or expelled by the superintendent, immediate notice of which shall be given to the parent or guardian; and shall be re-admitted into the public schools only by the superintendent in case of suspension, and by vote of the board in case of expulsion.

9. No child who comes to school without proper attention having been given to the cleanliness of his person and of his or her dress, or whose clothes are not properly repaired, shall be permitted to remain in school, but shall be sent home to be prepared for school in a proper manner.

10. Whenever any parent or guardian feels aggrieved by the action of any teacher, it shall be his duty to give information thereof to the superintendent; and in case the matter is not satisfactorily adjusted by him, such parent or guardian may appeal to the board. —*Wisconsin Journal of Education.*

The Book We are all Writing.

When you begin your writing books at school, you know they are all very much alike. The same picture may be on the covers, and the same white ruled paper inside—but when you take them home from school, how different! One, perhaps, is written in a clear, handsome hand, each page better than the one before it, even to the very end. All that see it admire and praise it.

Another is brought home scrawled and blotted and soiled and torn. They were nearly alike once; there was nothing to choose between them; but how different now.

Such a book each of us is writing. It is the book of our lives. We have already written many pages. Every sin is a blot. There is only one Being that can take out all those blots, and make the pages all clean, and help us to write out a good, fair book, growing better and better to the end. That one Being is JESUS CHRIST.—*The Child's World.*

WIFE AND LADY.—The Providence *Post* says: "It is certainly not in good taste for a gentleman to speak of his wife as his 'lady,' or to register their names upon the books of a hotel as 'John Smith and lady,' or to ask a friend, 'How is your lady!' This is all fashionable vulgarity, and invariably betrays a lack of cultivation. The term wife is far more beautiful, appropriate, and refined, whatever may be said to the contrary. Suppose a lady were to say, instead of My husband, My gentleman, or suppose we were to speak of Mrs. Fitz Maurice and her gentleman. The thing would be absolutely ludicrous, and its reverse is none the less so, if rightly considered. A man's wife is his wife, and not his lady; and we marvel that this latter term is not absolutely tabooed in such a connection, at least by intelligent and educated people."

LEATHER BONNETS.—Dame Fashion now endorses the generally received opinion that for some things there is "nothing like leather." The Philadelphia *Gazette* says:—

We yesterday were shown ladies' bonnets made of leather. What is more, they are very pretty. In a week or so they will be in the market. We also examined very beautiful artificial flowers, the foliage of which was of the same material. The colors are almost the natural hue of the material —russet, in different shades. The price is about the same as for flowers with foliage of muslin or velvet.

The New York *Commercial Advertiser* says it is a fact well worth noting, that for the first time in many years the congress coming into life in the middle of a presidential term is, in its political aspects, friendly to the president. For a quarter of a century, if we are not mistaken, an opposition speaker has been elected in every last congress of a presidential term. That the next congress is not merely union, but republican, is a strong testimony to the popular estimate of the fidelity, honesty, and patriotism of Abraham Lincoln and his advisers.

The Lynn (Mas.) *Reporter* says: "A couple were joined in marriage in this city a few days since, whose united ages were one hundred and fifty-two years. The blushing bride had passed her seventy-fourth summer, while the snows of seventy-eight winters rested upon the bride groom's youthful brow. He had once, and the bride twice, before entered into the marriage obligation.

In every noble heart burns a perpetual thirst for a nobler; in the fair for a fairer; it wishes to behold its ideal out of itself in bodily presence, with glorified or adopted form, in order the more easily to attain to it, because the lofty mass can ripen only by a lofty one, as diamond can be polished only by diamond.—*Jean Paul.*

When you say, in a phrase which is now Americanized, such and such a man "is a brick," do you think of, or do you know the origin of it? It is this: an eastern prince, on being asked, "Where are the fortifications of your city?" replied, pointing to his soldiers, "Every man you see is a brick."

A Massachusetts judge has decided that a husband may open his wife's letters, on the ground, so often and tersely stated by Theophilus Parson, of Cambridge, "that the husband and the wife are one, and the husband *is that one!*"

Two friends meeting, one remarked, "I have just met a man who told me I looked like you."

"Tell me who it was, that I may knock him down," replied the friend.

"Do n't trouble yourself," said he, "I did that myself immediately."

A leading publishing house in London is about to bring out a series of educational works especially for the schools of the Confederate States of America. We would humbly suggest that the first lesson should be on the subject of allegiance to their country and flag.

"Well, what next?" said Mrs. Partin, as she interrupted Ike who was reading the war news—"the pickets were driven in five miles. Bless my poor soul, that will make a strong fence. I suppose they had to be driven in deep to keep the seccessionaders from digging out under them."

AGRICULTURAL.

Wet Weather Work.

Under the above title, one of the purest and pleasantest of American writers—Donald G. Mitchel, better known perhaps as Ik Marvel—is writing a series of articles for the Atlantic Monthly about his researches among the agricultural literature of the Ancients. Many are the quaint old ideas, still more quaintly expressed, that he exhumes from his musty volumes. He shows us that many of the latter day theories of agriculturists were not unknown in the better days of Rome and Greece, and gives us many sage words from Virgil and Tasso and Columella. In his last article he introduces to the early writers on British Husbandry, quoting pertinently from their wise or otherwise sayings, couched in the ludicrous language of our early progenitors.

Mr. Mitchell tells us that Sir Anthony Fitzherbert is the first duly accredited writer in British Husbandry. His work is called a "Boke of Husbandrie." Some of the topics treated were.

"Whether is better a plough of horses or a plough of oxen."

"To carry out deunge & muck, & to sprede it."

"The fyrste furrying of the fallowes."

"To make a ewe to love hir lambe."

"To buy lean cattle."

"A shorte information for a younge gentylman that entendeth to thryve."

What a wife oughte to doos generally."

(*Sey*) "To kepe measure in spendynge."

"What be God's commandments."

He advises "young gentlemen that entendeth to thryve" to rise early and "if he fyndeth a gap in his hedge, or any water standynge in his pasture uppon his grasse, whereby he may take double harte, bothe losse of his grasse, & rotting of his shepe, & calves; or if he fyndeth or seeth anything that is amisse, & would be amended, let him take out his tables & write the defautes; and when he cometh home to dinner, supper, or at night, then let him call his bayley, & soo shewe him the defautes. For this," says he, "used I to do x or xi yeres or more; dyf he cannot wryte, lette him nycke the defautes uppon a stycke."

THE ROLLER.—There is no better pulverizer to follow the plow than the roller. We have evidence enough of this fact. No matter how cloddy the ground lifts, if the roller follows, crushing the clods as they are freshly turned, the action of the sun and air will do more towards completely pulverizing these clods than a thorough harrowing and cross harrowing. This is of importance to farmers who may have occasion to turn dry stubble land the present and next month with a view to seeding it with fall grain. Let the roller follow the plow before seeding. It will scarcely be necessary to touch it with the harrow, if the rolling is done the same day the soil is turned. The soil is left with a smooth surface on which the grain falls and which is likely to insure its being covered to a uniform depth; or if to be drilled in, this work is better done; but more important than all, an excellent seed bed is secured in which the seed will germinate and grow quickly and continuously without the aid of a shower. For a packed surface secures moisture generally.

ECONOMY OF FARM-HOUSE LIGHTS.—This is a very important question for the consideration of farmer's wives, who may find that it will not always be good economy to burn their own tallow. Certainly not, if it can be exchanged for a light-producing substance that will save the hard unpleasant labor of candle-making, and at the same time afford a much better and more pleasant light. Unfortunately, we have no standard of comparative cost of tallow, the almost universal source of farm-house light, with fluid substances. Kerosene oil is the least expensive of all fluid light producing substances; and as it is now refined and burned in improved lamps, we believe it to be a very agreeable substitute for tallow candles; but whether cheaper or not, can only be determined by actual experiments in different households, comparing the cost per gallon with the value per pound of tallow, and the light produced, or the light required. As a general thing, farm house lights are very inferior, and many a bright pair of eyes dimmed in consequence. It is on this account that the question of light should be more discussed and experimented upon. Do not continue to use candles, nor any particular form of lamps, nor kind of oil, because you have long been in the practice, if there is really something better.

INFORMATION.—It may be convenient to know that a quart of flour weighs one pound; a quart of cornmeal one pound two ounces; a quart of butter one pound and one ounce; a quart of best sugar one pound; a quart of white sugar, powdered, one pound and one ounce; a quart of best brown sugar one pound and two ounces; that ten eggs weigh one pound, though this depends somewhat on the size; sixteen large table spoonfuls make a pint.—*Ohio Farmer.*

With what care and attention do the feathered race wash themselves, and put their plumage in order? And how neat, clean, and elegant do they appear. Among the beasts of the field, we find that those who are the most cleanly are generally the most gay and cheerful, or are distinguished by a certain air of tranquility and contentment, and singing birds are always remarkable for the cleanliness of their plumage. So great is the effect of cleanliness upon man, that it extends even to his moral character. Virtue never dwelt long with filth; nor do I believe that ever was a person scrupulously attentive to cleanliness who was a consummate villain.—*Count Rumford.*

BATCHELDER'S COLUMN.

THE CONSERVER.

Published every Tuesday Morning at HASTINGS, DAKOTA COUNTY, MINNESOTA.

Terms.

Single copy one year	$2 00
" " six months,	1 00
" " three months,	50
Five copies, to one address,	8 75
Ten " " "	15 00
Twenty " " " and one to getter up of club,	30 00

Payment invariably in advance.

Address IRVING TODD, Publisher.

RATES OF ADVERTISING.

1 square	1 week	$1 00		2 squares	6 months	9 00
1 "	2 weeks	1 50		2 "	1 year	15 00
1 "	3 "	1 75		3 "	1 week	2 25
1 "	4 "	2 00		3 "	2 "	3 00
1 "	5 "	2 25		3 "	3 "	4 00
1 "	6 "	2 50		3 "	4 "	5 00
1 "	7 "	2 75		3 "	3 months	9 00
1 "	2 months	3 00		3 "	6 "	12 00
1 "	3 "	3 75		3 "	1 year	20 00
1 "	4 "	4 50		¼ col	6 months	15 00
1 "	5 "	5 25		¼ "	1 year	25 00
1 square	6 months	6 00		½ "	6 months	18 00
1 "	1 year	10 00		½ "	1 year	30 00
2 squares	1 week	1 75		¾ "	6 months	25 00
2 "	2 "	2 50		¾ "	1 year	40 00
2 "	3 "	3 00		1 "	1 year	50 00
2 "	4 "	4 00		1 "	1 year	70 00
2 "	3 months	6 00				

One inch in space will be counted as a square of solid matter.

Business cards on second page, not exceeding seven lines, seven dollars per year; each additional line one dollar.

Legal advertisements inserted at the rates prescribed by statute, and attorneys ordering such advertisements will be held responsible.

Special notices 15 cents per line for first insertion and ten cents for each subsequent insertion.

Transient advertisements must be paid in advance—all others quarterly.

Advertisements not otherwise ordered, will be continued until they are ordered out, and charged accordingly.

The Living Dead.

We are surrounded by the living dead,
Men whose lives seem purposeless and vain.
They're bubbles in the air, husks 'mid the grain,
Mere walking flesh-pipes without heart or head.
They'er dead as those on whose old grave we tread
Long years companioned with the flesh-fat worm.
To show they're men, they've nothing but the form.
They are not worth their daily meat and bread.
The marvels of creation move them not;
As well preach God unto a fleshless skull.
Surrounded by the grand and beautiful,
They're cold as ice stone of mossy grot.
Their life's a dream, a festering in the sun.
Snatched from this working earth, who'd miss them? None!

This Hand Never Struck Me.

We recently heard the following most touching incident. A little boy had died. His body was laid out in a darkened retired room waiting to be laid away in the grave.

His afflicted mother and bereaved little sister went in to look at the sweet face of the precious sleeper, for his face was beautiful even in death. As they stood gazing on the form of one so loved and beautiful, the little girl asked to take his hand. The mother at first did not think it best; but as the child repeated the request, and seemed very anxious about it, she took the cold hand of her sleeping boy, and placed it in the hand of his weeping sister.

The dear child looked at it for a moment, caressed it fondly, and then looked up to her mother through the tears of affection and love, and said; "Mother *this little hand never struck me.*"

What could be more touching and lovely!

Young readers, have you always been so gentle to your brothers and sisters, that were you to die, such a tribute could be paid to your memory? Could a brother or sister take your hand, were it cold, and say: "This hand never struck me!"

What an alleviation to our grief, when we are called to part with friends, to be able to remember only words and actions of mutual kindness and love! How bitter must be the sorrow, and how scalding the tears of remorse, of an unkind child, as he looks upon the cold form, or stands at the grave of a brother or sister, a father or mother, toward whom he had manifested unkindness.

Let us all remember, whatsoever we sow, in this respect, that we shall also reap.—*Well Spring.*

Mr. Noyes, in his book of Sketches of the War, tells the best story we have seen, of the way Yankee coolness puts down female insolence in rebeldom. A splendidly bosilked and befeathered female of the Jeff Davis flock, in passing one of our soldiers, gave the skirt of her dress the usual flirt to show her contempt for the tribe, and the soldier replied by the following bit of torture: "Why, marm, how dirty your stockings are! Just look at 'em!" Down went female skirts and female pride at the same instant, while a hearty laugh from his old comrades winged the sarcastic shaft and sent it well home.

Two loafers coming home late at night from a grog shop and instead of getting into their own beds, both got into one bed when the following dialogue ensued:

"I say, Sam, there's somebody in my bed."

"There's some one in my bed, too," replied Sam. "Let's kick them out."

After kicking awhile, Sam called out, "I say, Jim, I've kicked my fellow out."

"Better luck than me, by gracious, my fellow has kicked me out."

A Dutchman describing a rainy night, said: "Vell, last Friday night vash de vorst as never vash. I thought to go down der hill to mine housh, but de fashter I valks the fashter I stand still, for de dark he vash so tick dat I could not stir mine poots, and de rain—dunder and blixen—in more as dree minnets mine skin vas vet to mine close. But after von lettle vile he stop quitten to rain someding, so I keep feelin for mineself all de vay long, and ven I comes to my own house to valk in, vat you tink—mine Cot! he belongs to somebody else!"

A rascally old bachelor says the most difficult surgical operation is to take the jaw out of a woman.

HARDWARE.

PRINTING.

FURNITURE.

MISCELLANEOUS.

BOOKS AND STATIONERY.

PUBLICATIONS.

PATENT MEDICINES

BATCHELDER'S COLUMN.

GREAT ATTRACTIONS

AT THE

OLD STAND.

GEO. F. BATCHELDER,

(Successor to North & Carll)

WHOLESALE

AND

RETAIL

Dealer in

DRY GOODS,

GROCERIES,

Boots and Shoes,

HARDWARE, ETC.,

HASTINGS, MINN.

Having laid in an unusually heavy stock of staple wares, would invite the attention of the public to my large assortment of

GOODS,

Consisting of Imported and Domestic

SILKS, DELAINES,

LAWNS AND

CALICOES,

also to my stock of Foreign and Domestic

SHEETINGS,

These goods were purchased at exceedingly low rates, and am therefore enabled to sell at prices to suit the times.

A well assorted stock of

Hats and Caps,

for Men and Boys, of the latest styles.

READY-MADE

CLOTHING,

a fine assortment, custom made, from the best of cloths, bought expressly for this market, and will be sold at reasonable figures, for cash only.

A choice stock of pure and fresh

GROCERIES

Just received from the East, where especial attention was paid to their selection.

A fine lot of assorted

Boots and Shoes,

comprising Gent's, Ladies', Boy's, and Misses', of all varieties. The especial attention of farmers is invited to a large and complete stock of

HARDWARE.

The celebrated MolinePlow always on hand.

A long experience in and close supervision of the business, and personal attention to the buying of goods, gives confidence that entire satisfaction will be rendered to patrons. Customers will be waited on by experienced and accommodating salesmen, and their wishes promptly attended to. All goods warranted as represented.

GEO. F. BATCHELDER.

Hastings, June 8, 1863. 5-tf

THE CONSERVER.

Published every Tuesday Morning at
HASTINGS, DAKOTA COUNTY, MINNESOTA.

Terms.

Single copy one year $2 00
" " six months 1 00
" " three months 50
Five copies, to one address 8 75
Ten " " " 15 00
Twenty " " " and one to getter up of club 30 00
Payment invariably in advance.
Address IRVING TODD, Publisher.

RATES OF ADVERTISING.

1 square	1 week	$1 00		2 squares	6 months	9 00
[illegible]				[illegible]		
1 "	3 months	[illegible]		1 "	1 year	70 00

One inch in space will be counted as a square of solid matter.

Business cards on second page, not exceeding seven lines, seven dollars per year; each additional line one dollar.

Legal advertisements inserted at the rates prescribed by statute, and attorneys ordering such advertisements will be held responsible.

Special notices 15 cents per line for first insertion and ten cents for each subsequent insertion.

Transient advertisements must be paid in advance —all others quarterly.

Advertisements not otherwise ordered, will be continued until they are ordered out, and charged accordingly.

The Living Dead.

We are surrounded by the living dead,
Men whose lives seem purposeless and vain.
They're bubbles in the air, husks 'mid the grain,
Mere walking flesh-pipes without heart or head.
They'er dead as those on whose old grave we tread
Long years companioned with the flesh-fat worm.
To show they're men, they've nothing but the form.
They are not worth their daily meat and bread.
The marvels of creation move them not;
As well preach God unto a fleshless skull.
Surrounded by the grand and beautiful,
They're cold as ice stone of mossy grot.
Their life's a dream, a festering in the sun.
Snatched from this working earth, who'd miss them? None!

This Hand Never Struck Me.

We recently heard the following most touching incident. A little boy had died. His body was laid out in a darkened retired room waiting to be laid away in the grave.

His afflicted mother and bereaved little sister went in to look at the sweet face of the precious sleeper, for his face was beautiful even in death. As they stood gazing on the form of one so loved and beautiful, the little girl asked to take his hand. The mother at first did not think it best; but as the child repeated the request, and seemed very anxious about it, she took the cold hand of her sleeping boy, and placed it in the hand of his weeping sister.

The dear child looked at it for a moment, caressed it fondly, and then looked up to her mother through the tears of affection and love, and said: "Mother *this little hand never struck me.*"

What could be more touching and lovely!

Young readers, have you always been so gentle to your brothers and sisters, that were you to die, such a tribute could be paid to your memory? Could a brother or sister take your hand, were it cold, and say: "This hand never struck me!"

What an alleviation to our grief, when we are called to part with friends, to be able to remember only words and actions of mutual kindness and love! How bitter must be the sorrow, and how scalding the tears of remorse, of an unkind child, as he looks upon the cold form, or stands at the grave of a brother or sister, a father or mother, toward whom he had manifested unkindness.

Let us all remember, whatsoever we sow, in this respect, that we shall also reap.—*Well Spring.*

Mr. Noyes, in his book of Sketches of the War, tells the best story we have seen, of the way Yankee coolness puts down female insolence in rebeldom. A splendidly besilked and befeathered female of the Jeff Davis flock, in passing one of our soldiers, gave the skirt of her dress the usual flirt to show her contempt for the tribe, and the soldier replied by the following bit of torture: "Why, marm, how dirty your stockings are! Just look at 'em!" Down went female skirts and female pride at the same instant, while a hearty laugh from his old comrades winged the sarcastic shaft and sent it well home.

Two loafers coming home late at night from a grog shop and instead of getting into their own beds, both got into one bed when the following dialogue ensued:

"I say, Sam, there's somebody in my bed."

"There's some one in my bed, too," replied Sam. "Let's kick them out."

After kicking awhile, Sam called out, "I say, Jim, I've kicked my follow out."

"Better luck than me, by gracious, my follow has kicked me out."

A Dutchman describing a rainy night, said: "Vell, last Friday night vash de vorst as never vash. I thought to go down der hill to mine housh, but de faster I valks the fashter I stand still, for de dark he vash so tick dat I could not stir mine poots, and de rain—dundor and blixen—is more as dree minnets mine skin vas vet to mine close. But after von lettle vile he stop quitten to rain someding, so I keep feelin for mineself all de vay long, and ven I comes to my own house to valk in, vat you tink—mine Cot! he belongs to somebody else!"

A rascally old bachelor says the most difficult surgical operation is to take the jaw out of a woman.

HARDWARE.

ATTENTION EVERY BODY!

Buy Where You Can Buy Cheapest and get Good Articles.

If you want good hoes and forks, go to Thomas' Hardware Store.

If you want good scythes and snaths cheap, go to Thomas'.

HARDWARE.

If you want fine table and pocket cutlery, go to Thomas' Cheap Store.

If you want nails or iron cheap, go straight to Thomas', and no where else.

If you want any kind of tools cheap and good, go to Thomas.

If you want hatchets or axes of the best quality, go to Thomas' Cheap Store.

If you want kerosene oil cheap and good go to Thomas.

HARDWARE.

If you want stoves and tinware of the best quality and cheap as the cheapest, go to the cheap hardware store of John Thomas.

If you want locks, latches, butts and screws, or any kind of house trimmings, Thomas' is the place to buy.

If you want sheep shears, gopher traps, smooth irons, iron bench screws, augurs, augur bitts, hand bells, cow bells, or any article kept in a hardware store, go to Thomas' and get it cheap and of the best quality.

HARDWARE.

Try it and see if you cannot make money at it.

JOHN THOMAS.

Hastings, May 14, 1863. 5-tf

HARDWARE.

M. MC HUGH,

Dealer in

HARDWARE,
TINWARE,
STOVES, ETC.,

Corner of Second and Vermillion Streets, Hastings, Minnesota,

has on hand and is constantly receiving a general assortment and a full supply of

Iron,
Nails,
Tinware,
Glass,
Sash,
And
Putty,

Also the best stock of

CUTLERY

ever before exhibited in this market. These goods have been bought expressly for this trade, and will be sold on the most reasonable terms for cash.

I am also agent for, and have on hand, the celebrated

STEWART COOKING STOVE,

known to be the best cooking stove manufactured.

Hastings, May 14, 1863. 5-tf

H. H. PRINGLE,

Wholesale and Retail Dealer in

HARDWARE, IRON, NAILS,

STOVES AND TINWARE,

Mechanics' Tools,

Building Materials,

AGRICULTURAL IMPLEMENTS,

PAINTS, OILS, GLASS,

SASH, DOORS, BLINDS, ETC

HASTINGS, MIN.

TIN,

SHEET IRON & COPPER W'K

ON HAND OR MADE TO ORDER.

BRICK DRUG STORE,

R. J. MARVIN,

Dealer in

DRUGS,
MEDICINES,
CHEMICALS,
ETC., ETC.

On hand a large stock of

PAINTS,
OILS,
COLORS,
GLASS, AND
PAINTERS'
STOCK GENERALLY.

Also

Garden and Field

SEEDS.

Please give me a call before purchasing. Try my goods and prices, which is a better test than *blowing.*

May 1, 1863. 5-tf

PRINTING.

ALL KINDS OF

PRINTING

Neatly and Cheaply Executed

AT THE

CONSERVER OFFICE.

Cards,

Programmes,

Bill-Heads,

Circulars,

Posters,

Etc.,

Printed to Order and at

SHORT NOTICE.

Having received a choice supply of

NEW MATERIAL

from the East, am prepared to do

PLAIN AND FANCY WORK,

in styles to defy competition.

Orders from the country promptly attended to.

IRVING TODD.

FURNITURE.

H. BUTTURFF,

Manufacturer and Dealer in

FURNITURE, UPHOLSTERY,

DOMESTIC-WILLOW WARE,

CRIBS, HOBBY HORSES,

PROPELLERS, BABY-JUMPERS,

FEATHERS, PILLOWS, MATRESSES

COMFORTERS, WINDOW SHADES,

TABLE and FLOOR OIL CLOTH,

CARPETS, CURLED HAIR, etc. etc.

PARLOR FURNITURE,

Cane Seat and Common Chairs, Extention, Dining and Centre Tables, Rocking Chairs, Bedsteads, Wardrobes, Bureaus, Tin Safes, Picture Frames and Looking glasses.

I keep employed the best of workmen, and manufacture to order, with neatness and dispatch.

N. B. Coffins on hand and made to order.

Hastings, Nov. 20, 1862. 32-tf

THE LIVING AND THE DEAD CAN be supplied at

Herzog & Corson's

with all kinds of

Sash, Doors,
Blinds, Chairs,
Cabinet Ware,
Planing, Matching,
Sawing, Turning.
Etc., Etc.

Coffins of all kinds and styles, a large lot always on hand. Sole agents for

THE METALLIC BURIAL CASES.

Come and buy a good article cheap for cash or produce. Wood, Lumber, Pork, etc. taken in exchange for work.

Sale Rooms and Factory corner of Second and Eddy Streets, west of S. Roger's store. HERZOG & CORSON.

Hastings, Jan. 1, 1863. 38-tf

P. VAN AUKEN. W. H. LANGLEY

VAN AUKEN & LANGLEY,

STORAGE.

FORWARDING & COMMISS'N MERCHANTS,

Dealers in Produce, and Agents for

Threshing Machines and Reapers,

RAILROAD & STEAMBOAT TICKET AGENTS.

EQUITABLE LIFE ASSURANCE SOCIETY,

OF NEW YORK.

CASH CAPITAL, ... $300,000
NETT SURPLUS, ... $150,000

Dividends on capital limited by its charter to seven per cent per annum—the entire profits go to the policy holders.

R. W. MONTGOMERY, Agent.

Hastings, Minn. Office on First Street in Gardner's new stone block. 42-1y

MISCELLANEOUS.

BLACKSMITH SHOP.

PLOWS! PLOWS!! PLOWS!!

I have just established myself in the above business on Second Street, above Herzog & Corson's Furniture Factory, and am prepared to do all kinds of Blacksmithing.

Also, constantly on hand all kinds of plows of the most approved patterns and made of the best material. I shall be obliged for a share of public patronage, and shall always warrant my work to be of the best quality. JOHN BATEMAN.

Hastings, Nov. 20, 1862. 32-tf

BOOKS AND STATIONERY.

W. F. STANLEY,

DEALER IN

Books and Stationery,

Paper Hangings, Curtains, Fixtures, Cord, and Tassels; buff and green Holland, all green cloth for shades; Photographs of our generals and other distinguished individuals and albums to put them in; Yankee Notions, all the leading Magazines and Newspapers, Eastern and Western, St. Paul Dailies; agent for Prince & Sons Melodeons. 41-tf

CAPITAL NEW BOOKS, JUST PUBLISHED BY

JOHN BRADBURN,

(Successor to M. DOOLADY,)

Bookseller, Publisher, and Wholesale Book Jobber,

49 WALKER STREET,

(near Broadway.)

NEW YORK CITY.

Leaves from the Diary of an Army Surgeon.

By DOCTOR THOS T. ELLIS,

Late Post Surgeon at New York, and acting Medical Director at White House, Va.

Cloth. 350 pages. 12mo. Price $1.

A Liberal Discount to the Trade.

Each copy contains an autograph letter from Gen. McClellan.

DR. CUMMING'S REPLY TO BISHOP COLENSO.

Bishop Colenso Fully Answered.

His Errors refuted, and the Mosaic authorship of the Pentateuch clearly established, by the Rev. John Cumming, D. D., in a series of lectures.

Cloth. 271 pp. Price $1.

The Actress in High Life.

AN EPISODE IN WINTER QUARTERS

By a lady of South Carolina.

Cloth. 461 pp. 12mo. $1 25.

Adventures by Sea and Land of the Count de Gonzay

OR, THE DEVOTION AND FIDELITY OF WOMAN

An Episode of the Colonization of Canada.

By H. EMILE CHEVALIER.

Cloth. 312 pp. $12mo. $1.

Les Miserables.

By VICTOR HUGO.

Five Volumes in One.

Fantine, Marius, St. Denis.
Cosette, Valjean.

Cloth. 476 pp. 8vo. $1 50.

Hans of Iceland;

THE DEMON OF THE NORTH.

A Romance.

By VICTOR HUGO.

Cloth. 187 pp. 8vo. 50c.

Arbitrary Arrests in the South.

SCENES IN THE EXPERIENCE OF AN ALABAMA UNIONIST.

By R. S. THARIN, A. M.

Native of Charleston; for thirty years a resident of the Cotton States; and commonly known in the West as "the Alabama Refugee."

Cloth. 245 pp. 12mo. $1.

Lives and Letters of Abelard and Heloise.

By O. W. WIGHT.

Cloth. 319 pp. 12mo. $1.

Three Years in Chili.

Cloth. 158 pp. 12mo. 75c.

Woods and Waters.

THE SARANACS AND RACKET.

By ALFRED B. STREET.

Cloth. 341 pp. 12mo. $1 25.

Stories of Frontier Adventure in the South and West.

By W. T. COGGESHALL,

Author of Home Hits and Hints, Poets and Poetry of the West, etc.

Cloth. 318 pp. 12mo. $1.

The Battle of Waterloo.

By VICTOR HUGO.

Paper Covers. 75 pp. 16mo. 15c.

Trips in the Life of a Locomotive Engineer.

Paper Covers. 224 pp. 12mo. 50c.

Cloth, $1.

Our Farm of Four Acres,

AND THE MONEY WE MADE BY IT.

From the 12th London Ed. by Harriet Martineau.

Paper Covers. 148 pp. 12mo. 25c. Cloth 38c.

These Books may be obtained at Retail, in this town, from the store of W. F. STANLEY, on Ramsey Street. 16-1m

THE ATLANTIC MONTHLY.—BEGINNING of a new volume. The number for January, 1863, begins the eleventh volume of the *Atlantic Monthly.* From the commencement, in 1858, the *Atlantic* has rapidly increased in circulation, and it now has the largest class of readers since its beginning, five years ago. Its prosperity steadily augments, and it continues, amid all the fluctuations and dangers incident to our national crisis, to gain ground in the estimation of the public. At a time so pregnant with events which touch the future destinies of America in every vital particular, the publishers and editors do not deem it necessary to promise that its pages will never swerve from the honest paths of loyal patriotism and universal freedom. It opinions have always been on the side of Liberty, Progress, and Right, and the course it first adopted in its early career will ever be faithfully maintained.

The staff of writers regularly contributing to the *Atlantic Monthly* embraces many of the best known authors in American literature, and warrants the publishers in promising to its readers the best essays, the best stories, the best poems, which American talent can furnish.

LIST OF REGULAR CONTRIBUTORS.

In prose and poetry the *Atlantic* staff of writers is unequaled. The following authors are still among the regular contributors: James Russell Lowell, Henry W. Longfellow, Louis Agassiz, Ralph Waldo Emerson, Nathaniel Hawthorne, T. W. Higginson, Author "Margret Howth," Oliver W. Holmes, John G. Whittier, E. P. Whipple, Bayard Taylor, George S. Hillard, Mrs. H. B. Stowe, "The Country Parson," Rose Terry, Harriet E. Prescott. The *Atlantic's* list of contributors includes many of the leading writers of America.

TERMS.—The *Atlantic* is for sale by all book and periodical dealers. Price 25 cts a number. Subscriptions for the year $3, postage paid. Yearly subscriptions received or single numbers supplied by any dealer, or by the publishers. Specimen numbers sent gratis on application to the publishers. Inducements for subscribing, list of premiums, etc., furnished on application to the publishers.

TICKNOR & FIELDS, Publishers,
135 Washington Street,
44-tf Boston, Mass.

PUBLICATIONS.

THE CONTINENTAL MONTHLY.—The readers of the *Continental* are aware of the important position it has assumed, of the influence which it exerts, and of the brilliant array of political and literary talent of the highest order which supports it. No publication [illegible] has, in this country, so [illegible] combined the energy and freedom of the daily newspaper with the higher [illegible] of the first-class monthly [illegible] certain that the magazine [illegible] range to its contributors, [illegible] self so completely from the [illegible] ences of party or faction. In times like the present, such a journal is either a power in the land or it is nothing. That the *Continental* is not the latter is abundantly evinced by what it has done—by the reflection of its counsels in many important public events, and in the character and power of those who are its staunchest supporters.

Though but little more than a year has elapsed since the *Continental* was first established, it has during that time acquired a strength and a political significance elevating it to a position far above that previously occupied by any publication of the kind in America. In proof of which assertion we call attention to the following facts:

1. Of its political articles republished in pamphlet form, a single one has had, thus far, a circulation of one hundred and six thousand copies.

2. From its literary department, a single serial novel, Among the Pines, has, within a very few months, sold nearly thirty-five thousand copies. Two other series of its literary articles have also been republished in book form while the first portion of a third is already in press.

No more conclusive facts need be alleged to prove the excellence of the contributions to the *Continental*, or their extraordinary popularity; and its conductors are determined that it shall not fall behind. Preserving all "the boldness, vigor, and ability" which a thousand journals have attributed to it, it will greatly enlarge its circle of action, and discuss, fearlessly and frankly, every principle involved in the great questions of the day. The first minds of the country, embracing the men most familiar with its diplomacy and most distinguished for ability, are among its contributors; and it is no mere flattering promise of a prospectus to say that this magazine for the times will employ the first intellect in America, under auspices which no publication ever enjoyed before in this country.

While the *Continental* will express decided opinions on the great questions of the day, it will not be a mere political journal: much the larger portion of its columns will be enlivened, as heretofore, by tales, poetry, and humor. In a word, the *Continental* will be found, under its new staff of editors, occupying a position and presenting attractions never before found in a magazine.

TERMS TO CLUBS.

Two copies for one year,	$5 00
Three copies for one year,	6 00
Six copies for one year,	11 00
Eleven copies for one year,	20 00
Twenty copies for one year,	36 00

Paid in advance. Postage 36 cents a year, to be paid by the subscriber. Single copies $3 a year, in advance. Postage paid by the publisher. 12-tf

JOHN F. TROW, 50 Greene St., N.Y.,
Publisher for the Proprietors.

ONLY $1 25 A YEAR IN CLUBS OF 4.

Arthur's Home Magazine,

For 1863. Vols. XXI. and XXII. Edited by T. S. Arthur and Virginia F. Townsend. Contains novelets, stories, poetry, fashions, steel and wood engravings, needlework patterns in great variety, a mother's department, children's department, housekeeper's and health department, with literary reviews, and all the accessories of a first-class magazine.

The Lady's Book bears this flattering testimony to the character of *Arthur's Home Magazine*:

[illegible]

A new serial by T. S. Arthur will be commenced in the January number entitled Out in the World.

Rare and elegant premiums are sent to all who make up clubs: 1. A large photographic copy of that splendid engraving Shakspeare and his Cotemporaries. 2. A large photographic copy from an engraving of Huntington's celebrated picture Mercy's Dream. 3. A similar copy of Herring's Glimpse of an English Homestead.

TERMS.—$2 a year in advance and one premium plate. Two copies $3. Three for $4. Four for $5. Eight and one to getter up of club for $10. One of the premium plates is sent to every getter up of a club, small or large. Three red stamps must be sent to pay the postage on each premium. Address

T. S. ARTHUR & Co.,
323 Walnut Street, Philadelphia.

THE INDEPENDENT, EDITED BY *Henry Ward Beecher*, is a religious newspaper, and a real newspaper. It affords its readers fair and thoughtful editorial discussions of the most important facts and occurrences and interests of this nation and of the world. A comprehensive record of facts, men and movements of the religious world. A full and careful weekly history of the progress of the rebellion. Ample chronicles of the important general news; home and foreign. Fair and careful accounts of new books; made on the express principle of serving as a safe guide to buyers. Interesting correspondence from Washington; from the West; from the army; from abroad. Six columns a week of carefully selected matter for family reading; being prose and poetry, suited to interest both the old people and the young people. A full chronicle of the progress of business and of the current prices of merchandise, produce and live stock in New York City

ONE SERMON EVERY WEEK

By Rev. Henry Ward Beecher. The following eminent writers are special contributors to its columns:—

Mrs. Harriet Beecher Stowe,
Rev. Theodore L. Cuyler,
Rev. Robert M. Hatfield,
Rev. George B. Cheever,
Horace Greely,
Bayard Taylor,
John G. Whittier.

TERMS.—$2 per annum, paid in advance. Specimen numbers sent gratis.

JOSEPH H. RICHARDS, Publisher,
No. 5 Beekman Street, New York.

For sale by news agents.

PATENT MEDICINES.

ARE NOT TO BE EXCELLED AS A STOMACHIC AND Regulator OF THE DIGESTIVE ORGANS.

These Bitters are not offered to the public as a medicine which will cure all the "ills which flesh is heir to," but as a remedial agent —a great regulator of the system.

In the Bilious districts of the West and South there has, for a long time, been much needed an article of Stomach Bitters, which, if taken in proper quantities, and at the proper time, are a sure preventive of

Bilious Fever,
Fever and Ague,
Liver Complaint,
Dyspepsia,
Indigestion,
Jaundice,
Kidney Complaints,

and all diseases of a similar nature.

These Bitters are composed of rare and powerful roots and herbs, which make them Highly Tonic.

Dr. Roback's Stomach Bitters are the poor man's friend.

Dr. Roback's Stomach Bitters save the poor man many Doctor's Bills.

Dr. Roback's Stomach Bitters are the rich man's Solace and Comfort.

Dr. Roback's Stomach Bitters invigorate the weak and debilitated.

Dr. Roback's Stomach Bitters drive away melancholy and make Life enjoyable.

Dr. Roback's Stomach Bitters are the Soldier's Friend, by preventing Diarrhea, Dysentery, Rheumatism, etc.

These Bitters are put up in quart bottles, of which the above is a facsimile. The label is finely engraved, and is provided with a safe-guard from counterfeiters. Price $1 per bottle, or six for $5.

C. W. Roback, *Proprietor, No. 4. East Fourth Street, Cincinnati, to whom all orders should be addressed.*

FOR SALE BY

A. M. Pett, Hastings, J. R. Tickner, Mankato, W. H. McCollum, Mankato, and by druggists and merchants generally throughout the United States, Canadas and Brazil.

For Rats, Mice, Roaches, Ants, Bed Bugs, Moths in Furs Woolens, etc., Insects on Plants, Fowls, Animals, etc. Put up in 25c, 50c, and $1 00 Boxes, Bottles, and Flasks. $3 and $5 sizes for Hotels, Public Institutions, etc.

"Only infallible remedies known."

"Free from Poisons."

"Not dangerous to the Human Family."

"Rats come out of their holes to die."

Sold wholesale in all large cities.

Sold by all druggists and retailers every where.

Beware! of all worthless imitations.

See that COSTAR'S name is on each Box, Bottle, and Flask before you buy.

Address HENRY R. COSTAR.

Principal depot 482 Broadway, N. Y.

Sold by A. M. PETT,
Wholesale and Retail Agent,
51-10m Hastings, Minn.

FRED. B. CURTISS. W. C. COWLES.

CURTISS & COWLES,

DEALERS IN

Shoe and Harness Leather,

saddlery hardware, shoe findings, etc., Ramsey Street, near Levee, and lumber of all descriptions at corner of Second and Eddy Streets.

Hastings, Feb. 19, 1863. 45-tf

THE CONSERVER.

Our Ticket—Opinions of the Press.

From the Mankato Union.

The nomination of Col. Stephen Miller, for the office of governor gives entire satisfaction throughout the state. A better selection could not have been made. The colonel is so well and favorably known for honesty, and integrity at home, capability and bravery on the field of battle; and his loyalty is so well established, that nothing we can say will add to his fame. He is bound to be our next governor, and will be elected by a rousing majority.

The selection of C. D. Sherwood; speaker of the House of Representatives last winter for the office of lieut. governor, is a good move, and the nomination will be ratified by the people this fall.

With Geo. F. Potter, the nomination for clerk of the supreme court, we are well acquainted. He is a good union man, and has the ability to discharge the duties of the office with credit.

Of the other nominations our readers are acquainted. They are the present incumbents of the offices for which they are nominated, and the satisfaction they have heretofore given is a guarantee of their re-election.

We have a good ticket in the field —one that cannot easily be beaten; and we expect every union man in the state will labor valiantly for its triumphant election.

From the Preston Republican:

At the head of the ticket appears the name of the gallant Col. Miller. His home is at St. Cloud. As a candidate for elector in 1860, he became well known to the citizens of the entire state, and was every where received with great favor as an elector. Since the war broke out he has been in service of his country, first as lieut. colonel, and then as colonel. In these situations he discharged his duty to his country with such fidelity and favor as to add to the well grounded reputation he had already gained. When another was sought as a candidate for the chair vacant by the expiration of the present gubernatorial, the eyes of the people turned instinctively to Col. Miller as the man whom they delighted to honor.

So he had no competitior and was nominated unanimously for the highest state office. No better choice could have been made. He is deservedly esteemed throughout the state as a man of ability and moral worth.

For lieut. governor the convention presented the Hon. Charles D. Sherwood of Filmore County. He has represented the county two or three terms in the lower house, and was chosen speaker at the last session. He has shown distinguished legislative ability, and as a presiding officer won the praise of all. He will discharge the duties of the office to which this nomination is so sure to secure his election, with integrity and ability.

The other candidates are well known throughout the state, and will meet a cordial support and a triumphant election.

From the Wabashaw Herald.

Most of the nominees are well known to the people of the state, having served the state heretofore in the positions for which they are again nominated, and have prooved good and efficient functionaries. Those persons placed in nomination are equally well known for worth and ability.

Col. Miller, nominee for governor, whose nomination we advocated previous to the convention, is well known through the state as a man of energy, ability, and moral worth, and one whose patriotism has been well-attested on the battlefield for the past two years. At the ouset of our national troubles he was one of the first to offer his services, and ever since he has stood in the vanguard of our country's defenders and has battled manfully in defense of the right, and has won lasting laurels in some of the most bloody engagements known in modern history. His patriotic service haco been acknowledged by all, wherever duty has called him. He is now before the loyal people of the state as a candidate for "an office justly his due, disdaining the support of the disloyal, but confidently expecting the vote of every lover of his country, whatever may have been his past party predilictions. The loyal people of our state know full well how to reward the valor of such a man. They have already risen above old party issues, and [illegible] adopted the immortal sentiments of Gen. Jackson:—"Our Country—may she ever be right; but right or wrong, our country."

From the St. Cloud Democrat.

While the ticket meets with general endorsement, it will be seen that the peculiar fitness of Col. Miller's nomination receives special mention.

The fact is full recognized at this time that Minnesota wants a good governor—one that is loyal, honest, and able —and in this part of the state, at least, there are very many who have always been democrats who will cast their vote for Col. Miller at the coming election. He has been known to them for years as an upright citizen, reliable and trustworthy in all business transactions, and as one who would make the welfare of the state his chief aim. His long services as a soldier, first in the well-tried First Regiment, and subsequently in this state, in command of the forces in garrison, are fully appreciated. So, look out for a big majority for Col. Miller, in Northern Minnesota, and Stearns County will not be found behind her neighbors in bestowing honor upon a faithful and loyal soldier, and former citizen.

HOPE.—A bright and beautiful word is hope. It will come to us amid the darkness, and sing the sweetest song when our spirits are saddest; and when the lone soul is weary, and longs to pass away, it warbles its cheerful notes, and tightens again the slender fibres of our heart that grief has been tearing away.

MONETARY QUOTATIONS OF FOLLETT & RENICK.

(CORRECTED WEEKLY.)

Bankable Funds.

New England,	Bank State of Indiana.
New York,	Iowa,
New Jersey,	Michigan,
Ohio,	U. S Demand Notes.
Canada,	Wisconsin,
Philadelphia,	Bank of Minnesota,
Marine Bank, Minn.,	Winona Co. Bank,
Bank of Chatfield,	State Bank of Minn.,
Peoples' Bank,	Pittsburg.

Exchange.

FOR BANKABLE FUNDS.

	Buying.	Selling
New York, Philadelphia, Boston,	¼ prem.	½ prem.
Chicago and Milwaukee,	par.	¼ prem.

PREMIUM FUNDS.

Gold,	25	30
Silver (large),	17	25
U. S. Demand Notes,	25	30
Canada,	20	25

RETAIL PRICES CURRENT.

CORRECTED WEEKLY BY G. F. BATCHELDER.

Hastings, Sept 22, 1863.

FLOUR, per sack,	$2 50
WHEAT, per bushel,	65a70
CORN, do	40a45
OATS, do	40
POTATOES, do	50
BEANS, do	1 50
ONIONS, do	80
CRANBERRIES,	2 00
HAY, per ton,	6 00a8 00
WOOD, per cord,	3 00a4 00
SALT, per bbl	3 75
EGGS, per doz	12
BUTTER, per lb,	10a15
CHEESE, per lb	8a12
PORK, per cwt,	3a4
BEEF, per cwt,	3 00
HAMS, per cwt,	8a9
SHOULDERS, per cwt,	5a6
DRIED APPLES,	9
DRIED PEACHES,	15a20
SUGARS, per lb	12a17
MOLASSES, per gal	70a1 00
COFFEE, Java,	40
do Rio,	33

MISCELLANEOUS.

P. VAN AUKEN. W. H. LANGLEY

VAN AUKEN & LANGLEY,

STORAGE,

FORWARDING & COMMISS'N MERCHANTS,

Dealers in Produce, and Agents for

Threshing Machines and Reapers,

RAILROAD & STEAMBOAT TICKET AGENTS.

NEW ENGLAND HOTEL RE-OPENED.

CHAS. DAMEREL.

Having leased the above property, has thoroughly cleaned and refurnished the above old established hotel at Hastings, and is ready to do all in his power to conduce to the comfort and satisfaction of the traveling community, and solicits a share of public patronage.

In connection with the hotel I keep a livery and sale stable and feel confident I can please the majority with pleasant driving horses and steady and obliging drivers.

Teaming done at fair prices. Please call and see me at New England House.

CHAS. DAMEREL, Proprietor.

Hastings, Aug. 10, 1863. 18-6m

W. D. FRENCH,

Wholesale & Retail GROCER,

Union Block, - - Hastings, Minn.

Having removed to the large new store two doors west of his old stand, will keep constantly on hand a

LARGE STOCK

Which will be offered at

Wholesale or Retail,

AT THE

Lowest Market Price for Cash.

Merchants, Farmers, and other purchasers are invited to call and examine his stock and prices.

W. D. FRENCH.

Sept. 15, 1863. 23-tf

WINONA AND HASTINGS

MARBLE WORKS.

The subscriber would respectfully give notice to the people of Hastings and elsewhere that he has constantly on hand the largest stock of Foreign and American Marbles ever brought west of Lake Michigan, consisting of all kinds of

LARGE SPIRE MONUMENTS,
SKELETON MONUMENTS,
GRAVE STONES, MANTELS,
FURNITURE MARBLE, ETC.,

which he will finish to order in the most approved styles and for the lowest cash price. Parties wishing to purchase will do well to wait till my agent comes around or to write to me, before purchasing elsewhere. C. J. ALDBACH.

Shop opposite the court-house, Winona, and on Second Street, below Tyler, Hastings, Minn. 16-tf

---

WILKES' SPIRIT OF THE TIMES.

Office 201 William-st., New York.

George Wilkes, Ed. and Pro.

Four Dollars a Year in Advance.

To Clubs—5 Copies,	$17 00
" 9 "	30 00

No subscriptions received for less than three months.

Rates of Advertising.

15 cts per line		each single insertion.
48 "	" "	One month.
$1 25 "	"	Three months.
$2 00 "	"	Six months.

Sinclair Tousey, No. 121 Nassau Street, New York, general wholesale agents for supplying dealers. T. B. Callender, agent for Philadelphia.

Postmasters are requested to act as agents, and retain 20 per cent for their trouble. This percentage is, however, not to be deducted from club rates.

MISCELLANEOUS.

J. W. PRATT & CO.,

Dealers in

Cloths, Cassimeres, Vestings, and Tailor's Trimmings.

Also, Hats, Caps, and Gents'

FURNISHING GOODS.

Hastings, Minn., May 14, 1863. 1-tf

E. & H. T. ANTHONY, MANUFACturer of Photographic Materials, 501 Broadway, New York.

CARD PHOTOGRAPHS.

Our Catalogue now embraces considerably over four thousand different subjects (to which additions are continually being made) of Portraits of Eminent Americans, etc., viz:

72 Major-Generals,	525 Statesmen,
190 Brig.-Generals,	127 Divines,
250 Colonels,	119 Authors,
84 Lieut.-Colonels,	30 Artists,
207 Other Officers,	112 Stage,
60 Navy Officers,	46 Prominent Women,

147 Prominent Foreign Portraits.

2,500 COPIES OF WORKS OF ART,

Including reproductions of the most celebrated Engravings, Paintings, Statues, etc. Catalogues sent on receipt of stamp. An order for One Dozen Pictures from our catalogue will be filled on receipt of $1 80, and sent by mail *free.*

Photographic Albums.

Of these we manufacture a great variety, ranging in price from 50 cents to $50. Our Albums have the reputation of being superior to any others. The smaller kinds can be sent safely by mail at a postage of six cents per oz. The more expensive can be sent by express.

We also keep a large assortment of Stereoscopes & Stereoscopic Views. Our Catalogue of these will be sent to any address on receipt of stamp.

E. & H. T. ANTHONY,
Manufacturers of Photographic Materials,
501 Broadway, New York.

Friends or relatives of prominent military men will confer a favor by sending us their likenesses to copy. They will be kept carefully and returned uninjured.

Fine Albums made to order for congregations to present to their pastor, or for other purposes, with suitable inscriptions.

17-6mo

THE ATLANTIC MONTHLY.—BEGINning of a new volume. The number for January, 1863, begins the eleventh volume of the *Atlantic Monthly.* From the commencement, in 1859, the *Atlantic* has rapidly increased in circulation, and it now has the largest class of readers since its beginning, five years ago. Its prosperity steadily augments, and it continues, amid all the fluctuations and dangers incident to our national crisis, to gain ground in the estimation of the public. At a time so pregnant with events which touch the future destinies of America in every vital particular, the publishers and editors do not deem it necessary to promise that its pages will never swerve from the honest paths of loyal patriotism and universal freedom. It opinions have always been on the side of Liberty, Progress, and Right, and the course it first adopted in its early career will ever be faithfully maintained.

The staff of writers regularly contributing to the *Atlantic Monthly* embraces many of the best known authors in American literature, and warrants the publishers in promising to its readers the best essays, the best stories, the best poems, which American talent can furnish.

LIST OF REGULAR CONTRIBUTORS.

In prose and poetry the *Atlantic* staff of writers is unequaled. The following authors are still among the regular contributors: James Russell Lowell, Henry W. Longfellow, Louis Agassiz, Ralph Waldo Emerson, Nathaniel Hawthorne, T. W. Higginson, Author "Margret Howth," Oliver W. Holmes, John G. Whittier, E. P. Whipple, Bayard Taylor, George S. Hillard, Mrs. H. B. Stowe, "The Country Parson," Rose Terry, Harriet E. Prescott. The *Atlantic's* list of contributors includes many of the leading writers of America.

TERMS.—The *Atlantic* is for sale by all book and periodical dealers. Price 25 cts a number. Subscriptions for the year $3, postage paid. Yearly subscriptions received or single numbers supplied by any dealer, or by the publishers. Specimen numbers sent gratis on application to the publishers. Inducements for subscribing, list of premiums, etc., furnished on application to the publishers.

TICKNOR & FIELDS, Publishers,
135 Washington Street,
44-tf Boston, Mass.

THE LIVING AND THE DEAD CAN be supplied at

Herzog & Corson's

with all kinds of

Sash, Doors,
Blinds, Chairs,
Cabinet Ware,
Planing, Matching,
Sawing, Turning-
Etc., Etc.

Coffins of all kinds and styles, a large lot always on hand. Sole agents for

THE METALLIC BURIAL CASES.

Come and buy a good article cheap for cash or produce. Wood, Lumber, Etc., taken in exchange for work.

Sale Rooms and Factory corner of Second and Eddy Streets, west of S. Leger's store. HERZOG & CORSON.

Hastings, Jun. 1, 1863. 38-tf

FARMING IMPLEMENTS.

DAKOTA WORKS.

AGRICULTURAL IMPLEMENT

MANUFACTORY.

MONTGOMERY & THOMPSON,

Hastings, - - Minnesota.

We are now manufacturing a number of the celebrated

Indiana Fanning Mills,

the very best mill of the age. All we ask is a fair trial to convince the most incredulous that it is the best mill for *all purposes ever invented.*

Farmers, call and see it tested.

We are now prepared to repair all kinds of agricultural implements in the best manner, and at short notice.

Thankful for the liberal encouragement we have received in the past we hope, by strict and prompt attention to business, to merit a continuation of it in the future.

Hastings, June 14, 1863. 10-tf.

COPARTNERSHIP NOTICE.

The undersigned, having formed a partnership connection under the firm name of Gardner & Meloy as dealers in all kinds of agricultural implements and the latest valuable and useful patents, to-wit:

J. H. Manny's Reaper and Mower.

The Ohio Reaper and Mower.

Haine's Illinois Harvester or Header.

Burson's Celebrated Binder—Warranted.

Montgomery & Thompson's Fanning Mills.

Corn Shellers, of Latest Improvement.

Revolving and Wheel Horse Rakes.

Wheeler & Wilson's Sewing Machines.

The Model Clothes Dryer.

Linen Grain Bags.

Garden Rakes and Hoes.

Scythe Snaths and Stones.

Two, Three, and Four Tine Forks.

Storage and Commission solicited.

A. W. GARDNER,
J. C. MELOY.

Office corner Sibley Street and Levee, Stone Block.

Hastings, May 14, 1863, 5-tf

RAILROADS.

ILLINOIS CENTRAL RAILROAD

The old reliable and

DIRECT ROUTE,

via Dunleith. Express passenger trains leave Dunleith morning and evening, making quick time and close connections to all points

EAST AND SOUTH.

No change of cars between Dunleith and Chicago. Elegant sleeping cars attached to night trains. Baggage checked through to all important points. Fare lower to southern points than any other railroad line, and as low to eastern cities as the lowest.

This is the only direct route to

St. Louis and Cairo,

and passengers will arrive at these points from eighteen to twenty-four hours quicker than by any route through Chicago.

Freight transported to Milwaukee, Chicago, or points South and East at as low rates and as quick time guaranteed as by any other route from the Mississippi River.

W. P. JOHNSON, Gen. Pass. Agt., Chi. W. R. ARTHUR, Gen. Supt. Chicago.
J. S. TILDESLY, Gen. Western Agent.

Inquire for tickets by Illinois Central Railroad.

SAMUEL BOGERS, JR., Agent,
Cor. Vermillion and 2d Streets,
16-3m Hastings, Minn.

1863. PRAIRIE DU CHIEN ROUTE 1863.

For Milwaukee, Chicago, and all points East. The only direct route making sure connections, ample time being allowed on the river to insure the connection beyond any probable contingency.

The splendid first-class steamers

MILWAUKEE, KEY CITY,
WAR EAGLE, ITASCA,
AND NORTHERN LIGHT,

unequalled in elegance, speed, and comfort by any other line, leave Hastings daily about 10 P. M., making direct connection with express train leaving Prairie du Chien at 7.45 A. M., arriving at Milwaukee at 3.50 P. M., and Chicago 5.50 P. M., making direct connections at both points with trains for the East.

The change from steamers to cars being made at 7.45 A. M., passengers get a full night's rest and breakfast on board; advantages that cannot be secured by any other route. Magnificent palace cars with patent ventilators and dusters, rendering cars free from dust, and keeping the air pure and cool.

Through from Prairie du Chien to Milwaukee and Chicago without change of cars. Passengers by this route arrive at La Crosse, and twelve hours than via Dunleith. Fare as low as by any other route. VAN AUKEN & LANGLEY, on Levee.

5-tf

LEGAL NOTICES.

STATE OF MINNESOTA.

Sale of School Lands.

In accordance with an act entitled "an act to establish the State Land Office and for other purposes," approved March 10th, 1862, the following parcels or tracts of land will be sold at public auction, at the office of County Treasurer, in the town of Hastings, on Wednesday, the fourth day of November, 1863, at 10 o'clock A. M.:

Lands on which Fifteen per cent of the Purchase Money must be paid down.

Part of Sec.	Sec.	Town.	Range	Appraised value per acre.	Appraised value of Improvements
DOUGLASS.					
[illegible]					$58 00
MARSHAN.					
[illegible]					
RANDOLPH—HAMPTON.					
[illegible]					
INVER GROVE.					
[illegible]					
VERMILLION.					
sw qr of sw qr	16	114	18	5 00	
WATERFORD.					
nw qr of se qr	16	112	19	5 00	
CASTLE ROCK.					
[illegible]					87 50
[illegible]					238 50
EMPIRE CITY.					
[illegible]					9 50
[illegible]					88 50
[illegible]					371 25
[illegible]					589 50
ROSEMONT.					
[illegible]					50 00
[illegible]					59 00
[illegible]					73 50
EUREKA.					
[illegible]					48 00
[illegible]					408 50
[illegible]					118 00
[illegible]					42 00
[illegible]					147 00
LAKEVILLE.					
[illegible]					
LEBANON.					
[illegible]					
LAKEVILLE.					
[illegible]					
EAGAN.					
[illegible]					
MENDOTA.					
[illegible]					

Lands on which Seventy-Five per cent of the Purchase Money must be paid down.

Part of Sec.	Sec.	Town.	Range	Appraised value per acre.	Appraised value of Improvements
[illegible]					
HASTINGS.					
lot 2, 30a ne qr	36	115	17	8 00	
lot 3, 9.71a ne qr	36	115	17	8 00	
lot 8, 3.32a ne qr	36	115	17	8 00	
lot 13, 3.05a ne qr	36	115	17	8 00	
INVER GROVE.					
lot 7, 10.60a nw qr	16	115	18	7 00	
lot 8, 14.21a nw qr	16	115	18	7 00	
lot 9, 19.93a nw qr	16	115	18	7 00	
lot 10, 9.97a nw qr	16	115	18	7 00	
lot 11, 10a nw qr	16	115	18	7 00	
lot 13, 9.06a nw qr	16	115	18	7 00	
lot 14, 9.53a nw qr	16	115	18	7 00	
lot 15, 10a nw qr	16	115	18	7 00	
lot 16, 10a nw qr	16	115	18	7 00	
lot 1, 10.21a sw qr	16	115	18	7 00	
lot 2, 10.15a sw qr	16	115	18	7 00	
lot 5, 10.15a sw qr	16	115	18	7 00	
lot 5, 10.09a sw qr	16	115	18	7 00	
lot 6, 10.05a sw qr	16	115	18	7 00	
lot 7, 9.79a	16	115	18	7 00	
lot 8, 9.79a	16	115	18	7 00	
lot 1, 10.20a se qr	16	115	18	7 00	
lot 2, 10.42a se qr	16	115	18	7 00	
lot 3, 10.14a se qr	16	115	18	7 00	
lot 4, 10.33a se qr	16	115	18	7 00	
lot 6, 10.27a se qr	16	115	18	7 00	
lot 7, 10.58a se qr	16	115	18	7 00	
lots 3,8,9 ne qr	16	27	22	6 00	
lots 6,7 ne qr	16	27	22	[illegible]	
lots 10,11,12 ne qr	16	27	22	[illegible]	
lots 1—12 inc se qr	16	27	22	[illegible]	
lots 13—18 inc se qr	16	27	22	[illegible]	
lots 1, 2, 3, 4, 15, 16 nw qr	16	27	22	6 00	
lot 9 nw qr	16	27	22	5 00	
lot 10	16	27	22	6 00	
lots 9, 10, 11, 12, 13 sw qr	16	27	22	4 00	
lots 13,14,15 sw qr	16	27	22	6 00	
WEST ST. PAUL.					
lot 1 ne qr	16	28	22	5 00	
lot 2, 5.50a se qr	16	28	22	5 00	
lot 3, 11.15a se qr	16	28	22	7 00	
lot 5, 10a	16	28	22	7 00	
lot 7, 10a	16	28	22	[illegible]	
lot 8, 10a	16	28	22	[illegible]	
lot 9, 10a	16	28	22	[illegible]	
lot 10, 10a	16	28	22	[illegible]	
lot 12, 10a	16	28	22	[illegible]	
lot 13, 4.07a	16	28	22	[illegible]	
lot 14, 10a	16	28	22	[illegible]	
lot 15, 10a	16	28	22	[illegible]	
lots 2—14 inc 10a sw qr	16	28	22	4 00	

The balance of the purchase money is payable any time within twenty years, at the option of the purchaser, if interest at seven per cent per annum is annually paid in advance.

Interest to the first day of June, 1864, must be paid at the time of purchase.

Persons purchasing land upon which other parties have made improvements will be required to pay the owner of the same the appraised value of his improvements, one half to be paid at the time of the sale and the balance six months thereafter, with interest at seven per cent per annum.

In case the person occupying or improving the land has damaged the same, the appraised amount of damage will be deducted from his improvements, and when the occupant is the purchaser the damage will be added to the price of the land.

No lands will be sold for less than the appraised value.

Purchase money payable in specie and legal tender notes. CHAS. McILRATH,

22-14 Commissioner of State Land Office.

MORTGAGE SALE.—WHEREAS DEfault has been made in the condition of a certain mortgage deed executed by Harvey Gillett and Georgie R. Gillett, his wife, of the county of Dakota, in the state of Minnesota to Allen E. Rich and Isaac B. Tozer, then and now partners in business under the firm name of Rich & Tozer, made, acknowledged, and delivered by said mortgagors to said firm of Rich & Tozer, mortgagees, and bearing date the 8th day of May, A. D. 1862, which said mortgage contains the usual power of sale to said Rich & Tozer and their assigns, and was duly filed for record with said mortgage in the office of the register of deeds of said county, on the 9th day of said May at four o'clock in the afternoon of that day, and was thereupon duly recorded in said office in book K of mortgages on pages 587, 588, and 589; which said mortgage was given to secure the payment of one hundred and twenty-three dollars and seventy-one cents with interest at ten per cent per annum according to the conditions of a certain promissory note made by said Harvey Gillett and bearing even date with said mortgage. And there is claimed to be due and is actually due and unpaid upon said note and mortgage, at the date of this notice the sum of one hundred and thirty-four dollars and fifty cents. And no suit or proceeding at law has been instituted to recover the debt secured by said mortgage or any part thereof. The mortgaged premises are described as follows, viz: All that tract or parcel of land lying and being in Dakota County, state of Minnesota, and described as follows, to wit: Lot number fourteen (14) in block number three (3) in H. G. Bailly's addition to Hastings, as per recorded plat thereof now on record in the office of register of deeds in said county.

Now, therefore, notice is hereby given that by virtue of the power of sale in said mortgage contained and pursuant to the statute in such case made and provided the said mortgage will be foreclosed by a sale of said mortgaged premises at public auction to the highest bidder at the front door of the office of said register of deeds in Hastings, in said county, on the 3d day of October, A. D. 1863, at one o'clock in the afternoon of that day, to satisfy said mortgage debt and the expenses of said sale.

19-7t RICH & TOZER, Mortgagees.

A. M. Hayes, Att'y for said Mortgagees.

Dated Hastings, Minn., Aug. 18, 1863.

STATE OF MINNESOTA, SECOND Collection District,

Assessor's Office, St. Paul, August, 1863.

Public Notice

is hereby given that the lists, valuations, and enumerations made and taken under the Excise Tax Law of the United States within division numbered three, comprising the county of Dakota, will be open for examination at the office of Eli Robinson, in the city of Hastings, in said county, on the 20th day of August, A. D. 1863, and will remain open for the space of fifteen days from said time.

Notice is also given that appeals will be received and determined relative to any erroneous or excessive valuations or enumerations by the assistant assessor of said division at the office of Eli Robinson, in said city of Hastings, in said county of Dakota, on the 8th day of September, A. D. 1863, and immediately thereafter until all appeals are disposed of.

H. G. O. MORRISON,
Assessor, 2d District.

Dated August, 21, 1863. 20-4w

ENVELOPES AND WRITING PAPERS, AT WHOLESALE.

To Booksellers, Stationers, Druggists, Dealers in Fancy Goods, Merchants, and all others who purchase Envelopes and Writing Papers.

SAMUEL RAYNOR,

No. 118 William St., New York,

Begs leave to call the attention of dealers in Envelopes to the extensive assortment and superior quality of those manufactured by him. His machinery for manufacturing Envelopes is the latest and best —folding and gumming them in the most perfect manner. The assortment embraces over 700 kinds, including every size, style, color, and quality. The subscriber now has facilities for manufacturing half a million Envelopes per day, so that all orders can be filled promptly. Also the Irving and Harrison Mills Writing Papers, by the case, or in any quantity to suit the purchaser. All offered at the lowest possible prices, on the usual credit, or a discount off for cash.

Samples, with trade list of prices, furnished, when requested, and sent by mail free of postage. SAMUEL RAYNOR.

For sale in Hastings by W. D. Stanley, on Ramsey Street. 18-1m

PUBLICATIONS.

1863. THE 1863.

MILWAUKEE WISCONSIN.

Daily, Semi-Weekly, Weekly.

The proprietors of the *Wisconsin,* begs leave to announce that owing to increasing expenditures for Special Telegraphic and War Correspondence, together with various improvements in contemplation for the coming year, he has felt compelled to make some changes in the scale of prices at which it is furnished to subscribers. By comparison with the prices of other journals, it will be seen that the *Wisconsin* is still, as it ever has been, the cheapest paper in the North-West.

We shall continue to print the *Wisconsin* upon the plainest type and the finest paper that can be made, thus retaining the name of the "handsomest paper in the state."

The present proprietor has conducted the paper over fifteen years, and it is unnecessary for him to speak of his ability or enterprise as a Live Independent Newspaper. He will only say that his journal is faithfully pledged to the suppression of the rebellion and the destruction of the rebels in arms, by every means in the power of the Government, and to the most cordial and active support of the President in his Proclamation of Freedom.

Our list of correspondence embraces every regiment of Wisconsin soldiers, as well as the several grand divisions of the Union Army. The Local and Commercial Departments will receive the undivided attention of the most competent Editors and Reporters.

We call particular attention to the Semi-Weekly *Wisconsin.* It will be a large thirty-two column paper, without advertisements, made up expressly for country circulation. All matter of the Daily *Wisconsin* will appear in this sheet; thus the subscriber will receive all the news of a daily paper for the price of the semi-weekly.

DAILY WISCONSIN—BY MAIL.

Published every day (except Sundays,) at 9 A. M., 12 M., and 3 P. M., at the following rates:

1 copy 12 months, in advance		$6 00
1 copy 6 months,	"	4 00
1 copy 3 months,	"	2 00

SEMI-WEEKLY WISCONSIN.

Published every Tuesday and Thursday morning, as follows:

1 copy 1 year, in advance	$3 00
1 copy 6 months, "	1 50
4 copies 1 year (in one order)	10 00
10 copies 1 year " "	22 50

Additional copies at the rate of the club. Specimen numbers sent to any address.

WEEKLY WISCONSIN.

Published every Wednesday morning, and mailed every Tuesday evening.

1 copy 8 mos, in advance		$ 1 00
1 copy 1 year,	"	1 50
10 copies 1 year,	"	13 00
20 copies 1 year,	"	25 00

Additional copies at the rate of the club.

An extra copy will be sent to persons getting up clubs of ten or more of the Weekly. Money in registered letters may be sent at our risk.

WM. E. CRAMER,

38-tf Milwaukee, Wis.

THE BEST, CHEAPEST, AND MOST successful Family Paper in the Union. A complete pictorial history of the times.

HARPER'S WEEKLY,

Splendidly Illustrated. Price six cents a number—$3 00 a year.

Critical Notices of the Press.

Its fresh leaves, its clear type, its entertaining variety, its severe but just criticisms upon the follies of the times, its elegantly written and instructive articles, and its able correspondence, all combine to make it the model newspaper of our country, and one that every family must prize. Its condensed weekly summary of foreign and domestic intelligence is altogether superior to that contained in any other journal. Being published, too, in a form for preservation and binding, if taken care of as it deserves to be, it will be found in future years as welcome a companion for the family and fireside as the day on which it was first perused.—N. Y. Evening Post.

We would not so often call attention to Harper's Weekly if we were not well satisfied that it is the best family paper published in the United States, and for that reason, and that alone, we desire to see it undermine and root out a certain kind of literature too prevalent, which blunts the morals of its readers, vitiates their taste for sensible reading, and is already [illegible] in its effects.—New London Advertiser.

Wherever we go—in rail cars and steamboats—we find it read with eagerness, because of its spirited sketches of passing events. We all like to look at the faces of men we have read of, and at ships and towns that have figured in the bloody scenes of war. Of all such men and places and events this paper furnishes the best illustrations. Our future historians will enrich themselves out of Harper's Weekly long after writers and painters and publishers are turned to dust.—N. Y. Evangelist.

TERMS.

One Copy for One Year,	$3 00
One Copy for Two Years,	5 00

An extra copy will be allowed for every club of ten subscribers, at $2 50 each, or 11 copies for $25.

Harper's Magazine and *Harper's* Weekly together, one year, $5 00. *Harper's* Weekly is electrotyped, and back numbers can be had at any time.

Vols. I., II., III., IV., V., and VI., for the years 1857 to 1862 inclusive, of *Harper's* Weekly, handsomely bound in cloth extra, price $4 38 each, are now ready. The postage upon *Harper's* Weekly, when paid in advance at the office where it is received, is twenty-six cents a year.

HARPER & BROTHERS,

48-tf Franklin Square, New York.

THE INDEPENDENT, EDITED BY *Henry Ward Beecher,* is a religious newspaper, and a real newspaper. It affords its readers fair and thoughtful editorial discussion of the most important facts and occurrences and interests of this nation and of the world. A comprehensive record of facts, men and movements of the religious world. A full and careful weekly history of the progress of the rebellion. Ample chronicles of the important general news; home and foreign. Fair and careful accounts of new books; made on the express principle of serving as a safe guide to buyers. Interesting correspondence from Washington; from the West; from the army; from abroad. Six columns a week of carefully selected matter for family reading; being prose and poetry, suited to interest both the old people and the young people. A full chronicle of the progress of business and of the current prices of merchandise, produce and live stock in New-York City.

ONE SERMON EVERY WEEK

By Rev. Henry Ward Beecher. The following eminent writers are special contributors to its columns:—

Mrs. Harriet Beecher Stowe,
Rev. Theodore L. Cuyler,
Rev. Robert M. Hatfield,
Rev. George B. Cheever,
Horace Greely,
Bayard Taylor,
John G. Whittier.

TERMS.—$2 per annum, paid in advance. Specimen numbers sent gratis.

JOSEPH H. RICHARDS, Publisher,
No. 5 Beekman Street, New York.

For sale by news agents.

THE HASTINGS CONSERVER.

VOLUME III.---NO. 25. HASTINGS, DAKOTA COUNTY, MINNESOTA, TUESDAY, SEPTEMBER 29, 1863. $2 00 PER YEAR.

THE CONSERVER.

BY IRVING TODD.

TUESDAY, SEPTEMBER 29, 1863.

Single copies of the CONSERVER may be obtained at this office, or at the Bookstore. Price Five Cents.

Republican Union Ticket.

For Governor,
STEPHEN MILLER,
of Stearns County.

For Lieutenant Governor,
CHARLES D. SHERWOOD,
of Fillmore County.

For Secretary of State,
DAVID BLAKELY,
of Olmsted County.

For Auditor of State,
CHARLES McILRATH,
of Nicollet County.

For State Treasurer,
CHARLES SCHEFFER,
of Washington County.

For Attorney General,
GORDON E. COLE,
of Rice County.

For Clerk of the Supreme Court,
GEORGE F. POTTER,
of Houston County.

Union County Ticket.

For Senator,
N. N. THOMPSON.

For Representatives,
P. VAN AUKEN.
S. C. HOWELL.

For Treasurer,
D. B. TRUAX.

For Sheriff,
H. J. TAYLOR.

For Judge of Probate,
I. M. RAY.

For Register of Deeds,
H. A. MONSER.

For District Attorney,
R. W. MONTGOMERY.

For Surveyor,
C. B. LOWELL.

For Coroner,
P. HARTSHORN.

For Commissioner—2d District,
HENRY SPRAGUE.

For Commissioner—3d District.
JOSIAH BURWELL.

Beware of Bogus Tickets.

The democrats of this county, despairing of succeeding by fair means, are printing what purports to be union tickets with the whole or part of their democratic county nominees substituted instead of the genuine. They are well calculated to deceive the unwary, and strict watch should be made that none are fooled by them. Let every man read his ticket carefully before delivering it at the polls. They are principally intended to be used in the army.

As we write we have a couple of specimens before us. One is headed "Republican Union Ticket," with our state ticket entire, and their county ticket substituted instead of ours. The other is called the "Union Ticket" with H. T. Welles for governor, the balance of our state ticket, and the democratic county ticket. They were printed on Friday night under cover of darkness, and on Saturday were forwarded to the commissioners at St. Paul in sealed envelopes. They were issued and circulated with the sole intention to deceive, and are well calculated for that purpose. We would remind them, however, that there is a little penalty attached to such proceedings, and which might not be very convenient for some of those concerned to undergo just at present. Chapter XV., section 71, of the General Laws of Minnesota for 1861 reads thus:

"Any person who shall furnish an elector who cannot read the language in which such ticket is printed or written, with a ticket informing him that it contains a name or names different from those which are written or printed thereon, with an intent to deceive and induce him to vote contrary to his inclination, or who shall fraudulently or deceitfully change a ballot of any elector, by which such an elector shall be prevented from voting for such candidates as he intended, shall, on conviction thereof, be imprisoned in the state prison, and kept at hard labor, not less than six months, nor more than one year."

In doing what they have they clearly violated the spirit of the law if not the letter, and we greatly mistake the spirit of the people of Dakota County if their perfidous acts do not meet with a merited rebuke at the polls next November.

This article should have appeared in our last issue, but was crowded out.

Change of Programme.

The democratic state central committee met in St. Paul last week, and succeeded in patching up the following ticket:

Governor—Henry T. Welles, of Hennepin County.

Lieut. Governor—James S. Norris, of Washington County, *vice* La Due declined.

Secretary of State—Amos Coggswell, of Steele County, *vice* Welch declined.

Treasurer—Joseph Edelbrock, of Stearns County, *vice* Wilkins declined.

Auditor—John H. McKenney, of Fillmore County.

Attorney General—William H. Grant, of Ramsey County.

Clerk Supreme Court—Jacob Mainzer, *vice* Petsholo declined.

One of these, the candidate for clerk, promptly declined, but was finally induced to run by placing himself upon the patriotic resolution introduced by Col. Robertson as a platform, which is as follows:—

Resolved, That we look to the army and navy of the union to regain every state in rebellion without any compromise with rebels in arms, that we look to the loyal and faithful people of the South when the rebellion shall be terminated to assume the administration of their state governments, and we look to the supreme court to settle definitely and finally the constitutional rights of communities and individuals as effected be the events of the war, and upon this broad and comprehensive basis of agreement among all good citizens, and in common with the loyal masses of the American people, we propose "to move upon the enemy's works, until we force an unconditional surrender."

This is about as pretty a specimen of sharp practice as we have seen, but it will avail little. No matter what any one of the candidates may avow, they are nominated on a copperhead platform and must, of necessity, subscribe to it. This has been done by Mr. Welles in a recent speech, and tacitly by all the rest, Mr. Mainzer included, in permitting their names to be used in connection with it. Too late in the day, gentlemen, to be endeavoring to hide the copper. The people have seen it, and are satisfied.

Bishop Whipple has recently had the opportunity of securing a valuable library and philosophical apparatus for the church college at Faribault. A southern college, which was broken up by the rebellion, has been obliged to sell its library, etc., to pay its debts. The trustees were church men and desiring to save the library to the church, were willing to sell it at a nominal price to the Diocese of Minnesota. Good judges think it worth $15,000; the Bishop pays it for $2500. The only question is, will those who have followed the Diocese and Bishop with their prayers and alms, aid him in securing the valuable library to the church of Minnesota? This cannot be doubted. Nothing would so gladden the Bishop's heart and cheer him in his work. Any of his friends in this state or in other states, who are willing to aid the Bishop, will please send their gifts to Mr. H. T. Welles, Treasurer of the Diocese, Minneapolis, or to Bishop Whipple, Faribault, and will receive the thanks and prayers of the church.

We are pleased to note that our friend, H. J. Taylor, esq., is the candidate on the union ticket for sheriff, and that the prospects of his election are fair. Mr. Taylor was formerly a resident of this city and a member of the board of aldermen from the fourth ward. Never an ultra partisan, he served the interests of the city and from the fourth ward with commendable fidelity. About two years since he removed to his farm in Dakota County, which he has for some years been operating. We are certain that the people of Dakota County can do no better than to elect Mr. Taylor, and can assure them that he will make an excellent sheriff.—*St. Paul Press.*

The false report of Rosecran's defeat is ascertained to have originated with a copperhead telegraph reporter at Louisville. Such infamous outrages should not be allowed to go unpunished. Latest from Rosecran's is very encouraging. He has been heavily reenforced, and will act again on the offensive. The enemy suffered severely in the late battles.

Col. Miller writes, in response to an inquiry from Gov. Swift, that seventeen and a half companies belonging to the regiments ordered South will meet at Fort Snelling on Saturday, October 3d, and will march down the river on the 7th. Twelve companies are ordered to rendezvous at Winona, October 6th, leaving for that place on the 8th.

What You Swallow When You Vote the Democratic Ticket.

To show what doctrines men profess, endorse, and encourage, when they vote the false democratic, or copperhead ticket, we select a few specimen sentences from copperhead authorities. No honest man can read them without shame that such doctrine can be professed in America:

"Negro slavery is the foundation of liberty and the essence of democracy."—*N. Y. Day Book.*

"There never has been anything called for by the South, and there can be, that I would not willingly consent to."—*Speech of State Senator Clark, of Wisconsin, March, 1862.*

"History will relate that we, the North, manufactured the conflict, forced it to hot-bed precocity, nourished, and invited it."—*Detroit Free Press, April 16, 1862.*

"We tell them (Congress) that a Cromwell will rise in their midst before they progress too far, who will bring their head to the block without delay or mercy."—*Free Press, March 24.*

"I say to you, my constituents, that as your representative, I will never vote one dollar, one man, or one gun to the administration of Abraham Lincoln to make war upon the South."—*D. W. Voorhies, M. C. 7th Dist. Ind., Apr. 1861.*

"The democracy will yet teach Abe Lincoln and his co-usurpers that the ways of the transgressors is not easy."—*Hon. A. C. Dodge, of Iowa.*

"This is a damned abolition war. We believe Abe Lincoln is as much of a traitor as Jeff Davis."—*Ashland (Ohio) Dem. Union.*

"The president and his cabinet were never worthy of the confidence of the nation. The democratic party should never have given its assent to the appeal to the sword after the affair at Fort Sumpter."—*Detroit Free Press.*

The *Crawford Co. Forum*, referring to our soldiers says:

"It (the administration) has put arms in the hands of outlaws, thieves, murderers, and traitors."

The *Democratic Press*, Taylorville, Ill., speaking of the republican party and the army, says:

"In power less than a year it has spent millions of the people's money, and five hundred thousand men are employed to steal negroes from their southern masters."

"If the north and south are ever re united, we predict it will be when the confederate states North shall adopt their new constitution, (of Jeff. Davis,) or something very near like it. There's a good time coming, boys."—*Van Buren Co. Press, at Paw Paw.*

"Why this expenditure of more blood and treasure in a hopeless enterprise—why blame men for being traitors? We cannot see why."—*Detroit Free Press.*

"There, sir, is the damnable abolitionist who administers the government. The people ought to rise up and by physical force hurl him from the chair of the government. In the eyes of God and men, the people would be justified. They should do it, and I will go with them."—*Judge Pratt's Speech in the Michigan Legislature, Feb. 12, 1863.*

Geo. W. Peck, of Ohio, in a speech before the Lansing Democratic Association, March, 1863, said:

"You black republicans begun this war. You have carried it on for two years. You have sent your bell hounds down south to devastate the country—and what have you done? You have not conquered the South. You never can conquer them. And why? because they are our brethren."

John H George, N. H., democratic nominee for Congress, declared:

"I won't do anything to sustain the President, Congress, or any of the piratical crew that have control of this government. I won't do anything that can, in any way, be interpreted as supporting this war."

Preparations are being made to withdraw the present postal currency and send out a new and an improved issue, of the uniform size of the ten cent scrip now in circulation. It is to be printed in different colors for each denomination, on much thinner and stronger paper, which is made on a new principle, which is a secret with the Treasury Department, and cannot be photographed.

The corps of colored troops organized under the auspice of Gen. Banks is rapidly filling up. Fifteen thousand colored soldiers have already been mustered into the service and recruits are still coming in very rapidly. The maximum strength of the corps is twenty-five thousand.

Adjt. Gen. Malmros, of this state, has issued an order increasing the bounty for the killing of Sioux warriors to two hundred dollars.

The Richmond *Whig* announces the death of Gen. Sam Houston, at his residence in Huntsville, Texas, on the 26th of July. He was seventy years of age.

EDUCATION.—Make home an institution of learning. Provide books for the centre-table, and for the library of the family. See that all the younger children attend the best schools, and interest yourself in their studies. If they have the taste for thorough cultivation, but not the means to pursue it, if possible provide for a higher education. Daniel Webster taught at the intervals of his college course to aid an elder brother in the pursuit of a classical education, and a volume of his works is dedicated to the daughter of that brother, who early closed a brilliant career. Feel that an ignorant brother or sister will be a disgrace to your family, and trust not the prevention of such a reproach to the casual influence of the press, existing institutions, and the kind offices of strangers. If the family becomes, as it may be, an institution of learning, the whole land will be educated.

NEW ADVERTISEMENTS.

MORTGAGE SALE.—WHEREAS DEfault has been made in the conditions of a certain mortgage, bearing date on the 29th day of May, A. D. 1857, executed by Alexander Rey and Elizabeth Rey, his wife, both of St. Paul, in the county of Ramsey and state of Minnesota, to *Horace* Smith and Samuel F. *Harris*, both of Bennington, in the county of Bennington and state of Vermont, which said mortgage was acknowledged on the said 29th day of May, A. D. 1857, and duly recorded in the office of the register of deeds in the county of Dakota and state of Minnesota, on the 4th day of June, 1857, at 12 o'clock at noon, in Book D of mortgages, on pages 291 and 292, by which said mortgage the said Alexander Rey and Elizabeth, his wife, granted, bargained, sold, and conveyed unto the said *Horace* Smith and Samuel F. *Harris*, their heirs and assigns, forever, all those certain tracts or pieces of land, lying and being in said county of Dakota and state of Minnesota, and described as follows, to-wit: [Lot no. 4 in section no. twenty-two (22), and lot no. 4 in section no. twenty-three (23), all in township no. twenty-eight (28), range no. twenty two (22), together with all the hereditaments and appurtenances thereunto appertaining, which said mortgage was given to secure to the said *Horace* Smith and Samuel F. *Harris*, their heirs and assigns, the payment of the sum of thirty-three hundred (3300) dollars, with the interest thereon, according to the conditions of a certain mortgage bond, given by said Alexander Rey, George W. Thompson, and Isaac Markley to said *Horace* Smith and Samuel F. *Harris*, payable in one year from the date thereof, with interest thereon payable semi-annually at the rate of thirty per cent per annum, and five per cent a month after due upon both principal and interest, and bearing even date with said mortgage. And whereas there is now claimed to be due, at the date of this notice, on said bond and mortgage the sum of five thousand eight hundred and eighty (5880) dollars. And whereas a suit at law was commenced and a judgment recovered on said bond against the said Alexander Rey, George W. Thompson, and Isaac Markley, defendants, and in favor of the said *Horace* Smith and Samuel F. *Harris*, plaintiffs, in the district court for the second judicial district of the state of Minnesota, in the county of Ramsey, which judgment was docketed in said county of Ramsey on the 19th day of March, 1859, and whereas an execution was issued on said judgment to the sheriff of said county of Ramsey and by him returned wholly unsatisfied, and whereas nothing has ever been paid on said bond or on said judgment—

Now, therefore, notice is hereby given that by virtue of a power of sale contained in said mortgage, and in pursuance of the statute in such case made and provided, the said mortgage will be foreclosed by a sale of the premises above described at public auction for cash, at the front door of the court-house in Hastings, in said county of Dakota, to the highest bidder, on Wednesday, the 18th day of November, A. D. 1863, at 12 o'clock at noon of that day, by the sheriff of said county of Dakota, to satisfy the amount which shall then be due on said bond and mortgage, together with the costs of such sale so far as the proceeds of said sale will satisfy the same.

Dated at St. Paul, Sept. 21, 1863.

HORACE SMITH.
SAMUEL F. HARRIS.
25-7w Mortgagees.
H. Hale, Atty. for Mortgagees.

LOCAL AFFAIRS.

P. O. Notice.—Summer Arrangement.
Mail going East closes at 11 o'clock, A. M.
Way mail down closes at 8 o'clock, P. M.
Mail for St. Paul closes on the arrival of the boat from below in the afternoon.
Faribault mail leaves at 6 o'clock A. M., closes at 9 o'clock P. M.
Office hours from 8 A. M. to 8 P. M.
WM. H. SKINNER, Post-Master.

ALEX. JOHNSON has disposed of the *Faribault Statesman* to Messrs. SENTELL & MOWATT, who will conduct it as heretofore.

SECESSION.—Secede from every name and kind of saleratus except the Chemical Saleratus. This is the kind to use on every occasion. For sale by all grocers.

POPULAR.—One of the most valuable and widest circulated photographs is that of Col. THORNE, engraved on his new bills, just issued, and a very good likeness it is. We would like a few copies for our album.

WALL PAPER.—STANLEY has just received a choice assortment of wall paper from New York, and those desirous of purchasing would do well to call around and see it. Also a large lot of school books.

NEW GOODS.—NEWMAN, at the new store, daily receiving lots of new goods, which he is displaying to good advantage. Call in, such of you as wish good bargains, and the opportunity will certainly be afforded.

READY MADE CLOTHING.—PRATT has just received one of the best stocks of ready made clothing ever brought into town, and is ready to dispose of it at reasonable rates. Call in and see if it is not so. Shop next door to post-office, Second Street.

RETURNED.—Mr. G. F. BATCHELDER, who has been on a lengthy visit at the East, has arived home, and the new goods are rapidly following him. There is no better place to trade in town than at the old stand of NORTH & CARLL'S, on the levee.

COMMENCED.—The Prescott Graded School began its fall session one week ago yesterday. That town, with half our population, finds five or six teachers necessary. We are more economical than to spend our money so; but whether wisely economical is an entirely different question.

SILVER WARE.—We would again call the attention of our readers to the large and costly assortment of this indispensable article now offered for sale at MACOMBER'S. It is just from the East, and of the very latest styles. He has also received numerous other things in his line, which are offered at reasonable prices, and warranted to be as represented.

CONFERENCE.—The Methodist Conference will be in session in this place to-morrow, 30th inst. Bishop AMES will open the exercises with prayer. It is expected that there will be one hundred and fifty preachers in attendance, many with their families. It will last during the week and till Monday following, when the appointments will be declared.

BOOTS AND SHOES.—Prepare for the piercing cold of winter by being well shod, and you will save a deal in the way of lost time and doctor bills. You can do this to good advantage at DRAPER & BALLARD'S, who have one of the largest assortments in town. Country merchants would do well to call around and replenish their stores.

COUNTY FAIR.—We were over at the Pierce County Fair at Prescott on Saturday. The exhibition of articles was tolerable, considering the unsettled state of the country and the unprecedented drouth, and the attendance good. There was quite a display of fast horses in the afternoon, and several trots were made, Mr. ARCHER, of Hampton, taking the lead.

PERSONAL.—We find the following notices of two of our boys in the Mankato *Union*. We are glad to see them so well spoken of; they certainly deserve it:

"We are pleased to greet our old friend L. W. Collins, 1st. Lieutenant of Co. F. 7th Regiment. 'Ren,' as we used to call him, looks hale and hearty, and likes the idea of going South. He possesses all the qualities requisite to make a good officer, and as he is in the line of promotion, we wish him all that prosperity to which true merit entitles him."

"R. D. Traver, hospital steward of the 7th, is stopping at the Clifton. He has come up to visit his many friends here, previous to his departure south. He is very popular with the regiment, and makes an excellent steward."

LADIES, have you seen those fine Balmoral Skirts, Waterloo Double Shawls, and Ladies' Furs? They are very attractive, and for sale very low at JOHN H. MUES'.

NEW STORE.—See advertisement of JOHN H. MUES, in another column. Mr. MUES is recently from Red Wing, and has opened a first class lot of goods in the building formerly occupied by THOMAS. Call and see him.

ATTENTION.—For engraving, repairing, and watch-cleaning go to ANDREW'S, on Second Street, and you will have your work well done and warranted. There is no better in town. Business promptly attended to.

THE ATLANTIC MONTHLY for October has the following table of contents:—Charles Lamb's Uncollected Writings; My Palace; The Deacon's Holocaust; The United States Armory; The Pewee; Mrs. Lewis; The Conquest of Cuba; Equinoctial; The Legend of Monte del Diablo; Life without Principle; Barbara Frietchie; Voluntaries; Our Domestic Relations; A Letter to Thomas Carlyle; Reviews and Literary Notices. For sale at STANLEY'S.

A RARE CHANCE.—The editor of the *Printer's Devil*, a handsome, illustrated, literary family journal, will send that paper on trial six months, free of postage, for the nominal price of twenty five cents.

This is one of the best papers in the country, and no one should lose this opportunity. Address Editor *Printer's Devil*, Box 2,900, New York.

Editors giving the above two or three insertions (including this notice) will receive the the P. D. six months free, on sending marked copy.

SEWING MACHINES.

FIRST OF THE SEASON.

Firemen's Ball.

Hope Company No. 1 will give a Grand Ball at *Teutonia Hall* on

MONDAY EVENING, OCT. 5th.,

the proceeds to be applied toward the purchase of an engine. *Tickets* for sale at the door.

Per order of committee.
Sept. 22, 1863. 24-2w

EDUCATIONAL.

BY PROF. T. F. THICKSTUN.

Up and Down the St. Croix.

Our recent trip up the St. Croix was a pleasant enterprise in more senses than one. In the first place we took the boat *Enterprise*, not by storm, but upon a superbly beautiful day at Prescott, put to sea upon the river, bound for Osceola and intermediate ports.

Of Hudson we learned nothing except that it is in its place yet. Its friends here will no doubt be gratified for the information.

Stillwater has a good graded school under the management of Mr. Joel Townsend—a man of good name as a teacher. The people of the town are endeavoring to make their schools places for the education of their children and not for their imprisonment. Their primary department being large—too large for their house—they have divided it into two sections. One of these is under drill during the forenoon of each day, the other during the afternoon. This is sensible.

The children everywhere are kept under fire too long. The reader will pardon the expression: these are military times. We have, from the bottom of our hearts, a thousand times pitied the poor creatures. They are drawn up in rank and file usually, if our observation is correct—although we have seen them in platoons and companies—and then battery after battery, broadside after broadside, shot, shell, grape—sometimes direct, sometimes by an enfilading fire—are poured in upon them. If the Minnesota First were to pass through such an ordeal we would fall down and lick the very dust beneath their feet, but when the Minnesota Least have heroically borne the weight of so many and so fearful blows we are more apt to "lick" the dust off their backs, because they cannot bear more.

The fact is we abuse the children with excess of labor in the school room. We expect them to do—to endure many times as much as God ever made them capable of doing. We recommend to other towns the practice of Stillwater. We are satisfied that they cannot do a better thing than to go and do likewise.

The Taylor Falls' paper is pushing its readers on the subject of school visitation. It urges them from many different stand points. A good thing it would indeed be, if all the patrons of a school would regularly visit their teacher and his pupils in the midst of their labors. During the millenium, we suppose it will be done, if not sooner.

Osceola has a good school, and a teacher they greatly love and respect. Wisconsin has a good school system, a superintendent of public instruction; and county superintendents. The schools are consequently healthful; they feel the effects of those stimulating agencies. Polk County has been fortunate in securing the services of Rev. S. T. Catlin as county superintendent. Her schools have consequently risen in point of discipline and educational effectiveness. We hope he may be reelected to the office this fall. Partisan politics should be suffered to meddle with the office. Let the best, the most experienced man be chosen.

Of self let us say just this simple word. We went to help dedicate a Baptist Church, and we did it as best we knew how. We commend the people to the New Jerusalem as well as to their meeting house.

Our journey home was by way of the same enterprising line. We arrived safely at Prescott, though at rather a late hour. We felt no disposition to wait for a Mississippi boat in which to ride up to Hastings after so successful a sail down the lake. We started for home a foot and alone in the dark. We did not whistle a word through the woods to keep up our courage, but we have heard it slyly hinted that we walked as fast as we could run. We have no disposition to deny this; it is to any one a perfectly natural gait in dangerous places.

We found upon our return that our school had *Hatched* up to 75, and now at this writing it numbers eighty odd.

The public schools of this city opened yesterday. Mr. A. D. Haynes is principal and is we understand to have two assistants. This is an improvement on past seasons, but the board of trustees should have hired ten teachers instead of three. The latter number of teachers can do little else than worry their pupils, the former number might have some success in teaching them.

THE CONSERVER.

BY IRVING TODD.

Office Over the Bank of Hastings, Exchange Block, Second Street.

Our Platform.

Resolved, That we, chosen to represent in convention the unconditional union men of Minnesota, grateful to Almighty God for the success which has hitherto crowned the arms of our country and for the prospect thus opened of a speedy, honorable, and lasting peace, do hereby, for ourselves and our constituents, reaffirm our determination to support our government by every means in our power in the vigorous prosecution of this war, —on our part, holy, just, and forced upon us by the criminal acts of others,—until not an enemy in arms shall be found within our borders. And to this we pledge our lives, our fortunes, and our sacred honor.

2. That we tender our grateful thanks to the survivors of our glorious armies, and our warm sympathy to the relatives of their gallant dead, who have won for the country so glorious victories, for themselves imperishable renown, and for us all an assurance of liberty and safety, for ourselves and our children, under our beloved and now well-tried government.

3. That with especial pride we point to the gallant achievements on many a hard-fought battle-field, of our Minnesota regiments. Their bravery, discipline, and patriotism have won for them a name that shall never die, and made forever honorable to a citizen of Minnesota.

4. That, without claiming for it exemption from error, we heartily endorse the general policy and conduct of our national administration; and we point to the recent magnificent triumph of our armies as its best vindication from the charge of incapacity so freely brought against it by those who prefer national ruin to success under the present administration. *Especially* do we approve the emancipation proclamation, and the raising of black troops, as being among the best possible measures to weaken the enemy and strengthen ourselves.

5. That our state administration and congressional delegation deserve our hearty approbation for the zealous and efficient co-operation they have afforded the national authorities in carrying on the war.

6. That we call upon those in authority to take such measures, by retaliation or otherwise, as shall effectually prevent brutal and barbarous treatment by the enemy of our soldiers, of whatever color.

7. That it is due to our shattered armies in the field, as well as to the sacred cause which they uphold, that their ranks should as speedily as possible be filled up by every means in our power. It is due to the country that the mobs raised to resist and prevent the draft, should not even seem to have succeeded a day longer than is necessary to enforce the laws.

8. That the way to peace is, and ever has been, open to the rebels; the only condition we have ever sought to impose is that they should lay down their arms and submit to the authority of the general government. We protest against the making of any terms with them in advance as to their *status* in communities, when they shall have returned to their allegiance. Having been declared "public enemies" by a recent unanimous decision of the Supreme Court of the United States, they must accept the consequences that legitimately flow from having placed themselves in that position.

Spirit of the Times.

Mr. Seward has recently issued a diplomatic circular, No. 39, a review of our affairs and the progress of events, from which we extract the closing part. He says:

Jefferson Davis, the leader of the sedition, has since proclaimed a levy of all the able-bodied men within his military lines. This, if carried into effect, will exhaust the whole material of which soldiers can be made. The insurgents estimate the whole number of conscripts thus to be gained at from 70,000 to 95,000. Our armies now confront the insurgents at all points with superior numbers. A draft of 300,000 more is in progress to replace those whose term of service have expired, and to fill up the wasted ranks of our veteran regiments, and the people, just so fast as the evidence of the necessity for that measure is received and digested, submit with cheerfulness to the ascertained demands. Our armies everywhere are well equipped, abundantly fed, and supplied with all the means of transportation.

The soldiers of two years' service bear themselves as veterans, and show greater steadiness in every conflict. The men accustomed to the camp, and hardened by exercise and experience, make marches which would have been impossible in the beginning of the contest. The nation is becoming familiar with arms, and easily takes on the habits of war. Large voluntary enlistments continually augment our military force. All supplies are abundantly and cheaply purchased within our lines. The country shows no signs of exhaustion of money, material, or men. A requisition for 6,200 remount horses was filled, and the animals despatched from Washington, all in four days. Our loan is purchased at par by our own citizens, at the average rate of $1,200,000 daily. Gold sells in our market at $1,23 to $1,27, while in the insurrectionary region it commands 1,200 per cent premium.

Every insurgent port is either blockaded, besieged, or occupied by the national forces. The field of the projected confederacy is divided by the Mississippi. All the fortifications on its banks are in our hands, and its flood is patroled by our national fleet.

Missouri, Kentucky, Delaware, Maryland—all slave states—support the federal government. Missouri has already in convention ordained the gradual abolition of slavery, to take effect at the expiration of seven years. Four-fifths of Tennessee, two thirds of Virginia, the coasts and sounds of North Carolina, half of Mississippi, and half of Louisiana, with all their large cities, part of Alabama, and the whole sea-coast of Georgia and South Carolina, and no inconsiderate part of Florida, are held by the United States. The insurgents, with the slaves they now hold in defiance of the president's proclamation, are now crowded into the central and southern portions of Virginia, North Carolina, South Carolina, Georgia, and Alabama, while the pioneer slaveholding insurgents beyond the Mississippi are cut off from the main force. On the other hand, although it is less than six months since the laws of custom of the United States would allow a man of African descent to bear arms in defense of his country, there are now in the field 22,000 regularly enlisted, armed, and equipped soldiers of that class, while fifty regiments of 2,000 each are in process of organization, and 62,800 persons of the same class are employed as teamsters, laborers, and camp-followers. These facts show that, as the insurrection continues, the unfortunate servile population, which was at the beginning an element of its strength, is being transferred to the support of the union.

You will use the facts presented in this paper in such a way as may be most effective to convince those who seek a renewal of commercial prosperity through the restoration of peace in America, that the quickest and shortest way to gain that desirable end is to withdraw support and favor from the insurgents, and to leave the adjustment of our domestic controversies exclusively with the people of the United States. I am, sir, your obedient servant,

WM. H. SEWARD.

COMPLIMENT.—In an account of the siege of Vicksburg, written by an English officer in the rebel service, who participated in the defense of that great stronghold, and published in the Edinburgh *Scotsman*, the following praise is bestowed upon the federal gunners:

"The enemy, who had access to all the appliances and improvements that science has invented to carry on modern warfare, can boast first class guns, the best of ammunition, and magnificent artillerymen. Besides this, they have everything they require in abundance, not to say profusion. For instance, whenever we dared to fire a shot from, say a 12-pounder howitzer, the enemy would concentrate upon it perhaps ten to fifteen 20-pounder Parrott guns, and would maintain a fire of perhaps two to three hours duration, throwing several hundred shot and shell into, around, or over the offending battery. They fire with the utmost precision, and they had attained such an excellent position, and such close proximity, that their rifle projectiles flew, in many cases, right through ten feet of earth, to strike and burst on whatever might be in the work. We had no resource but to run the guns out of the work, to keep them from being disabled, and reserve them to fire canister or grape in the event of a charge being made."

KANSAS INDIANS.—Commissioner Dole has made a treaty with the Osage Indians, by which, says the Leavenworth *Times*, the government purchases thirty by fifty miles off the east end of their reservation, adjoining the Cherokee neutral lands. This tract is to be devoted exclusively to colonizing Kansas Indians, according to the act of Congress. The government agrees to sell "in trust" to settlers, a tract twenty miles wide off the north side of their reservation.

Of the Creeks the government purchases a wedge-shaped strip, adjoining the state of Kansas, forty miles in length along the north line, and embracing the bulk of their reservation north of the Arkansas River. This tract is also to be devoted to the colonization of Kansas Indians.

The commissioner is negotiating with the Sac and Fox Indians for their removal, with a fair prospect of success. —*Missouri Republican*.

THE INFAMOUS FIVE.—When the bill for raising money for paying our soldiers in the field was put upon its final passage in the United States House of Representatives, it received a vote of 150 in favor to 5 members who voted against it. The names of those five members who voted against paying our brave troops, are:

Clement L. Vallandigham, of Ohio, an exile now in Canada, having been expatriated for complicity with the enemy.

Benjamin Wood, of New York, editing a secession newspaper.

H. C. Burnett, of Kentucky, expelled from the House of Representatives for treason, now in the rebel army.

John W. Reid, of Missouri, expelled from the House of Representatives for treason, and now, or lately in the rebel army.

The Austrian government has published the official catalogue of its school books, which are all printed at the Imperial office, at Vienna (one of the wonders of the world), in an admirable style. It is interesting to note that they are printed on paper made of "corn shucks," or of the leaves which protect the ear of maize. This material gives the page a yellow color, which medical men hold to be less fatiguing to the eye than our snowy pages.

VERMONT ELECTION.—In the late election in Vermont, the copperheads managed to elect two or three representatives in the legislature, but it now turns out that in nearly every case their success was achieved by fraud. In a fair election, probably not a single copperhead would have been elected in the entire state.

Rank and fashion may be all very fine in time of peace, but rank and file must have precedence of them in time of war.

A single firm pays one hundred and fifty thousand dollars a year to the London *Times* for advertising.

Everywhere endeavor to be useful, and everywhere you are at home.

Kitty's Wager.

"It's against my principles," said Parker Pelham, buttoning his pockets, and inclining his chair at an angle of forty-five degrees against the piazza railing. "Taxes, taxes, nothing but taxes. Government must suppose a man made of money; and then, right on top of that, every woman of your acquaintance expects you to pay funds into her private treasury. It's all nonsense—and I, for one, won't be victimized. Besides, I do n't consider it fair for us men to be bled at every pore, while the women keep their own purses intact. If you women kind are so vitally interested in the hospitals, and all that sort of thing, why do n't you lend a helping hand yourself?"

Mr. Pelham screwed up his lips, tapped his fingers on the railing, and nodded his head, as one who should say, "I rather guess you'll find that argument unanswerable." Kitty Brace, standing among the roses that shut out the June sunshine, turned round so suddenly, that the tinted petals showered softly down around her like a pink snowstorm. Parker instinctively moved his chair back, as he caught the dangerous sparkle of her hazel eyes, and saw the crimson pennon of defiance fluttering across her cheeks.

"Please to explain yourself, Mr. Pelham," said Kitty, clasping a sprig of roses very tightly in her two little hands, lest they should descend wrathfully on Parker's ears, in spite of her determination to be very "proper" and dignified. "Have we not denied ourselves every unnecessary luxury? Nay, have we not even parted with our jewels and trinkets to send aid to those who suffer in our country's behalf?"

"That's all very fine," said Parker turning up his nose in lofty disregard of feminine logic. "Smooth sailing, smooth sailing! You may talk as much as you like, Miss Kitty, but you'll never persuade me you are in earnest until I see you make some sacrifice worth boasting of."

"I do n't want to boast," said Kitty indignantly; but oh! if I were only a man—if I could only earn money!"

"You'd do unheard of things, I've no doubt," said Mr. Parker, sarcastically. "But you can earn money if you choose to try."

"How, pray?"

"Well, for instance, those crimson sprinkled strawberry beds on the side-hill—a man would turn 'em into money quick enough, a woman do n't choose to take that trouble—it's easier to beg."

"Yes," said Kitty, taking no notice of the covert sneer, "but nobody wants strawberries here—there's no market for them."

"There is in the city I suppose. Ah, yes—that's right, Miss Kitty—curl your lips and toss your head. Come now—here's an exemplification of my assertion, that you shrink from the slightest effort in this cause. You expect us to do everything, while you are willing to do nothing. Now, I'm not afraid to wager fifty dollars that you would n't sell five dollars' worth of strawberries to keep your soldier heroes from want."

Kitty was silent for a moment—then she drew out her little morocco pocket-book with solemn emphasis.

"I'll call witnesses, sir, and the wager shall be registered."

Parker Pelham eyed the little beauty as if he scarcely understood her.

"Mind, you are to sell them yourself, Miss Kitty, no manœuvering."

"Set your heart at rest, Mr. Pelham, all the conditions of your bargain shall be complied with."

"But, Miss Kitty, have you reflected? Such a very unladylike thing—"

"I see nothing unladylike in endeavoring to serve my country's defenders," said Kitty, quietly, a lambent smile sparkling in her eyes as she noted Parker's perturbed brow. "Fifty dollars, it is a very neat little sum. And now I must go to see about some baskets for my berries—there's no time to be lost."

"Fifty dollars!" feebly muttered Mr. Pelham, as the light dress fluttered down the garden walk. "What a confounded fool I was! why could n't I have said five instead. But of course I'm perfectly safe—she'll never do such a thing—never!"

"Strawberries. Who'll buy my strawberries?"

Mrs. Leclere was reading in her cool, quiet parlors as the silvery voice echoed through the street. Instinctively she rose and pushed aside the curtains.

A slender figure in a brown calico dress, her face shaded by a blue-ribboned bonnet, was leaning over the area railings, on which she dextrously balanced a basket of ripe strawberries, glowing scarlet through their covering of fresh vine leaves.

Mrs. Leclere shaded her eyes with her hand, and looked again.

"Why Kitty Brace, can it be possible that it is you?"

"I myself, and no other," laughed Kitty. "I'm selling strawberries on a wager—will you buy some?"

"Buy some! of course. Give me a dozen baskets, and then come in, you little witch, and tell me about it."

"Not just now—have n't time," answered Kitty demurely. "But you shall hear of it by-and-by."

Mrs. Leclere thought Kitty had never looked so pretty in tule and pearls as she did under the quaint shadow of that shaker bonnet—her eyes dancing with suppressed mischief, and the brown curls tucked behind her ears; and the old maid behind the window blinds of the opposite house thought it "very queer" to see Mrs. Leclere lean from her casement to kiss the strawberry girl.

"Strawberries? how much be they a basket?"

Mrs. Jones rubbed the soapsuds from her sodden fingers, and polished them off on her check apron, as she opened the basement door.

"Five cents? that's too much; I won't give but four. James Adolphus, if you do n't keep your hands out o' that strawberry basket, I'll skin you. I'd calcula'ted to get a few for preservin' but sugar's so awful high. Julius Alexander, come in out of the street this minute, or I'll come after you. I'd put up two jars o' pineapples, but James Adolphus got at one, and t'other blowed up with a bang on Easter Sunday. Can't ye give me four baskets for a shillin'? Them baskets is the biggest cheats—don't hold half they pretend to. Take postage stamps? Well, pour 'em out. My gracious, if here ain't a strawberry leaf in one of the baskets. Look here, young woman, do n't you ever show your face here again selling strawberries. A leaf—just to fill up, I'll warrant. Where do you expect to go to when you die, I'd just like to know?"

The door was slammed in Kitty's face with more emphasis than politeness. Strawberries had its unpleasant aspects as well as most other occupations in this world; but our little heroine was undismayed. It takes a good deal to daunt a courageous woman.

Late in the afternoon, Mr. Parker Pelham's clerk came softly into the back office, where his master was busily engaged in writing.

"I beg you pardon, sir, but do you wish to buy any strawberries.

"Strawberries—no," said Mr. Pelham abstractedly.

"I told the young person so, sir, but —dear me, here she is now."

There was a defiant little tap on the door, and Miss Kitty Brace walked in, her hazel eyes sparkling like two stars under the shaker bonnet.

"You do n't wish to purchase, Mr. Pelham? That's fortunate, for I've sold every berry. Please to count my change—I believe it amounts to nine cents over and above the specified five dollars.

Parker Pelham stared at the double handful of postage currencies in blank astonishment and dismay.

"You do n't mean to say, Miss Kitty, that——"

"I do mean to say that I have won the wager, sir."

How pretty she looked in that moment of bright animation. Ordinarily Parker Pelham would have hesitated long, ere parting with a red cent of his hoarded money, but beauty is a wonderful subduer. All the treasured hopes of months leaped up in that one moment of fascination.

"I own myself vanquished, Miss Kitty," he said, handing over a neatly folded fifty dollar bill. "Take it—and——"

He paused a moment, in awkward uncertainty.

"Kitty, will you take my heart too?"

Thank you, sir," said Kitty demurely, "but I should scarcely know what to do with the article. *My* promised husband is fighting under the stars and stripes; and one heart is all I can take care of at one time. Good evening, sir."

Alas, for the humiliated and discomfited Parker Pelham, was it not hard enough to loan fifty dollars, but he must lose a sweetheart, too?" But all the Rothschilds never felt so rich as Kitty Brace when she enclosed that fifty dollar bill to purchase comforts for the soldiers.

MASCULINE BELLES.—I often wonder what would be the effect upon a man's vaunted constancy of such a bourse of flattery as any average pretty woman is subject to. Imagine an individual of good sense and calm judgment, surrounded constantly by a set of fascinating ladies, who were only too happy to be his slaves, complimenting him perpetually on his "fine eyes" his "faultless complexion," and his "superb dancing;" fancy him serenaded by night, visited by day, presented with bouquets, and receiving an honest offer of marriage from persons whose happiness was but too plainly bound up in a favorable answer.

What, I say, would be the probable result of such an intoxicating process on the character of any young man? Would it not render him so utterly conceited and heartless that he would be quite unendurable? Yet the successful belle is blamed for an innocent fondness of gayety and admiration. I do not mean to imply that I think such an ordeal favorable to the development of the best qualities of a woman's nature, but considering that, from the necessities of the case, it is utterly impossible for a beauty to avoid this adulation, fair allowance ought to be made for its effects, and credit given for resisting its evil results.—*Lillie D. Umsted.*

THE RISE OF THE ROTHSCHILDS.—When George III. came to the throne, there was a little boy at Frankfort, who did not dream of ever having to do personally with the sovereigns of Europe. He was in the first stages of training for the Jewish priesthood. His name was Meyer Anselem Rothschild. For some reason or other he was placed in a counting-house at Hanover, and he soon discovered what he was fit for. He began humbly as an exchange broker, and went on to be the banker of the Landgrave of Hess, whose private fortune he saved by his shrewdness when Napoleon overran Germany. How he left a large fortune and a commercial character of the highest order, and how his five sons settled in five great cities of Europe, and have had more authority over war and peace, and the destinies of nations, than the sovereigns themselves, the world pretty well knows. Despotic monarchs must be dependent on money-lenders and command unlimited revenues for untold purposes, which is never true of domestic sovereigns.

The single man who does not save money on six dollars a week, will not be apt to on sixty; and he who does not lay up something in the first year of independent exertion will be pretty apt to wear a poor man's hair into his grave.

BATCHELDER'S COLUMN.

GREAT ATTRACTIONS

AT THE

OLD STAND.

GEO. F. BATCHELDER,

(Successor to North & Carll)

WHOLESALE

AND

RETAIL

Dealer in

DRY GOODS,

GROCERIES,

Boots and Shoes,

HARDWARE, ETC.,

HASTINGS, MINN.

Having laid in an unusually heavy stock of staple wares, would invite the attention of the public to my large assortment of

GOODS,

Consisting of Imported and Domestic

SILKS, DELAINES,

LAWNS AND

CALICOES,

also to my stock of Foreign and Domestic

SHEETINGS,

These goods were purchased at exceedingly low rates, and am therefore enabled to sell at prices to suit the times.

A well assorted stock of

Hats and Caps,

for Men and Boys, of the latest styles.

READY-MADE

CLOTHING,

a fine assortment, custom made, from the best of cloths, bought expressly for this market, and will be sold at reasonable figures, for cash only.

A choice stock of pure and fresh

GROCERIES

Just received from the East, where especial attention was paid to their selection.

A fine lot of assorted

Boots and Shoes,

comprising Gent's, Ladies', Boy's, and Misses', of all varieties. The especial attention of farmers is invited to a large and complete stock of

HARDWARE.

The celebrated Moline Plow always on hand.

A long experience in and close supervision of the business, and personal attention to the buying of goods, gives confidence that entire satisfaction will be rendered to patrons. Customers will be waited on by experienced and accommodating salesmen, and their wishes promptly attended to. All goods warranted as represented.

GEO. F. BATCHELDER.

Hastings, June 9, 1863. 9-tf

THE CONSERVER.

Published every Tuesday Morning at
HASTINGS, DAKOTA COUNTY, MINNESOTA.

Terms.

Single copy one year	$2
" " six months,	1
" " three months,	[illegible]
Five copies, to one address,	8 00
Ten " " "	15 00
Twenty " " " and one to getter up of club,	30 00

Payment invariably in advance.

Address IRVING TODD, Publisher.

RATES OF ADVERTISING.

1 square	1 week	$1 00	2 squares	6 months	9 00
1 "	2 weeks	1 50	2 "	1 year	15 00
1 "	3 "	1 75	3 "	1 week	2 25
1 "	4 "	2 00	3 "	2 "	3 00
1 "	5 "	2 25	3 "	3 "	4 00
1 "	6 "	2 50	3 "	4 "	5 00
1 "	7 "	2 75	3 "	3 months	9 00
1 "	2 months	3 00	3 "	6 "	12 00
1 "	3 "	3 75	3 "	1 year	20 00
1 "	4 "	4 50	¼ col	6 months	15 00
1 "	5 "	5 25	¼ "	1 year	25 00
1 square	6 months	6 00	½ "	6 months	18 00
1 "	1 year	10 00	½ "	1 year	30 00
2 squares	1 week	1 75	1 "	6 months	30 00
2 "	2 "	2 50	1 "	1 year	40 00
2 "	3 "	3 00	1 "	1 year	50 00
2 "	4 "	4 00	1 "	1 year	70 00
2 "	2 months	6 00			

One inch in space will be counted as a square of solid matter.

Business cards on second page, not exceeding seven lines, seven dollars per year; each additional line one dollar.

Legal advertisements inserted at the rates prescribed by statute, and otherwise ordering such advertisements will be held responsible.

Special notices 15 cents per line for first insertion and ten cents for each subsequent insertion.

Transient advertisements must be paid in advance—all others quarterly.

Advertisements not otherwise ordered, will be continued until they are ordered out, and charged accordingly.

Funeral Dirge.

Solemn strikes the funeral chime,
Notes of our departing time,
As we journey here below,
Through a pilgrimage of woe!

Mortals, now indulge a tear,
For mortality is near!
See how wide her trophies wave
O'er the slumbers of the grave!

Here another guest we bring!
Seraphs of celestial wing,
To our funeral altar come—
Waft this Friend and Brother home.

Lord of all—below—above—
Fill our hearts with Truth and Love!
When dissolves our earthly tie,
Take us to thy Lodge on high.

Here is Next.

A little Sunday school boy in Baltimore had been taught by his aunt Kate to repeat the twenty-third Psalm, so generally learned by children, and which, among other beautiful declarations, inculcates the lesson, "Thy rod and thy staff they comfort me." But our little friend sadly failed to get the hang of this part, as the following will show:

His mother having occasion to administer to him a little "whaling," in reply to his remonstrances urged also that for his good she ought not to "spare the rod." He stood the infliction with great fortitude, but at the close, with big tears in his eyes and hopping about like a parched pea, he gave vent in this impassioned strain, half soliloquy and half directed to his astonished parent—"There now; it ain't so; Aunt Kate said it would, but it don't comfort me a bit!"

"What doesn't comfort you, my dear?" asked the mother.

"Why, the rod don't. I don't feel any better, and there ain't any comfort 'bout it, and I'll just tell her so."

The "points" of this speech were not fully comprehended until, on summoning "Aunt Kate," it was discovered that our young friend had only got things a little "mixed;" and confounded the rod spoken of by the Psalmist with the sturdy little stick just then so uncomfortably applied to him.—*Harper's drawer.*

Our Ohio corn-growing readers will understand and enjoy the following:

During the last Ohio State Fair, at Cleveland, the city was visited by thousands from the adjacent rural districts to witness the exhibition. As a consequence, at the close of the third day of the fair the commissary departments of the hotels and eatinghouses were reduced to short rations, and the number that had to retire supperless was not a few. At one of the hotels a famishing countryman, of brawny proportions, and apparently not afflicted with any such complaints as indigestion or loss of appetite, had worked his way through the crowd that was packed about the dining-hall door, and found a vacant seat at a table. For a few minutes he indulged in "the pleasure of hope," expecting soon to be able to appease his wolfish appetite. All about him, and far beyond the range of knife, fork, or digitals, was a waste of empty dishes. After having been seated for a weary half hour a knife and fork were placed at his side, which revived his sinking hopes. Then came another aggravating delay, the hurrying waiters passed to and fro utterly regardless of his importunities for something to eat. Finally he turned half around in his chair, and calling a waiter to him, he looked at him as only a despairingly hungry man can look, and in a loud voice exclaimed: "I am terribly hungry!—*have you got any corn in the shock?*"—*Ib.*

A Portland (Maine) paper tells an amusing story in which a democratic politician and minister are the heroes. By mistake they exchanged carpet bags, and the one arrived at a democratic mass meeting with a sermon, and the other where he was to preach with a political speech and a bottle of whisky.

Josey being rather remiss in his sunday school lesson the teacher remarked that he hadn't a very good memory. "No ma'am," said he, hesitating; but I have got a first-rate forget-ery."

What is that which is ever before us, can never be seen, and yet all are looking toward it? To-morrow.

In returning thanks, in an after dinner speech, Brown declared that he was "too full for utterance."

She who can compose a cross baby is greater than she who composes books.

HARDWARE.

ATTENTION EVERY BODY!

Buy Where You Can Buy Cheapest and get Good Articles.

If you want good hoes and forks, go to Thomas' Hardware Store.

If you want good scythes and snaths cheap, go to Thomas'.

HARDWARE,

If you want fine table and pocket cutlery, go to Thomas' Cheap Store.

If you want nails or iron cheap, go straight to Thomas', and no where else.

If you want any kind of tools cheap and good, go to Thomas.

If you want hatchets or axes of the best quality, go to Thomas' Cheap Store.

If you want kerosene oil cheap and good go to Thomas.

HARDWARE.

If you want stoves and tinware of the best quality and cheap as the cheapest, go to the cheap hardware store of John Thomas.

If you want locks, latches, bolts and screws, or any kind of house trimmings, Thomas' is the place to buy.

If you want sheep shears, gopher traps, smooth irons, iron bench screws, augurs, augur bitts, hand bells, cow bells, or any article kept in a hardware store, go to Thomas' and get it cheap and of the best quality.

HARDWARE.

Try it and see if you cannot make money at it.

JOHN THOMAS.

Hastings, May 14, 1863. 5-tf

HARDWARE.

M. MC HUGH,

Dealer in

HARDWARE,
TINWARE,
STOVES, ETC.,

Corner of Second and Vermillion Streets, Hastings, Minnesota,

has on hand and is constantly receiving a general assortment and a full supply of

Iron,
Nails,
Tinware,
Glass,
Sash,
And
Putty,

Also the best stock of

CUTLERY

ever before exhibited in this market. These goods have been bought expressly for this trade, and will be sold on the most reasonable terms for cash.

I am also agent for, and have on hand, the celebrated

STEWART COOKING STOVE,

known to be the best cooking stove manufactured.

Hastings, May 14, 1863. 5-tf

H. H. PRINGLE,

Wholesale and Retail Dealer in

HARDWARE, IRON, NAILS,

STOVES AND TINWARE,

Mechanics' Tools,

Building Materials,

AGRICULTURAL IMPLEMENTS,

PAINTS, OILS, GLASS,

SASH, DOORS, BLINDS, ETC

HASTINGS, MIN,

TIN,

SHEET IRON & COPPER W'K

ON HAND OR MADE TO ORDER.

BRICK DRUG STORE,

R. J. MARVIN.

Dealer in

DRUGS,
MEDICINES,
CHEMICALS,
ETC., ETC.

On hand a large stock of

PAINTS,
OILS,
COLORS,
GLASS, AND
PAINTERS'
STOCK GENERALLY,

Also

Garden and Field

SEEDS.

Please give me a call before purchasing. Try my goods and prices, which is a better test than *blowing.*

May 1, 1863. 5-tf

PRINTING.

ALL KINDS OF

PRINTING

Neatly and Cheaply Executed

AT THE

CONSERVER OFFICE.

Cards,

Programmes,

Bill-Heads,

Circulars,

Posters,

Etc.,

Printed to Order and at

SHORT NOTICE.

Having received a choice supply of

NEW MATERIAL

from the East, am prepared to do

PLAIN AND FANCY WORK,

in styles to defy competition.

Orders from the country promptly attended to.

IRVING TODD.

FURNITURE.

H. BUTTURFF,

Manufacturer and Dealer in

FURNITURE, UPHOLSTERY,

DOMESTIC WILLOW WARE,

CRIBS, HOBBY HORSES,

PROPELLERS, BABY-JUMPERS,

FEATHERS, PILLOWS, MATRESSES

COMFORTERS, WINDOW SHADES,

TABLE and FLOOR OIL CLOTH,

CARPETS, CURLED HAIR, etc. etc.

PARLOR FURNITURE,

Cane Seat and Common Chairs, Extention, Dining and Centre Tables, Rocking Chairs, Bedsteads, Wardrobes, Bureaus, Tin Safes, Picture Frames and Looking glasses.

I keep employed the best of workmen, and manufacture to order, with neatness and dispatch.

N. B. Coffins on hand and made to order.

Hastings, Nov. 20, 1862. 32-tf

THE LIVING AND THE DEAD CAN be supplied at

Herzog & Corson's

with all kinds of

Sash, Doors,
Blinds, Chairs,
Cabinet Ware,
Planing, Matching,
Sawing, Turning,
Etc., Etc.

Coffins of all kinds and styles, a large lot always on hand. Sole agents for

THE METALLIC BURIAL CASES.

Come and buy a good article cheap for cash or produce. Wood, Lumber, Pork, etc. taken in exchange for work.

Sale Rooms and Factory corner of Second and Eddy Streets, west of S. Koger's store. HERZOG & CORSON.

Hastings, Jan. 1, 1863. 36-tf

MISCELLANEOUS.

P. VAN AUKEN. W. H. LANGLEY

VAN AUKEN & LANGLEY,

STORAGE,

FORWARDING & COMMISS'N

MERCHANTS,

Dealers in Produce, and Agents for

Threshing Machines and Reapers,

RAILROAD & STEAMBOAT

TICKET AGENTS.

EQUITABLE LIFE ASSURANCE SOCIETY,

OF NEW YORK.

CASH CAPITAL,	$100,000
NETT SURPLUS,	$125,000

Dividends on capital limited by its charter to seven per cent per annum—the entire profits go to the policy holders.

R. W. MONTGOMERY, Agent.

Hastings, Minn. Office on First Street in Gardner's new stone block. 42-1y

---

BLACKSMITH SHOP.

PLOWS! PLOWS!! PLOWS!!

I have just established myself in the above business on Second Street, above Herzog & Corson's Furniture Factory, and am prepared to do all kinds of Blacksmithing.

Also, constantly on hand all kinds of plows of the most approved patterns and made of the best material. I shall be obliged for a share of public patronage, and shall always warrant my work to be of the best quality. JOHN BATEMAN.

Hastings, Nov. 20, 1862. 32-tf

PUBLICATIONS.

1863. THE 1863.

MILWAUKEE WISCONSIN.

Daily, Semi-Weekly, Weekly.

The proprietors of the *Wisconsin*, begs leave to announce that owing to increasing expenditures for Special Telegraphic and War Correspondence, together with various improvements in contemplation for the coming year, he has felt compelled to make some changes in the scale of prices at which it is furnished to subscribers. By comparison with the prices of other journals, it will be seen that the *Wisconsin* is still, as it ever has been, the cheapest paper in the North-West.

We shall continue to print the *Wisconsin* upon the plainest type and the finest paper that can be made, thus retaining the name of the "handsomest paper in the state."

The present proprietor has conducted the paper over fifteen years, and it is unnecessary for him to speak of his ability or enterprise as a Live Independent Newspaper. He will only say that his journal is faithfully pledged to the suppression of the rebellion and the destruction of the rebels in arms, by every means in the power of the Government, and to the most cordial and active support of the President in his Proclamation of Freedom.

Our list of correspondence embraces every Regiment of Wisconsin soldiers, as well as the several grand divisions of the Union Army. The Local and Commercial Departments will receive the undivided attention of the most competent Editors and Reporters.

We call particular attention to the Semi-Weekly *Wisconsin.* It will be a large thirty-two column paper, without advertisements, made up expressly for country circulation. All matter of the Daily *Wisconsin* will appear in this sheet; thus the subscriber will receive all the news of a daily paper for the price of the semi-weekly.

DAILY WISCONSIN—BY MAIL.

Published every day (except Sundays,) at 9 A. M., 12 M., and 3 P. M., at the following rates:

1 copy 12 months, in advance	$8 00
1 copy 6 months, "	4 00
1 copy 3 months, "	2 00

SEMI-WEEKLY WISCONSIN

Published every Tuesday and Thursday morning, as follows:

1 copy 1 year, in advance	$3 00
1 copy 6 months,	1 50
4 copies 1 year (in one order)	10 00
10 copies 1 year " "	22 50

Additional copies at the rate of the club, Specimen numbers sent to any address.

WEEKLY WISCONSIN.

Published every Wednesday morning, and mailed every Tuesday evening.

1 copy 8 mos, in advance	$ 1 00
1 copy 1 year, "	1 50
10 copies 1 year, "	13 00
20 copies 1 year, "	25 00

Additional copies at the rate of the club.

An extra copy will be sent to persons getting up clubs of ten or more of the Weekly. Money in registered letters may be sent at our risk.

WM. E. CRAMER,

38-tf Milwaukee, Wis.

THE BEST, CHEAPEST, AND MOST successful Family Paper in the Union. A complete pictorial history of the times.

HARPER'S WEEKLY,

Splendidly illustrated. Price six cents a number—$3 00 a year.

Critical Notices of the Press.

"Its fresh leaves, its clear type, its entertaining variety, its severe but just criticisms upon the follies of the times, its elegantly written and instructive articles, and its able correspondence, all combine to make it the model newspaper of our country, and one that every family must prize. Its condensed weekly summary of foreign and domestic intelligence is altogether superior to that contained in any other journal. Being published, too, in a form for preservation and binding, if taken care of as it deserves to be, it will be found in future years as welcome a companion for the family and fireside as the day on which it was first perused.—N. Y. Evening Post.

We would not so often call attention to Harper's Weekly if we were not well satisfied that it is the best family paper published in the United States, and for that reason, and that alone, we desire to see it undermine and root out a certain kind of literature too prevalent, which taints the morals of its readers, vitiates their taste for sensible reading, and is already ... its effects.—New London Advertiser.

Wherever we go—in rail cars and steamboats—we find it seized with eagerness, because of its spirited sketches of passing events. We all like to look at the faces of men we have read of, and at ships and forts that have figured in the bloody scenes of war. Of all such men and places and events this paper furnishes the best illustrations. Our future historians will enrich themselves out of Harper's Weekly long after writers and painters and publishers are turned to dust.—N. Y. Evangelist.

TERMS.

One Copy for One Year,	$3 00
One Copy for Two Years,	5 00

An extra copy will be allowed for every club of ten subscribers, at $2 50 each, or 11 copies for $25.

Harper's Magazine and *Harper's* Weekly together, one year, $5 00. *Harper's* Weekly is electrotyped, and back numbers can be had at any time.

Vols. I., II., III., IV., V., and VI., for the years 1857 to 1862 inclusive, of *Harper's* Weekly, handsomely bound in cloth extra, price $4 38 each, are now ready. The postage upon *Harper's* Weekly, when paid in advance at the office where it is received, is twenty-six cents a year.

HARPER & BROTHERS,

43-tf Franklin Square, New York,

AMERICAN AGRICULTURIST.—FOR the Farm, Garden, and Household. A thorough-going, reliable, and practical journal, devoted to the different departments of soil culture—such as growing field crops; orchard and garden fruits; garden vegetables and flowers; trees, plants, and flowers for the lawn or yard, care of domestic animals, etc., and to household labors. It has also an interesting and instructive department for children and youth, alone worth the cost of the paper. A full calendar of operations every month. Three to four hundred, or more, illustrative engravings appear in each volume. Over twelve hundred plain, practical, instructive articles and useful items, are given every year. The editors are all practical working men. The teachings of the Agriculturist are confined to no state or territory, but are adapted to the wants of all sections of the country—it is, as its name indicates, for the whole American Continent.

TERMS—INVARIABLY IN ADVANCE.

(For either the English or German Edition)

One copy, one year	$1 00
Six copies, one year	5 00

Ten or more, copies one year 80 cents each.

Add to the above rates postage to Canada 6 cents; to England and France 24 cents; to Germany 36 cents. Postage anywhere in the United States and territories must be paid by the subscriber, and is only six cents a year, if paid in advance at the office where received. All business and other communications should be addressed to the editor and proprietor.

ORANGE JUDD,

41 Park-Row, New York City.

PUBLICATIONS.

THE CONTINENTAL MONTHLY.—The readers of the *Continental* are aware of the important position it has assumed, of the influence which it exerts, and of the brilliant array of political and literary talent of the highest order which supports it. No publication of the kind has, in this country, so successfully combined the energy and freedom of the daily newspaper with the higher literary tone of the first-class monthly; and it is very certain that the magazine has given wider range to its contributors, or preserved itself so completely from the narrow influences of party or faction. In times like the present, such a journal is either a power in the land or it is nothing. That the *Continental* is not the latter is abundantly evinced by what it has done—by the reflection of its counsels in many important public events, and in the character and power of those who are its stanchest supporters.

Though but little more than a year has elapsed since the *Continental* was first established, it has during that time acquired a strength and a political significance elevating it to a position far above that previously occupied by any publication of the kind in America. In proof of which assertion we call attention to the following facts:

1. Of its political articles republished in pamphlet form, a single one has had, thus far, a circulation of one hundred and six thousand copies.

2. From its literary department, a single serial novel, Among the Pines, has, within a very few months, sold nearly thirty-five thousand copies. Two other series of its literary articles have also been republished in book form while the first portion of a third is already in press.

No more conclusive facts need to be alleged to prove the excellence of the contributions to the *Continental*, or their extraordinary popularity; and its conductors are determined that it shall not fall behind. Preserving all "the boldness, vigor, and ability" which a thousand journals have attributed to it, it will greatly enlarge its circle of action, and discuss, fearlessly and frankly, every principle involved in the great questions of the day. The first minds of the country, embracing the men most familiar with its diplomacy and most distinguished for ability, are among its contributors; and it is no mere flattering promise of a prospectus to say that this magazine for the times will employ the first intellect in America, under auspices which no publication ever enjoyed before in this country.

While the *Continental* will express decided opinions on the great questions of the day, it will not be a mere political journal: much the larger portion of its columns will be enlivened, as heretofore, by tales, poetry, and humor. In a word, the *Continental* will be found, under its new staff of editors, occupying a position and presenting attractions never before found in a magazine.

TERMS TO CLUBS.

Two copies for one year,	$ 5 00
Three copies for one year,	6 00
Six copies for one year,	11 00
Eleven copies for one year,	20 00
Twenty copies for one year,	36 00

Paid in advance. Postage 36 cents a year, to be paid by the subscriber. Single copies $3 a year, in advance. Postage paid by the publisher. 12-tf

JOHN F. TROW, 50 Greene St., N.Y.,
Publisher for the Proprietors.

ONLY $1 25 A YEAR IN CLUBS OF 4.

Arthur's Home Magazine,

For 1863. Vols. XXI. and XXII. Edited by T. S. Arthur and Virginia F. Townsend. Contains novelets, stories, poetry, fashions, steel and wood engravings, needlework patterns in great variety, a mother's department, children's department, housekeeper's and health departments, with literary reviews, and all the accessories of a first-class magazine.

The Lady's Book bears this flattering testimony to the character of *Arthur's* Home Magazine:

"As we have often before said, it is, without controversy, the best $2 magazine published in the country; and this is the strongly ... , many everywhere given by the press. We know of no periodical that so well deserves the praise bestowed. The editors never tire in their endeavors to give each month a rich and varied literary repast to their readers. Their work is kept fully up to the standard of their promise, is never dull, yet always full of instruction. We have often said, and repeat it again, that it should make a part of the reading of every household. We know of no better educator of the people, young and old. Of the editors we need not speak; their names are household words all over the country. In their hands no periodical can fail to reach the highest point of excellence."

A new serial by T. S. Arthur will be commenced in the January number entitled Out in the World.

Rare and elegant premiums are sent to all who make up clubs: 1. A large photographic copy of that splendid engraving Shakspeare and his Cotemporaries. 2. A large photographic copy from an engraving of Huntington's celebrated picture Mercy's Dream. 3. A similar copy of Herring's Glimpse of an English Homestead.

TERMS.—$2 a year in advance and one premium plate; Two copies $3. Three for $4. Four for $5. Eight and one to getter up of club for $10. One of the premium plates is sent to every getter up of a club, small or large. Three red stamps must be sent to pay the postage on each premium. Address

T. S. ARTHUR & CO.,
323 Walnut Street, Philadelphia.

THE INDEPENDENT, EDITED BY Henry Ward Beecher, is a religious newspaper, and a real newspaper. It affords its readers fair and thoughtful editorial discussions of the most important facts and occurrences and interests of this nation and of the world. A comprehensive record of facts, men and movements of the religious world. A full and careful weekly history of the progress of the rebellion. Ample chronicles of the important general news; home and foreign. Fair and careful accounts of new books; made on the express principle of serving as a safe guide to buyers. Interesting correspondence from Washington; from the West; from the army; from abroad. Six columns a week of carefully selected matter for family reading; being prose and poetry, suited to interest both the old people and the young people. A full chronicle of the progress of business and of the current prices of merchandise, produce and live stock in New York City

ONE SERMON EVERY WEEK

By Rev. Henry Ward Beecher. The following eminent writers are special contributors to its columns:—

Mrs. Harriet Beecher Stowe,
Rev. Theodore L. Cuyler,
Rev. Robert M. Hatfield,
Rev. George B. Cheever,
Horace Greely,
Bayard Taylor,
John G. Whittier.

TERMS.—$2 per annum, paid in advance. Specimen numbers sent gratis.

JOSEPH H. RICHARDS, Publisher,
No. 5 Beekman Street, New York.

For sale by news agents.

PATENT MEDICINES.

DR. ROBACK'S
STOMACH
BITTERS
ARE NOT
TO BE EXCELLED
AS A
STOMACHIC
AND
Regulator
OF THE
DIGESTIVE ORGANS.

These Bitters

are not offered to the public as a medicine which will cure all the "ills which flesh is heir to," but as a remedial agent—a great regulator of the system.

In the Bilious districts of the West and South there has, for a long time, been much needed an article of Stomach Bitters, which, if taken in proper quantities, and at the proper time, are a sure preventive of

Bilious Fever,
Fever and Ague,
Liver Complaint,
Dyspepsia,
Indigestion,
Jaundice,
Kidney Complaints,

and all diseases of a similar nature.

These Bitters

are composed of rare and powerful roots and herbs, which make them

Highly Tonic.

Dr. Roback's
Stomach Bitters
are the poor man's friend.

Dr. Roback's
Stomach Bitters
save the poor man many Doctor's Bills.

Dr. Roback's
Stomach Bitters
are the rich man's Solace and Comfort.

Dr. Roback's
Stomach Bitters
invigorate the weak and debilitated.

Dr. Roback's
Stomach Bitters
drive away melancholy and make Life enjoyable.

Dr. Roback's
Stomach Bitters
are the Soldier's Friend, by preventing Diarrhea, Dysentery, Rheumatism, etc.

These Bitters are put up in quart bottles, of which the above is a fac-simile. The label is finely engraved, and is provided with a safe-guard from counterfeiters. Price $1 per bottle, or six for $5.

C. W. Roback, Proprietor, No. 4 East Fourth Street, Cincinnati, to whom all orders should be addressed.

FOR SALE BY

A. M. Pett, Hastings, J. R. Tigkcom, Mankato, W. H. McCollum, Mankato, and by druggists and merchants generally throughout the United States, Canadas and Brazil.

For Rats, Mice, Roaches, Ants, Bed Bugs, Moths in Furs, Woolens, etc., Insects on Plants, Fowls, Animals, etc. Put up in 25c, 50c, and $1 00 Boxes, Bottles, and Flasks. $3 and $5 sizes for Hotels, Public Institutions, etc.

"Only infallible remedies known."
"Free from Poisons."
"Not dangerous to the Human Family."
"Rats come out of their holes to die."

Sold wholesale in all large cities.
Sold by all druggists and retailers every where.
Beware! of all worthless imitations.
See that Costar's name is on each Box, Bottle, and Flask before you buy.
Address HENRY R. COSTAR.
Principal depot 482 Broadway, N. Y.
Sold by A. M. PETT,
Wholesale and Retail Agent.
51-1yw Hastings, Minn.

FRED. S. CURTISS. W. C. COWLES

CURTISS & COWLES,
DEALERS IN

Shoe and Harness Leather,

saddlery hardware, shoe findings, etc., Ramsey Street, near Levee, and lumber of all descriptions at corner of Second and Eddy Streets.

Hastings, Feb. 12, 1863. 45-tf

THE CONSERVER.

The Campaign Conserver.

To meet the seeming great demand this fall for political documents, the publisher of the CONSERVER has concluded to issue a campaign paper for the term of eight weeks, commencing with Sept. 22d and ending with Nov. 10th, the latter number containing the complete election returns. To place it within the reach of all, it will be afforded at the following low rates, barely paying for the white paper:

5 copies to one address, $1 50
10 copies to one address, 2 50

And any larger number in same proportion. No clubs smaller than five can be received. Send in your orders accompanied with the cash, as speedily as possible. Postmasters and others friendly to the cause are invited to act as agents in securing names. Address

IRVING TODD,
3-3w Hastings, Minn.

In the present juncture of affairs near Charleston, the following is of interest to the reader:

Fort Sumter is three miles and three-eighths from Charleston, one mile and one eighth from Fort Moultrie, three-quarters of a mile to the nearest land, one mile and three eighths to Fort Johnson, and two miles and five-eighths to Castle Pinckney. The last named fort is one mile from the town, and Fort Johnson is two miles and a quarter from the town. These measurements are from surveys from the United States Coast Survey Department.

A CONTESTED MAN.—A druggist was aroused by the ringing of his night bell, went down stairs, and had to serve a customer with a dose of salts. On his return his wife grumbled out, "what profit do you get out of that penny?" "A ha'penny," replied the meditative druggist. "And for that ha'penny you will keep both me and yourself awake for a long time," rejoined the wife. "Never mind," added the placid druggist, "the dose of salts will keep him awake much longer, let us thank Heaven that we have the profit and not the pain of the transaction."

The author of a paper lately read before a scientific association in England calculates that the yield of gold from California and Australia, during the next ten years, will amount to £200,000,000, and that not more than £60,000,000 can be absorbed in Europe without a depreciation in its value. He advises persons with fixed incomes to take precautions for avoiding disastrous effects.

MONETARY QUOTATIONS OF FOLLETT & RENICK.

[CORRECTED WEEKLY.]

Bankable Funds.

New England,	Bank State of Indiana.
New York,	Iowa,
New Jersey,	Michigan,
Ohio,	U. S Demand Notes.
Canada,	Wisconsin,
Philadelphia,	Bank of Minnesota,
Marine Bank, Minn.,	Winona Co. Bank,
Bank of Chatfield,	State Bank of Minn.,
Peoples' Bank,	Pittsburg.

Exchange.

FOR BANKABLE FUNDS.

	Buying.	Selling.
New York, Philadelphia, Boston,	¼ prem.	½ prem.
Chicago and Milwaukee,	par.	¼ prem.
PREMIUM FUNDS.		
Gold,	25	30
Silver (large),	18	25
U. S. Demand Notes,	25	30
Canada,	20	25

RETAIL PRICES CURRENT.

CORRECTED WEEKLY BY G. F. BATCHELDER,

HASTINGS, Sept 29, 1863.

FLOUR, per sack,	$2 50
WHEAT, per bushel,	65a70
CORN, do	40a45
OATS, do	40
POTATOES, do	50
BEANS, do	1 25
ONIONS, do	50
CRANBERRIES,	2 00
HAY, per ton,	6 00a8 00
WOOD, per cord,	3 00a4 00
SALT, per bbl	3 75
EGGS, per doz	12
BUTTER, per lb,	10a15
CHEESE, per lb	8a12
PORK, per cwt,	3a4
BEEF, per cwt,	3 60
HAMS, per cwt,	8a9
SHOULDERS, per cwt,	5a6
DRIED APPLES,	9
DRIED PEACHES,	16a25
SUGARS, per lb	12a17
MOLASSES, per gal	70a1 00
COFFEE, Java,	40
do Rio,	35

WANTED.

Two Marble Workers Immediately. Apply at the Winona Marble Works, or at this office.
Hastings, Aug. 18, 1863. 19-tf

ESTRAY.—TAKEN UP BY THE SUBscriber, on or about the 1st of September, a brindle Ox, five or six years old, white spot in face, four white legs, white on belly, and short white tail. The owner is requested to prove property, pay charges, and take him away.
CHAS. YEATER.
Nininger, Sept. 10, 1863. 23-4w

W. P. STANLEY,

DEALER IN

Books and Stationery,

Paper Hangings, Curtains, Fixtures, Cord, and Tassels; buff and green Holland; oil green cloth for shades; Photographs of our generals and other distinguished individuals and albums to put them in; Yankee Notions, all the leading Magazines and Newspapers, Eastern and Western, St. Paul Dailies; agent for Prince & Sons Melodeons. 41-tf

NEW ENGLAND HOTEL RE-OPENED.

CHAS. DAMEREL.

Having leased the above property, has thoroughly cleaned and refurnished the above old established hotel at Hastings, and is ready to do all in his power to conduce to the comfort and satisfaction of the traveling community, and solicits a share of public patronage.

In connection with the hotel I keep a livery and sale stable and feel confident I can please the majority with, pleasant driving horses and steady and obliging drivers.

Teaming done at fair prices. Please call and see me at New England House.
CHAS. DAMEREL, Proprietor.
Hastings, Aug 10, 1863. 18-6m

NEW ADVERTISEMENTS.

PRINTING TYPES.

AND ALL OTHER

PRINTING MATERIALS,

Are offered for sale at

BRUCE'S NEW YORK

Type-Foundry,

At the Lowest Prices.

Roman type, Fancy type, Script type, German type, Music type, Chess and Checker type, Brass and Metal Rules, Brass and Electro Circles and Ellipses, Labor-Saving Rules, Labor-Saving Leads, Labor-Saving Slugs, Wood type, Labor-Saving Quotations, Borders, Ornaments, Leads, Brass Dashes, Circular Quads, Corner Quads, Ornamental Corners, Metal Furniture, Brass Galleys, Compositor's Numbered Slugs, etc.

Printers can also be supplied with Presses from all the different manufactures.

Printing Ink of all colors, Composing Sticks, Stands, Cases, Imposing Stones, Chases, and all other printing materials, at the manufacturer's prices.

Any publisher of a newspaper who chooses to publish the advertisement, including this note, three times before the first of December, 1863, and forward me one copy of the papers containing it, will be allowed his bill at the time of making a purchase from me of my own manufactures of five times the amount of said bill.
GEORGE BRUCE,
24-3t No. 13, Chamber-st., N. Y.

RICH PRAIRIE LAND FOR SALE,

In Castle Rock and Eureka Townships.

NE qr sec 4, town 113, range 19 (Castle Rock). SW qr sec 12, town 113, range 20 (Eureka). These two are regarded as the garden townships of Dakota County. The soil is a black loam, of the finest quality. The land lies near the track of the Cedar Valley Railroad, now being rapidly constructed, and in the midst of splendid farms. Many of these farms produced 25 bushels of wheat per acre the present season, with not sufficient rain from seed-time to harvest to wet a man's shirt. This last statement is on the authority of the Right Reverend Bishop Willouby, of that vicinity.
HENRY MCKENTY,
Dealer in Real Estate.
St. Paul, Sept. 15, 1863. 23-4w*

WINONA AND HASTINGS

MARBLE WORKS.

The subscriber would respectfully give notice to the people of Hastings and elsewhere that he has constantly on hand the largest stock of Foreign and American Marbles ever brought west of Lake Michigan, consisting of all kinds of
LARGE SPIRE MONUMENTS,
SKELETON MONUMENTS,
GRAVE STONES, MANTELS,
FURNITURE MARBLE, ETC.,
which he will finish to order in the most approved styles and for the lowest cash price. Parties wishing to purchase will do well to wait till my agent comes around or to write to me, before purchasing elsewhere.
C. J. ALDBACH.

Shop opposite the court-house, Winona, and on Second Street, below Tyler, Hastings, Minn. 18-tf

WILKES' SPIRIT OF THE TIMES.

Office 201 William-st., New York,

George Wilkes, Ed. and Pro.

Four Dollars a Year in Advance.
To Clubs—5 Copies, - - - $17 00
" 9 " - - - 30 00

No subscriptions received for less than three months.

Rates of Advertising.

15 cts per line each single insertion.
48 " " " One month.
$1 26 " " Three months.
$2 00 " " Six months.

Sinclair Tousey, No. 121 Nassau Street, New York, general wholesale agents for supplying dealers. T. R. Callender, agent for Philadelphia.

Postmasters are requested to act as agents, and retain 20 per cent for their trouble. This percentage is, however, not to be deducted from club rates.

BRICK DRUG STORE,

R. J. MARVIN.

Dealer in

DRUGS,
MEDICINES,
CHEMICALS,
ETC., ETC.

On hand a large stock of

PAINTS,
OILS,
COLORS,
GLASS, AND
PAINTERS'
STOCK GENERALLY.

Also

Garden and Field

SEEDS.

Please give me a call before purchasing. Try my goods and prices, which is a better test than *blowing.*
May 1, 1863. 3-tf

EQUITABLE LIFE ASSURANCE SOCIETY,

OF NEW YORK.

CASH CAPITAL, - - - - $100,000
NETT SURPLUS, - - - - $138,000

Dividends on capital limited by its charter to seven per cent per annum—the entire profits go to the policy holders.

R. W. MONTGOMERY, Agent.
Hastings, Minn. Office on First Street in Gardner's new stone block. 42-1y

MISCELLANEOUS.

J. W. PRATT & CO.,
Dealers in
Cloths, Cassimeres, Vestings,
and Tailor's Trimmings.
Also, Hats, Caps, and Gents'
FURNISHING GOODS.
Hastings, Minn., May 14, 1863. 5-tf

E. & H. T. ANTHONY, MANUFACturers of Photographic Materials, 501 Broadway, New York.

CARD PHOTOGRAPHS.

Our Catalogue now embraces considerably over four thousand different subjects (to which additions are continually being made) of Portraits of Eminent Americans, etc., viz:

72 Major-Generals,	525 Statesmen,
190 Brig.-Generals,	127 Divines,
250 Colonels,	116 Authors,
84 Lieut.-Colonels,	30 Artists,
207 Other Officers,	112 Stage,
60 Navy Officers,	46 Prominent Women,

147 Prominent Foreign Portraits.
2,500 COPIES OF WORKS OF ART,

Including reproductions of the most celebrated Engravings, Paintings, Statutes, etc. Catalogues sent on receipt of stamp. An order for One Dozen Pictures from our catalogue will be filled on receipt of $1 80, and sent by mail *free.*

Photographic Albums.

Of these we manufacture a great variety, ranging in price from 50 cents to $50. Our Albums have the reputation of being superior to any others. The smaller kinds can be sent safely by mail at a postage of six cents per oz. The more expensive can be sent by express.

We also keep a large assortment of **Stereoscopes & Stereoscopic Views.** Our Catalogue of these will be sent to any address on receipt of stamp.

E. & H. T. ANTHONY,
Manufacturers of Photographic Materials,
501 Broadway, New York.

Friends or relatives of prominent military men will confer a favor by sending us their likenesses to copy. They will be kept carefully and returned uninjured.

Fine Albums made to order for congregations to present to their pastor, or for other purposes, with suitable inscriptions.
17-6mo

ONLY $1 25 A YEAR IN CLUBS OF 4.

Arthur's Home Magazine,

For 1863. Vols. XXI. and XXII. Edited by T. S. Arthur and Virginia F. Townsend. Contains novelets, stories, poetry, fashions, steel and wood engravings, needlework patterns in great variety, a mother's department, children's department, housekeeper's and health departments, with literary reviews, and all the accessories of a first-class magazine.

The Lady's Book bears this flattering testimony to the character of *Arthur's Home Magazine:*

"As we have often before said, it is, without controversy, the best $2 magazine published in the country; and this is the strongly outspoken testimony everywhere given by the press. We know of no periodical that so well deserves the praise bestowed. The editors never tire in their endeavors to give each month a rich and varied literary repast to their readers. Their work is kept fully up to the standard of their promise, is never dull, yet always full of instruction. We have often said, and repeat it again, that it should make a part of the reading of every household. We know of no better educator of the people, young and old. Of the editors we need not speak; their names are household words all over the country. In their hands no periodical can fail to reach the highest point of excellence."

A new serial by T. S. Arthur will be commenced in the January number entitled Out in the World.

Rare and elegant premiums are sent to all who make up clubs: 1 A large photographic copy of that splendid engraving Shakespeare and his Cotemporaries. 2. A large photographic copy from an engraving of Huntington's celebrated picture Mercy's Dream. 3. A similar copy of Herring's Glimpse of an English Homestead.

TERMS.—$2 a year in advance and one premium plate. Two copies $3. Three for $4. Four for $5. Eight and one to getter up of club for $10. One of the premium plates is sent to every getter up of a club, small or large. Three red stamps must be sent to pay the postage on each premium. Address

T. S. ARTHUR & Co.,
323 Walnut Street, Philadelphia.

HOWARD ASSOCIATION,

PHILADELPHIA.

A Benevolent Institution established by special Endowment, for the Relief of the Sick and Distressed, afflicted with Virulent and Epidemic Diseases, and especially for the Cure of Diseases of the Sexual Organs.

MEDICAL ADVICE given gratis, by the Acting Surgeon.

VALUABLE REPORTS on Spermatorrhœa, and other Diseases of the Sexual Organs, and on the New Remedies employed in the Dispensary, sent to the afflicted in sealed letter envelopes, free of charge. Two or three Stamps for postage will be acceptable.

Address, DR. J. SKILLIN HOUGHTON, Acting Surgeon, Howard Association, No. 2 South Ninth Street Philadelphia, P. By order of the Directors

BLACKSMITH SHOP.

PLOWS! PLOWS!! PLOWS!!

I have just established myself in the above business on Second Street, above Herzog & Corson's Furniture Factory, and am prepared to do all kinds of Blacksmithing.

Also, constantly on hand all kinds of plows of the most approved patterns and made of the best material. I shall be obliged for a share of public patronage, and shall always warrant my work to be of the best quality. JOHN DAYEMAN.
Hastings, Nov. 20, 1862. 8-tf

FARMING IMPLEMENTS.

DAKOTA WORKS.

AGRICULTURAL IMPLEMENT

MANUFACTORY.

MONTGOMERY & THOMPSON,

Hastings, - - Minnesota.

We are now manufacturing a number of the celebrated

Indiana Fanning Mills,

the very best mill of the age. All we ask is a fair trial to convince the most incredulous that it is the best mill for *all purposes ever invented.*

Farmers, call and see it tested.

We are now prepared to repair all kinds of agricultural implements in the best manner, and at short notice.

Thankful for the liberal encouragement we have received in the past we hope, by strict and prompt attention to business, to merit a continuation of it in the future.
Hastings, June 14, 1863. 10-tf.

COPARTNERSHIP NOTICE.

The undersigned, having formed a partnership connection under the firm name of Gardner & Meloy as dealers in all kinds of agricultural implements and the latest valuable and useful patents, to-wit:

J. H. Manny's Reaper and Mower.

The Ohio Reaper and Mower.

Haine's Illinois Harvester or Header.

Burson's Celebrated Binder—Warranted.

Montgomery & Thompson's Fanning Mills.

Corn Shellers, of Latest Improvement.

Revolving and Wheel Horse Rakes.

Wheeler & Wilson's Sewing Machines.

The Model Clothes Dryer.

Linen Grain Bags.

Garden Rakes and Hoes.

Scythe Snaths and Stones.

Two, Three, and Four Tine Forks.

Storage and Commission solicited.

A. W. GARDNER,
J. C. MELOY.

Office corner Sibley Street and Levee, Stone Block.
Hastings, May 14, 1863, 5-tf

RAILROADS.

ILLINOIS CENTRAL RAILROAD

The old reliable and

DIRECT ROUTE,

via Dunleith. Express passenger trains leave Dunleith morning and evening, making quick time and close connections to all points

EAST AND SOUTH.

No change of cars between Dunleith and Chicago. Elegant sleeping cars attached to night trains. Baggage checked through to all important points. Fare lower to southern points than any other railroad line, and as low to eastern cities as the lowest.

This is the only direct route to

St. Louis and Cairo,

and passengers will arrive at these points from eighteen to twenty-four hours quicker than by any route through Chicago.

Freight transported to Milwaukee, Chicago, or points South and East at as low rates and as quick time guaranteed as by any other route from the Mississippi River.

W. P. JOHNSON, Gen. Pass. Agt., Chi. W. R. ARTHUR, Gen. Supt. Chicago.
J. S. TILDESLY, Gen. Western Agent.

Inquire for tickets by Illinois Central Railroad.
SAMUEL ROGERS, JR., Agent,
Cor. Vermillion and 2d Streets,
16-3m Hastings, Minn.

1863. PRAIRIE DU CHIEN ROUTE 1863.

For Milwaukee, Chicago, and all points East. The only direct route making sure connections, ample time being allowed on the river to insure the connection beyond any probable contingency.

The splendid first-class steamers

MILWAUKEE, KEY CITY,
WAR EAGLE, ITASCA,
AND NORTHERN LIGHT,

unequalled in elegance, speed, and comfort by any other line, leave Hastings daily about 10 P. M., making direct connection with express train leaving Prairie du Chien at 7.45 A. M., arriving at Milwaukee at 3.50 P. M., and Chicago 5.50 P. M., making direct connections at both points with trains for the East.

The change from steamers to cars being made at 7.45 A. M., passengers get a full night's rest and breakfast on board; advantages that cannot be secured by any other route. Magnificent palace cars with patent ventilators and dusters, rendering cars free from dust, and keeping the air pure and cool.

Through from Prairie du Chien to Milwaukee and Chicago without change of cars. Passengers by this route arrive at Chicago and all points East at the same time as via La Crosse, and twelve hours than via Dunleith. Fare as low as by any other route. VAN AUKEN & LANGLEY.
9-tf Agents, on Levee.

LEGAL NOTICES.

STATE OF MINNESOTA.

Sale of School Lands.

In accordance with an act entitled "an act to establish the state Land Office and for other purposes," approved March 10th, 1862, the following parcels or tracts of land will be sold at public auction, at the office of County Treasurer, in the town of Hastings, on Wednesday, the fourth day of November, 1863, at 10 o'clock A. M.:

Lands on which Fifteen per cent of the Purchase Money must be paid down.

Part of Sec.	Sec.	Town.	Range.	App. val. pr acre.	App. val. of improv'ts
DOUGLASS.					
ne qr of ne qr	16	113	17	$5 00	$35 00
sw qr of ne qr	16	113	17	5 00	
sw qr of ne qr	16	113	17	5 00	
se qr of ne qr	16	113	17	5 00	
ne qr of nw qr	16	113	17	5 00	
nw qr of nw qr	16	113	17	5 00	
sw qr of nw qr	16	113	17	5 00	
se qr of nw qr	16	113	17	5 50	
ne qr of sw qr	16	113	17	6 00	
nw qr of sw qr	16	113	17	5 00	
sw qr of sw qr	16	113	17	5 00	
se qr of sw qr	16	113	17	5 00	
ne qr of se qr	16	113	17	5 00	
nw qr of se qr	16	113	17	5 00	
sw qr of se qr	16	113	17	5 10	
se qr of se qr	16	113	17	5 00	
ne qr of ne qr	36	113	17	5 00	
nw qr of ne qr	36	113	17	5 00	
sw qr of ne qr	36	113	17	5 00	
se qr of ne qr	36	113	17	5 00	
ne qr of nw qr	36	113	17	5 00	
nw qr of nw qr	36	113	17	5 00	
sw qr of nw qr	36	113	17	5 00	
se qr of nw qr	36	113	17	4 00	
ne qr of sw qr	36	113	17	5 00	
nw qr of sw qr	36	113	17	5 00	
se qr of sw qr	36	113	17	5 00	
ne qr of se qr	36	113	17	5 00	
sw qr of se qr	36	113	17	4 00	
se qr of se qr	36	113	17	5 00	
MARSHAN.					
ne qr of ne qr	36	114	17	5 00	
nw qr of ne qr	36	114	17	5 00	
sw qr of ne qr	36	114	17	5 00	
se qr of ne qr	36	114	17	5 00	
ne qr of nw qr	36	114	17	5 00	
nw qr of nw qr	36	114	17	5 10	
se qr of nw qr	36	114	17	5 00	
sw qr of se qr	36	114	17	5 00	
RANDOLPH—HAMPTON.					
sw qr of nw qr	36	113	18	5 00	
ne qr of sw qr	36	113	18	5 50	
se qr of sw qr	36	113	18	5 00	
ne qr of se qr	36	113	18	6 50	
nw qr of se qr	36	113	18	5 50	
sw qr of se qr	36	113	18	5 00	
se qr of se qr	36	113	18	6 50	
INVER GROVE.					
sw qr of sw qr	16	115	18	5 00	
se qr of sw qr	16	115	18	5 00	
sw qr of se qr	16	115	18	5 00	
se qr of se qr	16	115	18	5 00	
VERMILLION.					
sw qr of sw qr	16	114	18	5 00	
WATERFORD.					
ne qr of se qr	36	112	19	5 00	
CASTLE ROCK.					
[illegible]					
EMPIRE CITY.					
[illegible]					
ROSEMONT.					
[illegible]					
EUREKA.					
[illegible]					
LAKEVILLE.					
[illegible]					
LEBANON.					
[illegible]					
LAKEVILLE.					
[illegible]					
EAGAN.					
[illegible]					
MENDOTA.					
[illegible]					

Lands on which Seventy-Five per cent of the Purchase Money must be paid down.

Part of Sec.	Sec.	Town.	Range.	App. val. pr acre.	App. val. of improv'ts
[illegible]					
HASTINGS.					
lot 2, 10a ne qr	36	115	17	8 00	
lot 3, 9.71a ne qr	36	115	17	8 00	
lot 8, 5.25a se qr	36	115	17	8 00	
lot 13, 3.06a nw qr	36	115	17	9 00	
INVER GROVE.					
lot 7, 10.22a nw qr	16	115	18	7 00	
lot 8, 14.21a nw qr	16	115	18	7 00	
lot 9, 19.92a nw qr	16	115	18	7 00	
lot 10, 9.97a nw qr	16	115	18	7 00	
lot 11, 10a nw qr	16	115	18	7 00	
lot 13, 9.98a nw qr	16	115	18	7 00	
lot 14, 9.98a nw qr	16	115	18	7 00	
lot 15, 10a nw qr	16	115	18	7 00	
lot 16, 10a nw qr	16	115	18	7 00	
lot 1, 19.21a sw qr	16	115	18	7 00	
lot 2, 10.15a sw qr	16	115	18	7 00	
lot 3, 19.55a sw qr	16	115	18	7 00	
lot 5, 10.09a sw qr	16	115	18	7 00	
lot 6, 10.33a sw qr	16	115	18	7 00	
lot 7, 9.78a	16	115	18	7 00	
lot 8, 9.79a	16	115	18	7 00	
lot 1, 10.29a se qr	16	115	18	7 00	
lot 2, 10.42a se qr	16	115	18	7 00	
lot 3, 19.14a se qr	16	115	18	7 00	
lot 5, 10.37a se qr	16	115	18	7 00	
lot 6, 10.27a se qr	16	115	18	7 00	
lot 7, 19.58a se qr	16	115	18	7 00	
lots 3,5,9 ne qr	16	27	22	6 50	
lots 6,7 ne qr	16	27	22	7 00	
lots 10,11,12 ne qr	16	27	22	6 00	
lots 1—12 inc se qr	16	27	22	6 00	
lots 12—16 inc ne qr	16	27	22	7 00	
lots 1, 2, 3, 4, 15, 16 sw qr	16	27	22	6 00	
lot 9 sw qr	16	27	22	5 00	
lot 10	16	27	22	5 50	
lots 9, 10, 11, 12, 15 sw qr	16	27	22	5 00	
lots 13,14,16 sw qr	16	27	22	6 50	
WEST ST. PAUL.					
lot 7 ne qr	16	28	22	5 00	
lot 2, 5.50a se qr	16	28	22	5 00	
lot 3, 11.15a sw qr	16	28	22	7 00	
lot 5, 10a	16	28	22	7 00	
lot 7, 10a	16	28	22	6 00	
lot 8, 10a	16	28	22	7 00	
lot 9, 10a	16	28	22	6 00	
lot 10, 10a	16	28	22	6 50	
lot 12, 10a	16	28	22	7 00	
lot 13, 4.07a	16	28	22	6 00	
lot 14, 10a	16	28	22	7 00	
lot 15, 10a	16	28	22	6 50	
lots 2—14 inc 10a sw qr	16	28	22	6 00	

The balance of the purchase money is payable any time within twenty years, at the option of the purchaser, if interest at seven per cent per annum is annually paid in advance.

Interest to the first day of June, 1864, must be paid at the time of purchase.

Persons purchasing land upon which other parties have made improvements will be required to pay the owner of the same the appraised value of his improvements, one half to be paid at the time of the sale and the balance six months thereafter, with interest at seven per cent per annum.

In case the person occupying or improving the land has damaged the same, the appraised amount of damage will be deducted from the improvements, and when the occupant is the purchaser the damage will be added to the price of the land.

No lands will be sold for less than the appraised value.

Purchase money payable in specie and legal tender notes. CHAS. McILRATH,
23-4 Commissioner of State Land Office.

MORTGAGE SALE.—WHEREAS DEfault has been made in the condition of a certain mortgage deed executed by Harvey Gillett and Georgie B. Gillett, his wife, of the county of Dakota, in the state of Minnesota to Allen E. Rich and Isaac B. Tozer, then and now partners in business under the firm name of Rich & Tozer, made, acknowledged, and delivered by said mortgagors to said firm of Rich & Tozer, mortgagees, and bearing date the 8th day of May, A. D. 1862, which said mortgage contains the usual power of sale to said Rich & Tozer and their assigns, and was duly filed for record with said mortgage in the office of the register of deeds of said county, on the 9th day of said May at four o'clock in the afternoon of that day, and was thereupon duly recorded in said office in book K of mortgages on pages 587, 588, and 589; which said mortgage was given to secure the payment of one hundred and twenty-three dollars and seventy-one cents with interest at ten per cent per annum according to the conditions of a certain promissory note made by said Harvey Gillett and bearing even date with said mortgage. And there is claimed to be due and is actually due and unpaid upon said note and mortgage at the date of this notice the sum of one hundred and thirty-four dollars and fifty cents. And no suit or proceeding at law has been instituted to recover the debt secured by said mortgage or any part thereof. The mortgaged premises are described as follows, viz: All that tract or parcel of land lying and being in Dakota County, state of Minnesota, and described as follows, to wit: Lot number fourteen (14) in block number three (3) in H. G. Bailly's addition to Hastings, as per recorded plat thereof now on record in the office of register of deeds in said county.

Now, therefore, notice is hereby given, that by virtue of the power of sale in said mortgage contained and pursuant to the statute in such case made and provided the said mortgage will be foreclosed by a sale of said mortgaged premises at public auction to the highest bidder at the front door of the office of said register of deeds in Hastings, in said county, on the 3d day of October, A. D. 1863, at one o'clock in the afternoon of that day, to satisfy said mortgage debt and the expenses of said sale.

18-7t RICH & TOZER, Mortgagees.
A. M. HAYES, Att'y for said Mortgagees.
Dated Hastings, Minn., Aug. 18, 1863.

STATE OF MINNESOTA, SECOND Collection District,

Assessor's Office, St. Paul, August, 1863.

Public Notice

is hereby given that the lists, valuations, and enumerations made and taken under the Excise Tax Law of the United States within division numbered three, comprising the county of Dakota, will be open for examination at the office of Eli Robinson, in the city of Hastings, in said county, on the 29th day of August, A. D. 1863, and will remain open for the space of fifteen days from said time.

Notice is also given that appeals will be received and determined relative to any erroneous or excessive valuations or enumerations by the assistant assessor of said division at the office of Eli Robinson, in said city of Hastings, in said county of Dakota, on the 8th day of September, A. D. 1863, and immediately thereafter until all appeals are disposed of.

H. G. O. MORRISON,
Assessor, 2d District.
Dated August, 21, 1863. 20-4w

ENVELOPES AND WRITING PAPERS, AT WHOLESALE.

To Booksellers, Stationers, Druggists, Dealers in Fancy Goods, Merchants, and all others who purchase Envelopes and Writing Papers.

SAMUEL RAYNOR,

No. 118 William St., New York,

Begs leave to call the attention of dealers in Envelopes to the extensive assortment and superior quality of those manufactured by him, in machinery for manufacturing Envelopes is the latest and best—folding and gumming them in the most perfect manner. The assortment embraces over 700 kinds, including every size, style, color, and quality. The subscriber now has facilities for manufacturing half a million Envelopes per day, so that all orders can be filed promptly. Also the Irving and Harrison Mills Writing Papers, by the case, or in any quantity to suit the purchaser. All offered at the lowest possible prices, on the usual credit, or a discount off for cash.

Samples, with trade list of prices, furnished, when requested, and sent by mail free of postage. SAMUEL RAYNOR.

For sale in Hastings by W. D. Stanley, on Ramsey Street. 19-1m

PUBLICATIONS.

THE NEW YORK TRIBUNE.

1863.

The New York *Tribune*, first issued in 1841, now in its twenty-second year, has obtained both a larger and a more widely diffused circulation than any other newspaper ever published in America. Though it has suffered, in common with other journals, from the volunteering and departure of tens of thousands of its patrons to serve in the war for the union, its circulation on the 6th of December, 1862, is as follows:

Daily	50,125
Semi-Weekly	17,250
Weekly	148,000
Aggregate	215,375

Pre-eminently a journal of News and of Literature, the *Tribune* has political convictions which are well characterized by the single word Republican in its hearty adhesion to the great truth that "God has made of one blood all nations of men"—republican in its assertion of the equal and inalienable rights of all men to "life, liberty, and the pursuit of happiness"—republican in its steadfast, earnest, defiant and hostility to every scheme and effort of the Slave Power from the Annexation of Texas to the great rebellion, to grasp the empire of the New World and wield the resources of our country for its own aggrandizement—republican in its antagonism to the aristocrats and despots of the Old World, who fondly hail in the perils and calamities suddenly thrust upon us by their American counterpart the overthrow and ruin of the model republic; republican in its hope and trust, its faith and effort, that this atrocious rebellion must result in the signal overthrow of its blotters, and the firm establishment of equal rights and equal laws throughout the whole extent of our country, where liberty and union shall indeed be "one and inseparable" henceforth and forever.

The *Tribune* devotes attention in calmer times, and to some extent in these, to education, temperance, agriculture, inventions, and whatever else may minister to the spiritual and material progress and well being of mankind; but for the present its energies and its columns are mainly devoted to the invigoration and success of the war for the union. Its special correspondents accompany every considerable army and report every important incident of that great struggle which we trust is soon to result in the signal and conclusive triumph of the national arms and in the restoration of peace and thrift to our distracted bleeding country. We believe that no otherwise can a fuller or more accurate view of the progress and character of this momentous conflict be obtained than through the regular perusal of our columns. And we earnestly solicit the co-operation of all friends of the national cause, which we regard and uphold as that of universal humanity, to aid us in extending its circulation.

Terms.

The enormous increase in the price of printing paper and other materials used in printing newspapers compels us to increase the price of the *Tribune*. Our new terms are

DAILY TRIBUNE.

Single copy	3 cents
Mail subscribers, one year	$8

SEMI-WEEKLY TRIBUNE.

One copy one year	$3
Two copies one year	5
Five copies one year	12
Ten copies one year	22 50

An extra copy will be sent to clubs of twenty and over.

WEEKLY TRIBUNE.

One copy one year	$ 2
Three copies one year	5
Five copies one year	8
Ten copies one year	15

Any larger number, addressed to names of subscribers, $1 50. An extra copy will be sent to every club of ten. Twenty copies to one address, one year, $25, and any larger number at same price. An extra copy will be sent to clubs of twenty. To clubs of thirty the semi-weekly *Tribune* will be sent. To clubs of fifty the daily *Tribune* will be sent gratis.

Address THE TRIBUNE,
Tribune Buildings, New York.

When drafts can be procured it is much safer than to remit bank bills. The name of the post-office and state should in all cases be plainly written. Subscribers who send money by express must prepay the express charges, else it will be deducted from the remittance.

THE ATLANTIC MONTHLY.—BEGINning of a new volume. The number for January, 1863, begins the eleventh volume of the *Atlantic Monthly*. From the commencement, in 1857, the *Atlantic* has rapidly increased in circulation, and it now has the largest class of readers since its beginning, five years ago. Its prosperity steadily augments, and it continues, amid all the fluctuations and dangers incident to our national crisis, to gain ground in the estimation of the public. At a time so pregnant with events which touch the future destinies of America in every vital particular, the publishers and editors do not deem it necessary to promise that its pages will never swerve from the honest paths of loyal patriotism and universal freedom. It opinions have always been on the side of Liberty, Progress, and Right, and the course it first adopted in its early career will ever be faithfully maintained.

The staff of writers regularly contributing to the *Atlantic Monthly* embraces many of the best known authors in American literature, and warrants the publishers in promising to its readers the best essays, the best stories, the best poems, which American talent can furnish.

LIST OF REGULAR CONTRIBUTORS.

In prose and poetry the *Atlantic* staff of writers is unequaled. The following authors are still among the regular contributors: James Russell Lowell, Henry W. Longfellow, Louis Agassiz, Ralph Waldo Emerson, Nathaniel Hawthorne, T. W. Higginson, Author "Margret Howth," Oliver W. Holmes, John G. Whittier, E. P. Whipple, Bayard Taylor, George S. Hillard, Mrs. H. B. Stowe, "The Country Parson," Rose Terry, Harriet E. Prescott. The *Atlantic's* list of contributors includes many of the leading writers of America.

TERMS.—The *Atlantic* is for sale by all book and periodical dealers. Price 25 cts a number. Subscriptions for the year $3, postage paid. Yearly subscriptions received or single numbers supplied by any dealer, or by the publishers. Specimen numbers sent gratis on application to the publishers. Inducements for subscribing, list of premiums, etc., furnished on application to the publishers.

TICKNOR & FIELDS, Publishers,
135 Washington Street,
44-tf Boston, Mass.

WILLIAM ATHERTON

Veterinary Surgeon,

Office 1st Door South of Vermillion Street

HASTINGS, MINN.

CPSIA information can be obtained
at www.ICGtesting.com
Printed in the USA
BVHW040537101118
532319BV00026B/2022/P

9 780483 392519